A Captain's Duty

This Large Print Book carries the
Seal of Approval of N.A.V.H.

A Captain's Duty

SOMALI PIRATES, NAVY SEALS, AND DANGEROUS DAYS AT SEA

Richard Phillips with Stephan Talty

THORNDIKE PRESS

A part of Gale, Cengage Learning

Detroit • New York • San Francisco • New Haven, Conn • Waterville, Maine • London

Copyright © 2010 by Richard Phillips.
Front matter map of Somalia reprinted with permission from Britannica Concise Encyclopedia, © 2001 by Encyclopedia Britannica, Inc.
Special thanks to DCL for the use of *Somali Pirate Takedown: The Real Story*, courtesy Discovery Channel and Military Channel.
Thorndike Press, a part of Gale, Cengage Learning.

LIBRARY OF CONGRESS CATALOGING-IN-PUBLICATION DATA

Phillips, Richard, 1956–
    A captain's duty : Somali pirates, navy SEALs, and dangerous days at sea / by Richard Phillips with Stephan Talty.
        p. cm. — (Thorndike Press large print nonfiction)
    Originally published: New York : Hyperion, c2010.
    ISBN-13: 978-1-4104-2934-6 (hardcover)
    ISBN-10: 1-4104-2934-2 (hardcover)
    1. Phillips, Richard, 1956– 2. Hijacking of ships—Aden, Gulf of. 3. Maersk Alabama (Ship) 4. Merchant mariners—United States—Biography. 5. Ship captains—United States—Biography. I. Talty, Stephan. II. Title.
VK140.P45A3 2010b
364.16'4—dc22
[B]   2010016318

Published in 2010 by arrangement with Hyperion, an imprint of Buena Vista Books, Inc.

Printed in the United States of America
1 2 3 4 5 6 7 14 13 12 11 10

To all those who go to sea:
the U.S. Navy,
the Navy SEALs,
the Merchant Mariners.
I am proud to be among them.

To my family: my wife, Andrea, and my
children, Daniel and Mariah,
who helped teach me patience.

Last, to my mother and father,
who raised me to believe.

CONTENTS

ACKNOWLEDGMENTS

I wish to acknowledge the U.S. Navy and the Navy SEALs; without them, this story would have been told by someone else with a different ending.

My crew, for their ability to come together, think on their feet, and do the best job they could as U.S. Merchant Mariners.

To the companies we work for: LMS Ship Management of Mobile, Alabama, and Maersk Line Limited of Norfolk, Virginia, for the aid and support they gave to the crew and their families during and after our incident.

To my family, friends, and neighbors, who were there giving support: Paige and Emmett, Susan and Michael, Lea, Alison, and Amber just to name a few.

Last, to the many who sent prayers and support during and after this incident, which meant so much to Andrea and me.

If fear is cultivated, it will become stronger.
If faith is cultivated, it will achieve mastery.
— *John Paul Jones, merchant mariner and*
Revolutionary War hero

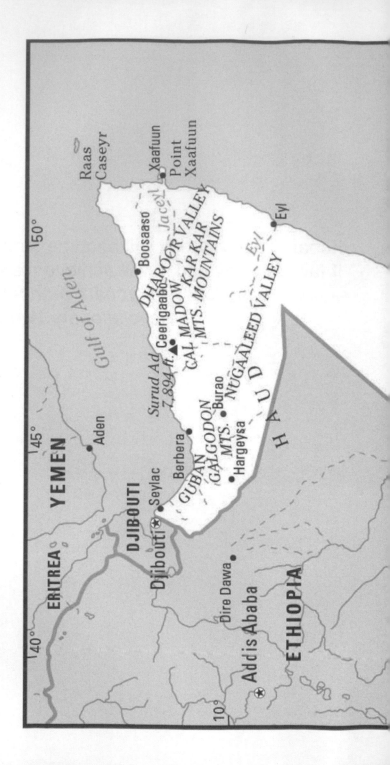

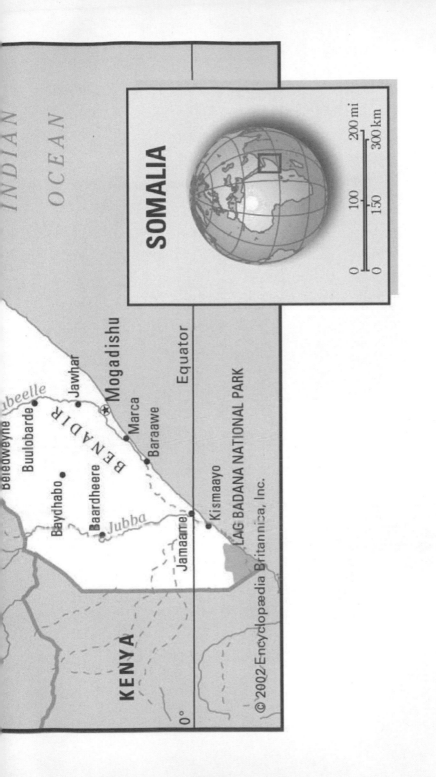

SOMALIA

INDIAN

OCEAN

Beledweyne
Buulobarde
Baydhabo
Baardheere
Jubba
Jamaame
Kismaayo
LAG BADANA NATIONAL PARK
Jawhar
Mogadishu
Marca
Baraawe
BENADIR
Shabeelle
Equator

KENYA

0°

© 2002 Encyclopædia Britannica, Inc.

0   100   200 mi
0   150   300 km

INTRODUCTION

The heat in the lifeboat had become completely unbearable. The last drops of cool ocean water from my escape attempt had evaporated off my skin hours ago and, even though it was two in the morning, the heat was radiating off the hull and pressing down on me. I felt as if I were sitting on top of the equator. I'd stripped down to my khakis and socks, but I couldn't even put my feet on the deck because it was boiling hot. My ribs and arms were aching, too, from the beating the pirates had given me, absolutely batshit furious that their million-dollar American hostage had almost gotten away.

I could see the lights of the navy ship through the aft hatch, dipping up and down on the ocean swells astern, about half a mile away. I'd almost made it. If the moon hadn't been so bright, the pirates would never have spotted me. I should have been drinking a cold beer in the captain's quarters right now, telling my adventure story to half the crew and waiting for my call home to go through.

The ship looked gigantic out there. It was like a piece of home floating so close it seemed unreal. It appeared to be a destroyer, which meant they had enough firepower to blow a thousand pirate ships back to Mogadishu. *Why hadn't they done anything?*

The hard plastic of the molded seats was digging into my back and causing my legs to cramp. I hung my head back, trying to relieve the stress on my neck. I was now trussed up like a deer in the middle of the lifeboat. The Somalis had lashed my hands to a vertical bar at the top of the lifeboat's canopy and bound my feet together. I couldn't even feel my fingers. The lanky pirate, the one I called Musso, had pulled the ropes so tight I'd lost sensation in less than a minute. My hands were starting to swell up like a pair of clown gloves.

I'd been better.

I stood there, panting, counting the minutes go by. I could hear the creaking of the boat and the slap of waves against the fiberglass hull.

Then, suddenly, the whole atmosphere in the boat changed. Nobody said a word, nobody moved. I couldn't see much anyway, just the eyes of the Somalis and their teeth when they smiled or spoke. There was a little moonlight coming in through the hatches, fore and aft, but I could feel the atmosphere change in a split second. It was like an electric switch had been flipped from positive to negative. When someone has a loaded AK-47 pointed at your face, you get to know his mood really well, believe me. If he's happy or annoyed, if his nose itches, if he's thinking about breaking up with his girlfriend, whatever. You *know*. And my skin just felt a change in the air — like something dangerous had slipped into the boat and was sitting right next to me.

I could catch glimpses of what was going on, but mostly it was what I heard. The first thing was a *click*. The sound was coming from the cockpit of the boat, where the Leader was sitting. *Click*. Silence. *Click*. Silence. *Click, click*. He was pulling the trigger of his 9mm, dry-firing it. In the darkness, I couldn't see if the gun was pointed at me, but I felt a cold sensation creep across my chest. The little bastard didn't have a clip in the gun, or my head would have exploded in a big red spray against the hull. No bullets in the chamber, either. Yet.

And then out of the darkness I heard the

17

chanting. From the cockpit, the Leader called out something in this droning voice and the other three — Tall Guy, Musso, and the crazy-eyed Young Guy — answered him. I leaned forward, trying to figure out what they were saying. It was obviously some kind of religious ceremony, like a Latin Catholic Mass back in Massachusetts when I was growing up. A few hours ago these guys had been laughing and telling jokes and boasting how they were "real Somali sailors, twenty-four/seven." You could almost forget they were pirates and I was their hostage. Now everything was different. It was like we'd gone back ten centuries and they were asking Allah for his blessing for what they were about to do.

I knew what was happening. But I didn't have to sit there and take it.

"What are you going to do now, kill me?" I yelled up to the Leader. In the darkness, I could hear him laugh — I saw the flash of his teeth — and then he coughed and spit. Then the four of them went back to the chanting. I tried to move my hands and loosen the rope, but I had to give it to Musso. He could tie a goddamn knot like nobody's business.

The prayers came to an end, just like that. The boat was quiet and I could hear the splashing of the waves again. I stared into the darkness, looking to see the muzzle of an AK-47 being raised toward me. Nothing.

"You have a family?"

The voice was mocking, self-assured. He was the Leader, no question.

"Yeah, I have a family," I said. I realized with a feeling of panic that I hadn't said my good-byes to them. I bit down on my lip.

"Daughter? Son?"

"I have a son, a daughter, and a wife."

Silence. I heard some rustling up near the cockpit. Then the Leader spoke again.

"That's too bad," he said. He was trying to rattle me. And he was doing a damn good job of it, actually.

"Yeah, that is too bad," I shot back. Whatever they did or said, I couldn't let them know they'd gotten to me.

Musso came toward me down the aisle of the lifeboat. He took some white cotton cloth that he'd torn from a shirt and laced it through the ropes around my hands. He didn't pull them tight, just twined them around the ropes. Then he took out some parachute-type lines, one red, one white, and started lacing those through. Slowly. His face was maybe a foot from mine and I could see him concentrating hard on what he was doing. The white and red lines were

19

looped around in this intricate pattern that he had to get exactly right.

It's a weird feeling, watching yourself being prepared to die. It was like they expected me to go along with my own murder, to be a good victim and not say a word. I felt a jolt of anger shoot through me. These guys were *not* going to take me away from my family, from everything and everyone I loved. No way.

When Musso was done, he walked back to the cockpit. The Somalis started talking again — regular conversation this time — and they seemed to come to some kind of an agreement. I saw the Leader hand his pistol to Tall Guy, who came walking down the aisle toward me. So he'd been chosen to do the job.

Tall Guy sat down behind me on the orange survival suit. For some reason, they had to be standing or sitting on something orange or red during the ritual. He checked the 9mm clip, slammed it back in, and then played with the gun. It was like he was toying with me. The one I called Young Guy, the one who'd been staring at me the whole two days, smiling like a deranged maniac, came over and dragged my feet onto the exposure suit. At the same time, Musso came down and started tugging hard on my arms. They were trying to get me in the right position, I guess, for a clean killing. The Leader was shouting at Musso, "Pull tight!" and then at the other guy, "Get him up!" Musso yanked on the line that tied my hands, trying to get my arms above my head. They wanted to stretch me out. *No goddamn way,* I said to myself. *I'm not going to be your fatted calf.*

As Musso pulled up, I jammed my fists under my chin. "You can't do it," I muttered to him through my teeth. "You're not strong enough." I thought if I could mess up their ceremony, I might survive a little longer. Musso started to get mad. His nostrils were flaring and he was getting exasperated with me. The sweat was popping off his face, and I started enjoying it — this badass Somali pirate with the automatic weapon couldn't get me to do his bidding. We came face-to-face. "You'll never do it," I whispered to him.

Musso finally let go of my arms and whacked me in the face. I grinned.

The Leader was getting hot, too, mixing his Somali and his English as he screamed at the guys. "Pull it tight!" he yelled. Musso studied me and then smiled. He put his hands on my arms and rested them there, like *Let's just chill out, pal.* I nodded, but I kept my fists jammed under my chin. Musso grabbed the line tethered to my wrists and yanked up hard. I was ready. My hands raised an inch as the rope creaked tight, but that was it.

Now the Somalis were really going for it, grunting with the effort, fighting me with everything they had. Musso tried to yank up on my hands; I held them down. One of them pulled my feet onto the orange suit, but I kicked them back. Another was standing behind me with the gun. I was breathing hard, mouthfuls of hot suffocating air, but I was holding my own. I thought in the back of my mind, *How long can you keep this up?* Not long, I knew. *Better say your good-byes.*

All of a sudden, there was an explosion near my left ear. I saw stars and my head kicked forward and dropped into my hands. My whole body went slack. I felt blood spurting out between my fingers and running down my face.

Holy shit, he really did it, I thought. *He shot me.*

My vision was blurred but I looked up at the vertical and horizontal green strut on the bulkhead wall. It looked like a cross, and just staring at it had settled my fears before. As I looked at the cross, the strangest thing came into my mind. *I'm going to see Frannie,* I thought. Frannie, my dang dog in Vermont, a nutcase from the pound who never once obeyed any of my commands. She'd been hit by a car in front of our farmhouse a month before I left. Now I was going to see her.

Then I heard Musso. "Don't do it!" he shouted. "No, no!" I looked up. Blood from my head had spilled onto the white knots. Musso was freaking out.

I took a deep breath. I didn't know if I'd dodged a bullet or what had just happened.

I really should have told the pirates: I'm too stubborn to die that easily. You're just going to have to try harder.

ONE:
-10 DAYS

PIRACY FIGURES UP 20 PERCENT IN FIRST QUARTER OF 2009: A total of 36 vessels were boarded and one vessel hijacked. Seven crew members were taken hostage, six kidnapped, three killed and one missing — presumed dead. In the majority of incidents, the attackers were heavily armed with guns or knives. The use and threat of violence against crew members remains unacceptably high. . . . Waters around Somalia continue to be notorious for hijacking of vessels and the abduction of crew for ransom.

— ICC International Maritime Bureau
Piracy Report, First Quarter, 2009

Ten days before, I'd been enjoying my last meal stateside with my wife, Andrea, in one of the most beautiful towns in Vermont. All you see from the front door of my converted farmhouse are rolling green hills, munching cows, and more rolling hills. Underhill is the kind of Vermont town where young farmers propose to their local sweethearts by spray-painting RACHEL, WILL YOU MARRY ME? on bales of hay. It's a place where you can walk for three minutes and be lost in a forest so deep and thick and silent you'd think you're going to trip over Daniel Boone. We have two general stores and one Catholic church, St. Thomas, and the occasional tourist up from Manhattan. It's as different from the ocean as the other side of the moon is, and I love that. It's like I get to live two completely different lives.

As a merchant mariner, I often work three months on and three months off. When I come home, I forget about the sea. I'm 100 percent into being a dad and husband. When our kids, Dan and Mariah, were young, from the moment they got up to the minute they went to bed, I'd take care of them. Neighbors and friends would ask me to babysit, so I'd have five or six kids in tow. I'd make dinner: French toast by candlelight, my specialty. I'd do Rich's Homework Club. I'd take the kids on class trips. Whatever I do, work or home life, I do with everything I have.

When I leave my family, it's for a long time. You need to do something special for them before you ship out, because it might be the last time you see them. When he was growing up, my son, Dan, would goad me, "Oh, I don't have a dad. He's never home. Guess he doesn't love me." We'd laugh about it — Dan is exactly like I was when I was nineteen: a smart aleck who will find your weakness and hammer it home until you give in and laugh. But what he said about my never being there would come back to haunt me. Because there's a kernel of truth there. My daughter, Mariah, and Dan would see me every day for three months and then I would be gone to some far-flung corner of the world. It didn't matter to them that there were other merchant mariners who stayed onboard even longer than I did, that I knew one guy, a radio operator, who was aboard one ship for two years straight.

As a sailor, you have to put your real life on your kitchen shelf and pick up your merchant marine life. Because on the job, you barely have a personal life. You're on call twenty-four hours a day to do whatever the ship needs. You eat and sleep and work and that's pretty much it. It's like you've died and gone to sea. Then you come back and take your real life off the shelf and start living it again.

You develop rituals to get through the transition from land to sea. Sailors have a phrase, "crossing the bar," which means leaving harbor for the unknown on the oceans (it also can refer to the death of a sailor), and you have to get yourself mentally prepared to go across. It's a stressful time when fears start creeping into the minds of your loved ones. It was probably the dangers of my job that were on Andrea's mind that cold March — pirates, rogue waves, desperate people in third-world ports. All the while, I'd be thinking like a captain, running through a checklist with a thousand things on it: What repairs do I need to see to? Are the guys on my crew dependable? I used to start doing this a month before I left, which would drive Andrea around the bend. Now, after thirty years at sea, I wait until I hit the deck of my ship.

Andrea and I have a tradition when I'm getting ready to leave. First, we argue. About nothing at all. In the weeks leading up to my leaving, Andrea and I always have arguments about little things, about the car or the weather or her hitting her head on the old ship's bell that hangs near the clothesline in our backyard. She must have smacked it three or four times while putting up fresh laundry to dry, and she always comes in and yells at me to take it down. (It's still up there, too — sentimental value.) But in those weeks before a job, we get on each other's nerves, which is nothing more than her being anxious about my leaving and me being anxious about leaving her.

Andrea is an emergency room nurse at a hospital in Burlington and she's a fierce, opinionated, loving Italian girl from Vermont. I love her to death. We'd met in a Boston dive bar, the Cask 'n Flagon, down near Kenmore Square, when she was in nursing school and I'd been around the world a few times already as a young sailor. I noticed this cute frizzy-haired brunette girl sitting at the bar, and I just had to talk to her. Andrea was talking with the bartender, since they'd just discovered they had mutual friends. Then, as she tells it, this tall guy with a beard appeared out of nowhere and sat down next to her.

"You have a problem," I said.

Andrea thought, Well, he's cute enough. I'll play along.

"What's that?" she said.

"Being the best-looking woman in every room you walk into."

"Thanks," she said. "There are three women in here. Not a huge compliment."

I laughed and stuck out my hand.

"I'm Rich," I said. "As in 'filthy.' " That was one of my better lines in the early eighties.

Andrea cracked up. Then she let me buy her a drink.

Years later, after we were married, Andrea told me that she thought I was funny and easy to talk to. Like most people's, her only knowledge of the merchant marine came from Humphrey Bogart movies. I guess that's why she let me tell her so many stories. "You made it sound intriguing," she said.

After we met, I had to ship out and Andrea didn't hear from me again for months. She moved to a new apartment after her first year at nursing school. Then one night at about 1 a.m., there was a rap on her door. When she opened it, there I was, smiling like I'd won the lottery. She was floored. She figured I must have walked all over Boston, trying to find her new address. She wasn't far off.

Andrea was twenty-five and very focused on school. Nursing was going to be her life. I was on her radar, but only a blip on the edge of the screen. I would ship out and she would get postcards and then letters from these ports all over the world. Then

I'd come back to Boston and take her out to dinner and the movies and pick her and her friends up at seven a.m. the next morning and drive them to their first classes. All the while, I'd have a new batch of stories to tell her about storms off Cape Hatteras or typhoons or good or crazy shipmates.

To me, it was just life on the seas. But she loved getting the postcards and the sudden reunions. "It was romantic," Andrea says to this day. "It really was."

The night before I shipped out for the *Maersk Alabama,* Andrea and I jumped in our car and went to our favorite restaurant, a place called Euro, in the nearby town of Essex. Andrea had the shrimp scampi and I had the seafood medley and we drank a bottle of red wine we brought with us. It's cheaper that way. I'm three quarters Irish and one quarter Yankee, but that one quarter controls the money. I've been known to be tight with a dollar, and I don't mind saying so.

The next day, March 28, Andrea dropped me at the airport, like she always did. There was nothing out of the ordinary in those last hours together. "Everything is going to be fine," I said. "I'm sure you're going to get a blizzard as soon as I leave, so just think of me lounging on deck in the hot sun." I love snow. There's nothing I like more than looking out my back window at the fields and trees covered in white. She laughed. "See you in June," she said and gave me a kiss. She usually stays until my flight leaves; that's a tradition that started when Mariah and Dan were young. They would stand at the window watching my flight take off and wave at their daddy, just milking that last moment of togetherness for everything it was worth. But the kids were in college now and Andrea was on her way to work and she couldn't wait. It was the first time that ever happened. I thought about that later.

I love the sea and being a merchant mariner, but you meet a lot of oddballs on ships. I think a lot of it has to do with leaving people behind for so long. It can mess up your head. Marriages break up. Girlfriends find new guys. Sailors get "Dear John" e-mails in the middle of the night on some lonely stretch of water miles from anywhere. Sometimes, a crew member will disappear, just jump overboard in the middle of the ocean, never to be found. A lot of it has to do with the strain that comes from being away from loved ones.

Merchant mariners always talk about

Jodie. Jodie's the guy who's at home screwing your wife while you're out on a ship. He's eating your food, driving your car, chugging your beer. Jodie's going to be sitting on your couch when you arrive home, asking, "Who are you?" When a guy calls his wife and she doesn't answer, we tell him, "She's out with Jodie." As much as we joke about it, Jodie is all too real. Guys get home and their apartment is cleaned out, their bank balance reads zero, and their fiancée is gone without leaving a note. It happens to some sailors over and over again. Every time I heard about Jodie it made me feel more thankful that I had Andrea at home. Jodie never visited my house.

But I'm not going to lie, some sailors just start out crazy — especially the cooks. I'm convinced there are very few normal, well-adjusted cooks in the entire U. S. Merchant Marine. Not one, except for my brother-in-law, Dave. But you do have your share of eccentrics among the rest of the crew, too. I've served under an old-salt captain named Port-and-Starboard Peterson who in fog as thick as pea soup would refuse to use radar *because it would hypnotize you into crashing into another ship.* The radar was evil, you see. One guy wore half a mustache for an entire three-month trip. Another demanded to be called Polar Bear when we sailed toward the North Pole and Penguin when we went toward the South Pole. This guy collected so many T-shirts from the different ports that you could barely push open the door to his quarters. I knew another seaman who showed up at the boat wearing a wolf-skin coat with the head still attached. Sailors are a breed apart, that's for sure.

It's been that way forever. The merchant marine is the first of the nation's services. We were founded in 1775, before the army and the navy. In all our wars, including World War II, guys who just couldn't live with the navy's regulations ended up onboard cargo ships. They didn't see the point of having a crease in their dungarees or saluting every officer onboard; they just weren't made that way. It's no accident that many of the Beat writers like Jack Kerouac and Allen Ginsberg were former seamen. The need to wander and the need to rebel go hand in hand. We're a bunch of misfits and renegades and damn good seamen.

When I'm taking ships from port to port, books on the history of the merchant marine or World War II are always piled by my bunk. We were the first to die in World War II — seventeen minutes before the attack on Pearl Harbor, a Japanese sub strafed the lumber hauler SS *Cynthia Olson* and sank it, over 1,000 miles north of Honolulu. Thirty-three sailors jumped into lifeboats but were never seen again, because all hell was breaking loose on navy ships a thousand miles away. And the merchant marine suffered more casualties than any other service in World War II. One in every twenty-six sailors died while doing his duty. Crewmen torpedoed along the Atlantic coast drowned in engine oil while sunbathers watched from the shore. Men in the North Atlantic froze solid to the floors of their lifeboats after their tankers went down. Enormous five-hundred-foot ships carrying ammunition and dynamite to the front lines were torpedoed, blowing up in explosions so violent they never found a trace of the tons of metal or the hundreds of men aboard. They just disappeared into thin air. Which is fitting, really. The merchant marine has always been the invisible service, the guys who brought the tanks to Normandy, the bullets to Okinawa, but no one ever remembers us. What General Douglas MacArthur said was true: "They brought us our lifeblood and paid for it with their own."

But when the boys from the cargo ships went home, there were no ticker-tape parades, no G.I. Bill, nothing like that. They're still trying to get recognition so they can live out their lives with dignity. There's a bill before Congress that will guarantee them standing as World War II veterans and pay them a small stipend, but it's taking so long to get through the political process that most of the guys will be dead before it's passed. That's a shame.

When I was coming up in the service, I met guys who'd served in World War II and had ships shot out from beneath them. And I remember what one guy told me: "I was in the merchant marine when the war broke out and I saw ships going down left and right. I got so scared I joined the navy." He was just playing the odds. Being a merchant mariner was a good way to meet your maker in those days.

A lot of us have a chip on our shoulder. We're patriots. We have a proud tradition. We're rugged individualists with a few mixed nuts thrown in to keep it interesting.

But we never make the headlines.

On that trip to the *Maersk Alabama,* I had one of those history books packed in my carry-on luggage, but I sat on the plane thinking about what I had to do once I got aboard. My flight left at 3 p.m. I was headed to Salalah, Oman, on the east coast of the

Arabian Peninsula, where the ship was loading up its cargo holds. I've flown as long as forty-two hours to get to a ship, and this time the journey was nothing unusual: Burlington to Washington, D.C., D.C. to Zurich, Zurich to Muscat, Oman, where I crashed at a hotel for ten hours. The next morning, I headed straight back to the airport for the flight to Salalah. I left Vermont on March 28 and arrived at my destination on the thirtieth. Wherever there's work as a merchant mariner, you go. Joining me on the trip was Shane, my chief mate and an able-bodied seaman, who was also headed to the *Maersk Alabama.*

I rolled out of bed on March 30, my brain cloudy from jet lag, and jumped in a car that took me to my ship. The *Maersk Alabama* was sitting at the dockside, its two cranes swinging containers onto the deck, when I walked up the gangway, boarded the ship, and went up to my office to meet the relieving captain, who debriefed me on what was going on. The captain left and I dumped my gear in my quarters, which were connected to an office, one floor below the bridge on the starboard side. To get from my room to the ship's bridge, all I would have to do is walk down the hallway to the center door. Opening it, I'd be in the

37

chimney, or central ladder way. One flight up and I'd be on the bridge, the command center for the whole ship.

The house was what we call the seven-story superstructure at the stern (or rear) of the ship. A small condolike structure, it contained our living quarters, our mess hall, and our hospital. The top level was the bridge, where large windows ran from the ceiling to about waist-high and were met by a metal wainscoting that dropped to a special antifatigue rubber floor. (Watches are kept on the bridge, where a mate and an AB, or able-bodied seaman, are constantly scanning the horizon, so you want them to stay alert.) It looked like a greenhouse in there, with views for miles in every direction. In the middle of the bridge was the conning station — that's where we steer the ship from — and a flat electronic console filled with navigation aids. That's where you'd find the radar. Radar doesn't look like the cathode tube setup you see in Humphrey Bogart movies. These days it looks more like a TV, with ships still appearing as a small blip, but now with data streaming down the right side of the screen: the speed of any vessels, CPA (closest point of approach, which tells you the point at which you're going to intersect with that approaching ship), and time to CPA. On the port side stood a chart table, where the second mate — the office man on a ship — does his work. There was a GMDSS, or Global Maritime Distress and Safety System, which gave us continuous weather updates, a small electronic station, which replaced the traditional radio operator, and a computer.

Starboard there was an all-important piece of equipment: the coffeepot, my first stop every morning.

Port and starboard, doors led off to the bridge wings, walkways eighteen feet long that we used while maneuvering or docking. These wings allow you to see down the sides of the ship and avoid banging into the piers or another vessel. Above the bridge was the flying bridge, an open platform that marked one of the the highest points on the ship.

Each deck below the bridge was designated by a letter. My quarters were housed on E deck. The chief engineer's, too. The engineers' and mates' rooms were on D deck. C deck held quarters for the crew, while B held more space for the ABs and the vessel lounges. A deck housed the mess, where we ate our meals, and the hospital. On the main deck was the ship's office.

Dropping below the deck into the belly of the ship, directly below the house, sat the engine room. Forward of that were the enormous cargo holds, with tanks holding ballast, fuel, and water underneath. Behind, or aft, of the engine room, under the main deck, was the after steering room.

I spent the next few hours going over the *Maersk Alabama* with a captain's eye. The first thing I noticed was that the ship had let the security slip a little. I could see doors open all over the ship. The engine door, the bridge door, the cargo scuttle that led into the holds — they were all key points of entry for any intruders and they were all standing wide open. Even though we were in port, they should have been secured. The pirate cages were unlocked, too. Pirate cages are steel bars over the ship's ladder ways that come up from the main deck to the superstructure on the exterior of the ship. After you climb up a ladder, you're supposed to lower this screen of welded bars over the hole you've just come through and lock it. These screens are designed to keep any intruders from ascending the ship to the bridge.

I'd captained the *Maersk Alabama* once before and I knew her pretty well. She was a container ship, one of the workhorses that carry the Toyota you're driving, the plasma TV you're watching, or the Reeboks you're wearing. (Without the merchant marine, there is no Walmart.) Merchant mariners don't get to sail the beautiful ships of the world, the yachts and sloops and the rum-runners. We don't get to stand at the helm with a gin and tonic in our hands. We work trawlers, barges, bulk carriers, tankers. The *Maersk Alabama* was built in China ten years ago; it was 508 feet long and 83 feet abeam and painted blue on the hull and beige on the superstructure, like all the ships owned by Maersk. Two 40-foot cranes, each six stories high, were placed fore and aft, which enabled us to quickly load and unload the containers that sat on top of the deck on any given trip. Her top speed was eighteen knots, powered by a single diesel engine, and her capacity was 1,092 TEUs, or twenty-foot equivalent units, which meant she could carry approximately 1,092 of the containers you see stacked at ports or being pulled by tractor trailers across America. This ship was like a thousand other vessels out there, but for the next three months it was going to be my home, my job, and my responsibility.

We were on the EAF4 run (East Africa 4),

which went from Salalah, Oman, to Djibouti in the Republic of Djibouti and Mombasa, Kenya, on the Indian Ocean. Sometimes we'd include Dar es Salaam on the trip, but this time it was only three stops. I'd always found East Africa to be a good run, relaxing even, compared with hauling cars from Yokohama to the United States on a nail-biting schedule. The trip promised sunny weather, interesting ports, a solid ship. It was one of the best runs I'd ever been on, and I felt lucky to have it.

We were carrying seventeen tons of cargo, including five tons of supplies for the World Food Programme, what we call "handshake food": grain, wheat, peas, the essentials for survival. From those ports the food would be trucked hundreds of miles into countries like Rwanda, Congo, and Uganda, landlocked places that can't get the stuff any other way. Every piece of merchandise — every lightbulb, every pair of shoes, and every gallon of gas — that ends up in those countries has to go through two ports, Mombasa or Dar es Salaam. I later heard from one Catholic relief outfit that had twenty-three containers onboard the *Maersk Alabama* destined for Rwanda. They told me it was their entire six-month supply for the refugees they cared for and if it was delayed or hijacked, some of those desperate men, women, and children would have starved to death.

When you get on a ship, you want to hit the deck running, but you can't. There are ten thousand things to get ready when you're setting sail, starting with the basics: What time do we eat? Are the cranes working? Are there any pipes leaking? Is the third mate sitting in his room saying "Redrum" over and over again? I've always said that all ships are different but working on a ship is always the same. You have to learn the vessel first, and you have to grab someone who's getting ready to leave. Even though they're dying to get off the ship and fly back to their family and kids or their girlfriend and a three-month supply of beer, you have to find out what's been happening or you're lost.

I met my crew. I'd worked with my chief mate, Shane Murphy, before. He was young, physical, and very hands-on. Shane was a straight shooter who looked like a Boy Scout and thought like a captain. We'd met in odd circumstances on our first trip together. He was going through the Oman airport heading to the ship when the customs officials decided to "temporarily confiscate" his CDs. It happens all the time, and the CDs often end up in the customs official's own collection. Shane blew up and was arrested for "insulting a public official." After three days in a roasting hot jail cell, we'd been able to get him out and onto our ship. He was a good shipmate and I knew I could count on him in an emergency.

Mike Perry was the chief engineer, a born-again Christian in his fifties who looked like a country-and-western singer and ran a tight engine room. I'd worked with him nearly three months before on the same EAF4 run. He was an ex-navy guy who was never afraid to argue with me if he thought he was right, which is something I've always respected, even encouraged, in a chief or any crew member. Things happen so fast on a ship that you have to know your duty automatically; when a typhoon's threatening to rip your ship apart, or a pirate is closing at twenty-five knots, you either perform or you're dead. So he and I were gung-ho about training. There was just one difference: Mike believed everyone could be trained to a high level, which is a navy thing. I believed some guys were just too far gone to absorb even the basics, and you had to work around that. You could only train some guys so much; perfection was just not possible.

I was relieved that Mike and Shane were sailing with me. They were both strong leaders, proactive about training the crew and getting jobs done right, qualities that are too often missing in sailors these days.

I met the rest of the crew. The third mate, Colin Wright, was a stout Southern guy I'd never met before. There was also an AB who was in his sixties and really should have been tending his gardenias in a retirement community. His best sailing days were behind him. You often had to explain the most basic things to him, and sometimes even then he wouldn't get it. And I met a new AB who introduced himself as ATM. I demanded he get his passport and prove he wasn't messing with me. Sure enough, there it was, "ATM Mohammed." He was a Pakistani who'd won the lottery for an American visa. ATM was young, bright-eyed, and looked capable. The rest of the guys I shook hands with as the day went on. Onboard a ship getting ready to leave port, there's no time for more than that. Most captains will make an initial assessment of the crew. This seemed like a good crew, with the exception of one of the senior sailors.

The command structure on a merchant marine ship is a lot like the military's. The captain is responsible for the crew, the ship, and everything on it. Period. Below him are three divisions: the deck department, run by the chief mate (simply called the mate on a ship); the engine department, run by the chief engineer (known as the chief onboard); and the steward department, run by the chief steward. The mate is responsible for cargo, security, medical, maintenance, storing, loading, safety operations, and anything short of a meteorite landing on the forward deck. Under him is the second mate (called the paper mate), who is responsible for navigation, maintaining charts, and seeing to the bridge's electronic equipment. He's the voyage planner, the guy who lays the courses down, labels them, and makes sure the light list (which gives us all the lighthouses along our route) and the Notice to Mariners are up to date. The third mate is in the entry-level slot. He takes care of the safety equipment and does anything the mate tells him to do. Beneath the third is the bosun, the leader of the able-bodied seamen and the foreman who actually puts the mate's orders into effect. The chief and his men (first, second, and third engineer) focus on what makes the ship go: the power plant and auxiliaries (compressors, pumps, and motors), as well as maintaining all the equipment on the ship.

Mark Twain said that going to sea is like going to jail with a chance of drowning, and he was spot on. You give up any idea of a normal, comfortable life when you step onboard. Merchant mariners aren't weekend warriors; we are there to work twenty-four hours a day, seven days a week. On the water, every day is like a Monday — a workday with more to come stretching out into the distance.

I have a tough reputation in the business. I'm known to be demanding, and I am. Each sailor has the lives of his crew in his hands, and I wouldn't allow them to be thrown away because someone wasn't prepared. Andrea's brother, who's also a sailor, told her once: "Onboard Rich is a different person from the fun-loving guy you know. You wouldn't even recognize him." I do like to have fun whenever I can, but not at the cost of neglecting what the ship needs. That's not going to happen on my vessel.

My first order of business was letting the crew know in no uncertain terms that we had to get the security profile right. The news out of Somalia was grim. Everyone knew that pirates there were wreaking havoc on the shipping lanes. The usual route around the Horn of Africa brings you within twenty miles of the Somali coast, but ever since 2005, when the pirates started terrorizing the merchant ships there, captains had been going out fifty miles, then one hundred, then two hundred miles to get away from these bandits. What was a five-day trip now takes ten. Ships don't double their sailing time unless there are some very dangerous people waiting for them. But no matter how far off shore ships were going, the pirates were finding and hijacking them.

As soon as I settled aboard the *Maersk Alabama,* I started getting e-mail bulletins from the Office of Naval Intelligence and various security firms about pirates: mysterious blips appearing on radar and giving chase, gun battles, the works. Ships, fishing boats, and yachts were being taken left and right. A great deal of the action was taking place around the Somali coast and in the Gulf of Aden, a deep-water basin 920 miles long and 300 miles wide that lies between Yemen and Somalia on the Horn of Africa. Something like 10 percent of all the world's petroleum supply is shipped via the Gulf of Aden, as tankers bring oil out of the ports of Saudi Arabia, through the Red Sea, into the Gulf, then out to the Arabian Sea and on to Europe and America. A trillion dollars' worth of goods passes by the Somali coast every year. Essentially, sailors are bringing the world's most vital resource through the world's most unstable region, which had turned the area around the Gulf of Aden and the Somali coast into a shooting gallery. Anyone sailing there would be under constant threat of attack from pirates, who were getting smarter and more violent by the month. The total ransoms paid were soaring into the tens of millions a year, attracting desperate young men to the gulf like bees to honey.

And this was exactly where we were headed. Our next destination was Djibouti, which lies at the far western end of the Gulf of Aden. We had to sail in, unload, and get back out before the bad guys could get a bead on us.

I sent Andrea a quick e-mail saying I'd made it to the ship safely and we were getting ready to embark. I'm not one for phone calls. Too damn expensive. But I let her know I was aboard and thinking of her.

Andrea misses the days when I wrote her long letters or postcards. I'd always send her at least one long letter written over a week's time, telling her what ocean I was crossing, what the weather was like, silly stuff the crew was up to. In the beginning, I signed the first postcards "Rich." That's when we'd decided we were "in deep like," not "in love." It took a while to get more. Andrea still remembers the time she got one letter, before we were married, and at the bottom, it said, "Love, R." She was so struck by it. I guess that's when she first thought, "Oh, maybe he *is* serious." Andrea has kept every letter I ever wrote her.

I did call a few times from around the globe, and I always used the same opening line. Andrea would be asleep and she'd pick up the phone and I'd say, in this low, Barry White voice, "Is your husband home?"

And she'd say, "No, as a matter of fact, he's not."

"Good. I'll be right over."

I don't know when that started, but it became our private joke.

But it was the letters she really loved, especially the ones where I'd get all romantic. I wrote in one that "I miss the inside of your arms." How could she resist that? And in another, I said, "I'll be seeing you in the moon." I explained to Andrea how the full moon was always good luck for sailors, and when I looked at one, I thought of her sleeping under it thousands of miles away. So the full moon became ours, a way to be in touch with each other. And when our children were young, they would all look up at the clear Vermont night sky and the kids would shout, "Look, it's Daddy's moon." And Andrea would say, "That's right." And Mariah and Dan would look up at the moon and say, "Good night, Daddy, wherever you are." Andrea did anything she could to keep me connected to the kids' daily lives.

I'd always loved kids. One of my jobs before joining the merchant marine was working with schizophrenic children and I'd really enjoyed it. "Dealing with kids is good preparation for dealing with crews," I told Andrea. And it was true. I even instituted something called the Crying Room on my ships, a little mediation club for crew members who were having problems with each other. I'd write and tell Andrea about every session, how one guy would come into the Crying Room and yell, "He pulled a knife on me!" and the other sailor would say, "Only after he swung at me with a wrench!" I'd listen patiently and nod and let the guys get their frustrations out. At the end I'd say, "Let's shake hands and get back to work." Not every captain does that, but I felt it made for a better ship.

When I left for the sea, Andrea always

posted a picture of me on the refrigerator, along with a photo of "Daddy's ship." Next to it, there was always a list of questions for Daddy that I'd have to answer when I got home. But most of all, we had the full moon to share. Andrea cherished it because it always brought me close to her.

Two:
-8 Days

GULF OF ADEN: Bulk carrier (TITAN) hijacked 19 Mar 09 at 1430 UTC while underway in position 12:35N — 047:21E. Six men in a speed boat armed with AK-47s and pistols boarded and hijacked the vessel. The pirates are in control of the vessel and sailing her to Somali coastal waters.

GULF OF ADEN: Cargo vessel (DIAMOND FALCON) fired upon 14 Mar 09 at 0629 UTC while underway in position 13:42N — 049:19E, approximately 50NM southeast of Al Mullikan, Yemen. Two skiffs with men onboard armed with automatic weapons and RPGs fired upon the vessel. The captain conducted evasive maneuvers and counter-piracy measures while a Turkish warship nearby dispatched two helicopters to provide assistance along with a Danish warship. The men in the two skiffs fled the scene after the warships' arrival.

— *East Africa bulletin, Worldwide Threats to Shipping Report, Office of Naval Intelligence, April 2009*

We were scheduled to depart Salalah on April 1. I woke up at five a.m., checked the weather, and then began my morning routine. I walk the entire length of the ship every day, to check for dents, leaks, anything out of the ordinary. The shore gantries had loaded the last container and we'd paid the departing crew, signed on the new members, brought aboard our supplies — food, new videos, and fuel — and were ready to sail. By six thirty a.m., I was on the bridge, drinking my first cup of coffee and looking out at the sun already burning the surface of the water. The boat was a beehive of cranes, men, and swinging containers in constant, frantic motion. But the seas were calm, with this great big sun hanging just over the horizon and a haze of mist just beginning to dissipate.

When you're a sailor, you return to an ancient rhythm. The sun tells you when to get up and when to go to bed. It bookends your day with these incredible sunrises and sunsets. I couldn't wait to get out on the water. *This is why you go to sea,* I thought, as I looked out over my ship. I knew that every day on the water would be different. It always is. The sea would never look the same, its color changing from a granite black to vivid blue to an almost transparent green. Men go to sea for a lot of reasons — for the chance to work in the open air, for love of the oceans, because their father and their grandfather did it, or because they think it's easy money (it's not). But if you don't like mornings like this, when the whole voyage is ahead of you, you might as well stay home and go to work in a factory making toasters. When you're a seaman, leaving port always reminds you why, despite the danger and the boredom and the loneliness, you wanted to be one in the first place.

As we got ready to depart, I was up on the bridge talking with the port pilot, who would guide us out of Salalah harbor. The pilot called out, "Dead slow ahead," and the third mate answered, while I watched the RPMs on the engine, wanting to keep it well under our maximum. Within half an hour, we'd cleared the harbor, dropped off the pilot, and were gliding out of Salalah into the glassy Indian Ocean.

Every time I left a port, I thought about

how I'd gotten into this profession, how unlikely it was that I'd become a sea captain. If it hadn't been for a sailor who wanted to meet some girls and have a good time, I might never have even heard of the merchant marine. In fact, growing up in Winchester, Massachusetts, outside Boston, there were plenty of people who doubted I'd get farther than the corner bar.

My main problem was that I was a little wild. My nickname in high school was Jungle, and I have to say I earned it. My friends and I would occasionally end up in bars in the rougher parts of Boston or Cambridge and sometimes have to fight our way out. Once, in the early seventies, my buddies and I had a few beers and were roaming around Boston when we came across this huge group of people. "Carnival!" we thought in our stupor. We waded through the crowd until we got to the front and realized we were at a Mau Mau rally where a militant loony was preaching revolution. When the speaker saw us, he just froze. We were lucky we made it out alive, but it was just another night for the boys from Winchester.

You had to be pretty rugged to survive in Boston in the sixties and seventies. I grew up in a neighborhood with its share of milquetoasts and bookish nerds. But it was also full of guys who were throwbacks to a different era, guys who had no problem smacking you in the face as a way of testing what you were made of. And I didn't flinch. I was known for being someone who didn't back down from a fight. If you were soft, you stayed in your room until it was time to go away to college.

Some of my tough-mindedness goes back to my paternal grandparents, I'm sure. They lived in the Fidelis Way projects in Brighton, which was a tough area then and still is today. They'd come over from County Cork and arrived in America just in time for the Depression. Those dark years had affected them deeply. My grandparents probably didn't have that much more growing up in Ireland, but what amazed me was that they made everything and wasted nothing. They made their own soap and their own bread and their own curtains and they probably took a shot at making their own clothes at one point. I was one of eight kids, four girls and four boys, and my brothers and sisters used to hate going to Grandma and Grandpa Phillips' house. There were no second helpings at dinner, so you'd better eat what you got because there wasn't going to be anything else. I seldom saw my grandmother smile.

It's funny. I never thought of it at the time, but seeing how hard my grandparents had worked just to survive must have sunk into my brain. They'd built a life from the scraps the world had given them. One thing that my family never lacked was a work ethic, and in them I saw where it had begun.

My mother was from West Roxbury, then a pretty well-to-do part of Boston. Her parents were both teachers and she brought to the family the belief that you get an education, no matter what. I wasn't much of a student but at least she made me into a reader, someone always interested in improving himself. Beyond sticking my nose in a book every chance she got, my mother was the proverbial glue that held the family together. She was a warm and sympathetic person, curious about everything — if I had a problem, I went to her. Andrea says my father was the wind in the sails and my mother was the keel. She kept the family balanced. Without her, we would have been thrown to the sharks for sure.

My father was more typical of the Irish-American men of that time: he did things for you but he didn't exactly smother you with affection. He was as tough as they come: six foot two and barrel-chested with the Phillips short legs and long torso. He was a big sports guy, having played football and basketball at Northeastern, where he met my mother. My father proved his love by going out and working like hell. You wanted that *and* a hug every night, too? Go talk to your mother.

Dad wasn't a great communicator. I loved him but he was very hard to please. "Do it right, do it once, or don't do it at all" was his motto, quickly followed by "you horse's ass." It seemed that no matter what I did, his response would be, "You can always do better." That infuriated me at times. Yeah, but what about a little credit now for what I did right? I learned how to do things right from my dad. I wanted to prove myself to him, but I wanted to do it my way.

My dad believed that, when it came to us kids, the best defensc is a good offense. In the mornings, he'd scream at us to get out of thc single bathroom we all had to use. "You're going to be late for school!" he'd yell in his deep, booming voice. We were so terrified we'd whittled our bathroom time to the absolute minimum. Then we'd grab our books, race out to the street, and meet our friends for the long walk to school. Two minutes later we'd see my father driving by. He worked at the very same school we were going to, but he'd never so much as turn his head as he passed.

My friends would say, "Hey, isn't that your dad? Why isn't he picking us up?"

"You don't want to know" would be my answer.

It was like growing up with Vince Lombardi in a bad mood.

My philosophy was always a blend of my dad's intensity and my mom's caring. She took the edges off, but in many ways I'm just as tough-minded as he is. You *can* always do better. I hate to admit it, but the old man made his mark on me. With certain exceptions. My dad never once told me that he loved me or that he was proud of me (though I knew he did and that he was). I tell my kids I love them all the time. You learn what to inherit and what to leave behind.

I was a wise-guy kid. I'd meet teachers who on the first day would shake my hand and say, "Oh you have so much potential!" *You don't even know me,* I thought. And even though everyone knew my parents as teachers, I didn't go in for education very much. My dad taught business and math and served as the assistant football coach and the head basketball coach at the high school near our house and my mom taught fourth and sixth grade in Massachusetts and New Hampshire schools, but I was lurking near the bottom of every class, just doing enough to get by. For me, school was a place to ogle girls, play sports, and see my friends. Sort of like church, with sports.

Rebellion came naturally to me. I couldn't fake an interest in things that didn't interest me. Plus I knew I had other abilities: I was tough, I was a hard worker, and I knew how to learn.

But I always felt like I was a very lucky guy and life was going to take me to some interesting places. Even my teachers sensed that. One day, my French teacher, Doc Copeland, went around the room and said, "Joey, you're going to make an excellent bricklayer. Mary, you're going to be a housewife. Joanie, maybe an architect." When he came to me, he stopped and said, "You're going to do a lot of traveling." I was happy with that.

Sports was the biggest thing in my life, growing up. I had three brothers, and I wanted to beat them at games just as much as they wanted to beat me. You competed against your friends at Bogues Court, the local basketball pit. Your street competed against the next street in games where the only fouls were the ones that drew blood. And your school lived or died by who won the big football game against your rival.

It was an atmosphere that bred a certain mental toughness. I learned about life, about leaders and followers, by playing sports. Hell, I learned *everything* by playing sports. One of my favorite athletes was Larry Bird, who was born average and made himself into a superstar athlete by sheer mental toughness. That's something I respected.

I played football, basketball, and lacrosse in high school and I was just average in all of them. Sophomore year, I caught the football coach's eye and he took an interest in me. Coach Manny Marshall would see me in the school hallways and he'd come up to me like I was on the verge of taking the team to the state championship. "Oh, how're you feeling today? Drink plenty of milkshakes, you've got to put on more weight. Oh, you don't have to go to gym, don't worry about gym, I can take care of that. How you feeling? Feeling strong?" Junior year, I was out with mono and after years of being obsessed with sports, I realized there were other ways of having fun — namely, partying. But Coach Marshall still zeroed in on me every time he spotted me. "Don't tell anyone else," he'd say. "But you could be captain next year."

I wasn't good enough to be the captain. I hadn't played all year. I didn't deserve the title.

Coach Marshall expected me to fit his system, which required players to live and die by the score. He couldn't understand the fact that I enjoyed myself whether we were winning or losing. "Why are you grinning?" he'd yell at me. "Because I'm having fun?" I'd answer. For him, football was a religion and if I was laughing with my friends when the team was losing, then I must be the Antichrist. I went from being his star prospect to riding the bench. I even quit the team before the final game of the season, against our archrival Woburn, just because the sport had stopped being fun. I watched the game as part of the band, where I played saxophone. I'd made the band leader deliriously happy: "It's the first time someone's told the football coach, 'Sorry, I can't play because I have to be in the band.'" Coach Marshall hated me after that.

I guess I did have something to learn about being part of a team.

I loved sports, but I bucked against the restrictions. It was the same with basketball.

The JV coach called me and a guy named Gunk Johnson after a practice early in the season and turned to me first and said, "Phillips, I'm not going to play you because your father didn't play me when I was a student. And Gunk, I'm not going to play you because I don't like you." He thought he'd run us out of there. When the coach asked us what we were going to do, Gunk and I looked at each other and then I said, "Coach, we're gonna stick."

That was my motto: I'm gonna stick. Especially if you try to push me.

I guess right then you'd have pegged me for the merchant marine. Every guy I met in the merchant marine had stories like that. We weren't the kids who made class president. We were the guys who rode beat-up motorcycles to school, played the offensive line, and drank in the Fells, the nearby woods where all the kids hung out. We went our own way. We were the square pegs someone tried to smash into a round hole and said, "Nope, not gonna do it."

In 1975, I was well on my way to fulfilling my detractor's prediction that I wouldn't do very much with my life. I'd had a few jobs, working as a security guard at Raytheon, shuttling checks to the Federal Reserve from the local banks, and driving a taxi. I was a hack in Arlington, a town north of Boston. It didn't have much of a future, but it was colorful. One time a guy I'd never seen before jumped in my cab, gave me an address, and told me he had to go in and get the money. I pulled around back, expecting him to try to pull a fast one on me, but within a minute a woman came screaming out the door and jumped in a car, followed by this maniac. He jumped in my cab and screamed, "I'll give you twenty bucks if you can catch her." It was clear to me that the man and the woman were caught up in some wild domestic drama — which I never got to the bottom of — and I'd suddenly landed in the middle of it. I hit the gas and we went through the streets of Arlington like the chase scene from *Bullitt.* Finally I pulled even with the woman and saw her terrified face through the window. That's when my fare yelled, "Run her off the road!" Apparently, he thought I was a hit man, not a cab driver. I pulled over, collected my $20 for catching her, then threw him out of the cab.

I learned a lot. It's a tough job and you can't go by the book; you have to use your imagination. But I had no real direction, no real plan for myself in life. I'd gone to the University of Massachusetts at Amherst, mainly because my parents were both teachers and wanted me to give college a shot. I'd studied animal science, because I wanted to be a vet. But one class, in which I had to use a slide rule, told me I wasn't cut out for college. I dropped out after my first semester, the victim of too much partying, too many girls, and not enough hitting the books. If there was anything wild going on at that campus in the fall of 1974, I was probably around it.

So I became a taxi driver. And one day I was coming out the back way of Logan Airport when I picked up a sharp-looking guy with pressed dungarees and a leather jacket that looked like it cost a thousand bucks. I was impressed. "Where you going?" I asked the guy. "I want some action," he said. Not an unusual request in the city of Boston in the mid-seventies.

"What kind of action are you looking for?"

"I want booze and I want broads," he said.

"Okay, I can do that," I said. I cranked the meter and headed for the Combat Zone, which in those days was a single street packed with college girl revues and blazing neon signs even during the day. You could get anything in the Combat Zone, and I mean anything. You want a double-jointed Romanian girl who plays Beethoven concertos and excels in field hockey? Done. You want a rocket-propelled grenade and an old-fashioned? Done. I mean, the place never let you down. It was Disney World for adults.

When we got to the Zone, the guy's eyes got big in my rearview mirror. "This'll do?" I said. He nodded. "This is good."

It was a $5 fare and he tipped me $5. I'd walked twenty bags up ten flights of stairs for an old lady and been handed a twenty-five-cent tip, so $5 got my attention. As he got out, I asked the guy what he did for a living. That was my personal form of career counseling. If I got someone in the back of my cab who looked like he was interesting and who threw money around like it was confetti, I asked him what his job was.

"I'm a merchant mariner," he said.

I nodded. "What's that?"

"Well, we carry cargo in ships."

"Sounds exciting."

Which it didn't. What sounded exciting is pulling into a port at ten thirty in the morning and going to a place like the Combat Zone with a pocketful of cash and the nicest leather jacket in Boston, looking for a good time all by himself.

As he was walking into some strip joint, I

yelled after him, "Hey, how do you get into that?"

The guy had probably been at sea for three months and he really didn't want to spend any more time talking to a male college dropout. "Here," he said, and he handed me a card with the address of a seaman's school in Baltimore. Then he was gone.

I wrote the school but never heard back. I forgot about it until my brother Michael came back to Boston and showed up at a keg party I was hosting in my apartment. He was at the Massachusetts Maritime Academy down in Buzzards Bay, and he gave it a glowing review. "It's not bad," he said, over a plastic cup of frosty cold Falstaff beer. "They don't shave your head. It's not really a military academy, there are not really any uniforms, there's not a lot of discipline and when you get out, you can stay home six months out of the year." I was working two jobs, making $220 a week, and I was ready for something new. I'd always liked Jack Kerouac and the idea of traveling the world looked better after every shift hauling prostitutes and businessmen around Boston. My neighbors Mrs. Paulson and Mr. Muracco worked hard and were instrumental in getting me accepted at the

68

Academy, and my high school varsity basketball coach wrote a letter to the coach there recommending me. A few months later, I was in. I couldn't wait to go.

I drove to the campus in my VW bus, nearly cross-eyed with a massive hangover from a final blowout my friends had thrown the night before. I rolled in feeling like John Belushi after an all-night toga party. The MMA's campus is tiny, a group of maybe six dorms, a training ship, a few classroom buildings, an administration center, and a library. When I first saw it, I thought, *This doesn't look too bad.* And the admiral who greeted us was very polite, especially to the parents. "Today you lost your boy," he said at one point. "When we return him to you, he'll be a man."

When the last parents' car had cleared the parking lot, the instructors turned and started screaming at us. We weren't these bright young men to be cherished anymore. We were "youngies," and youngies were worth about as much as spit on pavement. The instructors screamed at us as they herded us into a barbershop to get our heads shaved and screamed at us while they marched at double-time all over the campus before ending the day by screaming at us for no reason at all. The MMA turned out to be a true-blue military school where they broke you down before they built you into a merchant seaman. I had to give it to my brother. He'd gotten me good.

We went through a year of constant hazing. There was an admiral called Shakey who was supposedly in charge of the academy, but the upperclassmen ran the school. You'd be walking down the hall and a three-striper — a junior — would come around a corner and demand you list the twenty-five things found in all lifeboats, in alphabetical order. If you couldn't do it, you had to drop and give him twenty push-ups. On the summer cruise to Bermuda, they'd dress you in four layers of clothing including a winter coat, gloves, hat, and goggles and take you into the engine room on the training ship in the middle of summer, where the temperature hits 160 degrees, and work you until you dropped from dehydration. And you had to suck a lollipop through the whole thing, don't ask me why. If you ratted on a classmate, they'd cut a fire hose, slip the end under your door, and turn it on full blast. Say good-bye to your stereo equipment and your camera, pal. If you messed with a four-striper — a senior — the boys would have what they called a "blanket party." You'd be sleeping in your bunk, and all of a sudden a blanket would be thrown over your head and ten upperclassmen would pummel you to within an inch of your life. Or the upperclassmen would ambush you in a place called Four Corners. People had nightmares about that place. You'd turn the corner and there would be a gang of stripers lying in wait. They'd immediately begin screaming for us to "be a steam engine." One guy would be the vertical piston, another would be the prop and the shaft and the steam drum, which meant you were running in circles or pumping your body up and down or making a damn fool of yourself in some other way. For hours.

It'd all be illegal now. Back then, hazing was a character builder, but now it's not politically correct. I'm sure they have sensitivity training there the first week and you can get demerits for even implying that a youngie might tie a better knot. But in my time, some of the lieutenant commanders who lived on campus were afraid to walk into the dorms.

One senior, an upperclassman, made a special project of me. We just rubbed each other the wrong way, mostly because he was a stickler for rules and respect, and I don't give any unless I get it in return. It was like a chemical reaction. Instant dislike on both sides. He made it his mission to drive me out of the school.

Every time he saw me on campus, he would make my life miserable. "What are you, a virgin?" he'd scream at me. "What's the matter, never been laid?" I wasn't going to take that from a punk kid who was younger than me. "Way before you, loser," I said. And ever since that day, he'd had it in for me.

One time, close to the Christmas holidays, I was walking with some classmates from mess hall toward our dorm. Of course, he was waiting for me at the Four Corners.

"Goddamn it, Phillips, are you still here?" he yelled. Some of his friends snickered. Everyone knew the skinny bastard had it in for me. "Why don't you just go pack your bag, because you'll never make it out of here. I'm guaranteeing that right now."

If I'd ever had any doubts of making it out, they ended right there. My ancestors are from County Cork, and I'm told it's known as the Rebel County, for its opposition to British rule. I have their genes.

"I swear to God," I whispered under my breath, "you'll never get me out of here."

I smiled at him, a big, enthusiastic smile. He did not like that.

"Drop and give me twenty!" he yelled. Yeah, they actually said that.

I shook my head. "Sir, that ain't even worth going down for," I said.

He looked . . . well, I would say "shocked."

"What did you say, youngie?"

"I said, 'Sir, that ain't even worth going down for.' Give me forty."

Two hours later, I was soaked with sweat, doing push-ups and sit-ups. I was dirty and sweaty and my arms felt like ropes of wet noodles. He was watching the sweat rolling down my face, enjoying himself. All my classmates had gone back to the dorm.

Finally, he got hungry. He announced he was heading off for dinner.

"I want to come back and find you here, or it's two weeks' worth of demerits," he said. Demerits were worse than anything — you'd spend your entire weekend working them off.

When he was gone, one of his classmates came running out of the mess hall. I watched the upperclassman approach. He was one of the nicer guys in the senior class.

"That's it, Phillips. Dismissed."

I looked up. Then I dropped down for another twenty.

"No thank you, sir, I'm fine," I said, my face a few inches from his highly polished shoes. I felt like I was going to pass out, but I was pissed off. I wouldn't be the one to break.

I heard a sigh as I counted out twenty.

"Don't be a dickhead, Phillips, I'm cutting you a break here. Dismissed."

I stood up, out of breath, and looked him in the eye.

"Need to hear it from him, sir."

"He's an asshole. So that's not going to happen."

I thought for a minute, breathing hard. I didn't want to let the bastard win. But the admission by an upperclassman that this jerk was in the wrong was good enough for me. Besides, I thought another twenty push-ups would damn near kill me.

"Very good, sir." And I walked away. The thought of my tormentor coming to find an empty hall gave me a laugh. I owe the fact that I graduated partially to that numbskull.

For me, the best motivator in the world is idiocy administered by a bully.

Not everyone was so determined to gut it out. Out of 350 guys at the beginning of our freshman year, 180 graduated. Not one of them was a milquetoast, believe me.

But I liked the academy. First of all, there were no girls, and they had been one of my downfalls at college. They were a distraction I couldn't handle; at the time, crazily enough, I thought this was a plus (but not for long). And the school was filled with guys from a million different backgrounds but with a similar outlook on life: they wanted adventure, freedom, physical work, and independence. They were, for the most part, guys who had a wild sense of humor and too much imagination to work in an office. I could appreciate that.

The academy taught me discipline, which is something I needed in my life. I learned to stop messing around so much: when something needs to get done in the merchant marine, it gets done. It wasn't make-up work; every task had real value. It allowed you to stay safe on the ship and get to your next port of call. On a ship, there are no idle hands; everyone has a task that he has to accomplish. What you do affects every man on the ship.

But the clincher came in the summer of 1976, during my first training ship cruise. The tall ships were in Boston for the bicentennial and made it a spectacular time to be sailing in the harbor. My classmates and I got to work on the *Patriot State,* the training ship. We were painting, running lines, doing drills, all out in the fresh air during that summer. I loved it. It was physical and you dropped into your bunk at the end of the day knowing you'd accomplished something with a minimum of bullshit.

It was the first time since high school that I'd truly felt part of a team. But this time, something was different. I didn't feel the need to go my own way so much. There was a lifestyle and tradition here. Even a freedom, if you could stick it out. I wanted to be part of it.

It was at the academy that I started to hear the stories of the merchant marine: how during the Revolutionary War, American merchant sailors working as privateers captured or destroyed three times more than the navy ships did, and how from just one town in Massachusetts, a thousand sailors disappeared fighting the British. How the Barbary pirates kidnapped merchant mariners and sold them into "the awful fate of Moorish slavery." How pirates on the Spanish main would capture sailors, rob them blind, and lock the crew in the hold while they set fire to the deck and set the ship adrift. How America was really built on the backs of wooden ships sailing out of ports like Salem to the far reaches of the world, from Cádiz to the Antarctic, carrying everything from molasses, gunpowder, gold dust, Chinese silk, to, of course, African

76

slaves. The merchant marine always got there first — Java, Sumatra, Fiji. We blazed the trails across the oceans. The navy followed us. That's what you learned at the MMA.

But it wasn't all history. Seniors would ship out on commercial vessels and come back, their pockets bulging with money, and tell us stories about the stunning women in Venezuela or a brawl in Tokyo that destroyed an entire bar. Pirates were always lurking in these stories, as newly minted captains would gossip about how bad the Strait of Malacca had gotten or the best way to fight off bandits in Colombia. These guys made every trip sound like it was straight out of Robert Louis Stevenson.

I was dying to get out there and see it all for myself.

THREE:
-7 DAYS

The industry believes very strongly that it's not for the companies to train crews to use firearms and then arm them. . . . If you open fire, there's potential for retaliation. Crews could get injured or killed, to say nothing of damage to the ship.
— *Giles Noakes, chief maritime security officer for BIMCO, an international association of ship owners* Christian Science Monitor, *April 8*

The first day out of Salalah went smoothly. We were making good time down the east coast of the Arabian peninsula headed for the Gulf of Aden. So far, it was a normal run. I hoped it stayed that way.

I posted the standard procedures for a pirate attack in my night orders, which the mates read and put into practice. But that was just a paper reminder. I needed to see how the guys responded to a live-action threat. Salalah to Djibouti is a three- or four-day trip, but that first day, everyone is exhausted. A ship is like being in a womb: you have the water rushing by, making that gurgling sound, you have the rhythm of the engines, you have the whole ship vibrating to the turn of the screw. That's why sailors love that first day at sea. You've left your troubles behind and you've entered this comforting world you know so well. But the bad thing is, you get lulled into a sense of safety. I didn't want to crack down on the security lapses I'd seen until we were out on the bright blue. We were heading into the most dangerous waters in the world, and I wanted my ship to be ready.

The morning of April 2, I walked up to the bridge and grabbed my cup of coffee. The radar was clear. I looked over at Shane, the chief mate, who'd been up there since 4 a.m. We talked about our plans for the day, what kind of overtime was likely to be needed, what projects he was working on. Fairly quickly, the conversation turned to bullshitting about sports and the latest news. I'd told Shane before the trip began, "I'm going to start backing away on this run. You're going to step up and do more: overtime budgets, maintenance, safety and emergency stuff. You've already shown me you can do it." He was on his way to being a captain and I knew he was ready for more responsibility.

After a few minutes, I said, "We're running an unannounced security drill today."

A chief mate is by far the hardest-working man on a ship. He's running around fourteen hours a day, seven days a week, and a security drill just makes his life more complicated.

Most mates would say, "Damn it, Cap, do we have to?" But Shane was different. "Great, I love unannounced drills," he said. Music to my ears.

"Eat your breakfast and we'll do it at 9 a.m.," I said. "You won't finish any work today, but we have to do this."

"We're ready," he said. "Let's —"

"Don't tell me what you're going to do," I said. "Let's just see how we perform."

At two minutes to nine, I climbed up to the bridge. My third mate, Colin Wright, was there with an AB. I walked up to him and said, "There's a boat coming along, starboard side. Four men, with weapons, acting hostile." It was the start of the security drill.

He looked at me.

"Ohhhkay," he said.

I waited. He was just looking at me. "Well,

you've got to do something," I said.

"Oh! Okay," Colin said. And he rang the general alarm, which sounds all over the ship.

"No, we don't want to do the general alarm first," I explained. "We want to do the whistle first." You want the pirates to know you're aware of them and are getting ready to defend yourself. The general alarm rings only inside the ship, while the whistle can be heard up to five miles away.

Colin sounded the whistle. I watched the crew swing into action. Each man had a muster point that he was supposed to run to; about half of them were heading the wrong way. Not good.

"Fire pump," I called.

"Right," Colin answered. On a ship like the *Maersk Alabama,* you have probably thirty-five fire stations with hoses and nozzles. But the pirate hoses are specially placed to repel an attack. These five hoses — three on the stern and two facing back aft — are secured into position and left in the "On" position so that you can hit the pump switch from the bridge and *boom,* you're shooting water. You want to be able to control the fire hoses from the bridge during a pirate attack. Not only is it impossible for the pirates to advance up a ladder when that stream is hitting them full force, but the fact that the hoses are going full blast tells the intruders that we're ready for them, even if they're miles away.

When Colin hit the button, however, nothing happened. It turned out a valve on the fire pump had been left open, which meant no water could flow to the hoses.

An absent-minded able-bodied seaman was on the bridge, just standing there looking like he'd lost his dog. He needed to know the correct routines, as well, so I started going over them with him.

"We're under attack by pirates," I said. "What are you supposed to do?"

He looked at me. "I'm . . . supposed . . . to . . . ," he said slowly.

"You're supposed to give the security signal first."

Sounding the proper signal takes the right touch; you've really got to accentuate the horn or it's going to sound like "abandon ship" or another call. And this man could never do it. It always sounded like he was playing "The Star-Spangled Banner" on the thing. Another foul-up. I ordered him to hit the fire pump, which has a red "off" button and a green "on" button. Of course, he pushed red and walked away. "No," I said. "You have to push green and then check to make sure it's flowing."

"Got it," he said.

No you don't, I wanted to reply.

Next I sent the AB to lock the three bridge doors. If the pirates board the ship, all the key access points — engine room, bridge — should be locked. You want to prevent the pirates from gaining control of the ship. Because once they do, they can set course for the coast of Somalia, where there's no police presence, and stuff you into a safe house where Jack Bauer himself would never find you. Then they could sell you to the highest bidder, like Al Qaeda.

That was my deepest fear, and I knew it rattled my entire crew. To end up in some stinking hole with a blindfold on, chained to a post like an animal and at the mercy of fundamentalist militants, is the worst fate imaginable. Every one of us worried about being the next Daniel Pearl.

The AB ran off the bridge. Colin was doing all the right things. He'd switched the ship's radio to VHF, he'd hit the lights, he'd gotten the fire pump going, and he'd begun simulating evasive maneuvers.

"What's the nonduress password?" I called out. That would let anyone inside a locked door know the mate on the other side of the door didn't have a gun to his head.

"Mr. Jones," he said.

Wrong. "Mr. Jones," in fact, was the code for the SSA, or secret security alarm, which is a button the captain presses in the case of an emergency, instantly patching him via satellite to a rescue center manned around the clock. The agent there asks a question, "Is Mr. Jones there?" If you answer "no," you're not under threat and the agent will debrief you on the situation. If you answer "yes," you have an AK-47 at your back and the agent will break off contact because he knows you can't answer freely.

It is like the president's nuclear code. The third mate wasn't even supposed to know it.

"Not even close," I said. "It's 'suppertime.' "

Colin winced. We clearly had our work cut out for us.

Meanwhile, the AB arrived back on the bridge. He'd been tasked with closing the three bridge doors, which should have taken about twenty seconds. He'd been gone five minutes.

"Where've you been?" I already knew the answer.

"I went to close the doors."

"Which doors did you close?"

"Every door on every level."

"Did they have locks on them, these doors?"

"Ah," he said. "No."

The whole purpose of locking doors is to isolate decks against penetration by the intruders, to create safe zones where the crew can move in case their hiding places are breached. Unlocked doors don't offer much of a safe zone.

"So you were closing the doors, not locking them?"

"Yeah," he admitted, "I was just closing them."

"Which doesn't do much good, does it?"

"No, I guess not."

Colin shook his head. "I've gone over this with him six, seven times," he said.

I nodded.

"We are in search of excellence," I said, "but oh, we will accept so much less."

A few of the guys laughed. They knew that was one of my sayings.

The drill ended. I gathered all the crew except the third mate in the ship's office and broke down what had gone right and wrong. It hadn't gone perfectly by any means. I don't want to give the impression that this was a ship of fools. Most of these guys were good sailors, but every captain has their own way of doing things, and you have to teach the mates your approach. That first drill was a shake-out exercise. I knew the crew would step up and things would improve drastically.

During the critique, Mike, the chief engineer, called out, "What about a backup safe room in the after steering room?"

If pirates attacked, the chief engineer would go immediately to the engine room. The first and third engineer would go to the after steering room. The rest of the crew would run to the ship's office. But if the pirates breached that door, the crew would need a second safe room and after steering was a perfect candidate. It was hidden off a tiny corridor and would be nearly impossible for the pirates to find.

"Good point," I said. "Let's make it happen."

"What if they're listening in on the radio?" an AB asked.

"Unlikely," I said. "But it's a good point. So we won't mention locations. If I hear from the chief mate, I assume he's on deck. If I hear from the second mate, I assume he's at his muster point. Engineers in the engine room. If you don't have a muster point, I'll assume you're in the safe room. Everyone got that?"

The men nodded.

"What else have we got in case of pirate attack?" I asked.

"We've got twist locks and flares," somebody called out. A twist lock is a heavy metal lock used to secure containers to the deck. They were great for throwing down at pirates and braining them, but completely inaccurate. We had ten on the bridge ready to go.

"Okay, everyone know what they need to work on?"

More nods.

Whenever you get a bunch of sailors together to drill for pirate attacks, there's usually one guy who's seen just one too many John Wayne movies and wants to go toe to toe with the bastards. Usually, he's sixty-five years old and three hundred pounds and gets out of breath running to be first in the dinner line. Sure enough, as we were wrapping up the drill, this crusty old AB spoke up. "Cap, we got to have weapons," he said. "I want to fight." The motto of the United States Merchant Marine Academy is, after all, *Acta non verba,* or "Deeds, not words."

But it wasn't going to happen. This guy could barely climb a ladder and now he wanted to take on a group of young, fit pirates who would as soon gut him and throw him overboard as look at him.

"Listen," I said. "We don't want to bring a knife to a gunfight. Fighting is an option, but we have to play it by ear. First, we muster. Then we get the hoses and lights ready. Then we secure ourselves. Got it?"

Nods all around.

"Then, if we find out that all they have is knives and clubs, we can use hatchets and axes and lead pipes that we have stockpiled. We can use twist-lock poles" — long steel bars used to secure the containers — "as pikes." The image of doing battle with pirates like medieval warriors might seem ridiculous, but there had actually been cases where a crew charged out of their safe room waving poles and axes and the pirates freaked out and jumped over the side. It was a dangerous move, but the prospect of spending four months being held for ransom drove the sailors to desperation.

We also decided that if the pirates boarded, no one would walk outside with their keys. If the pirates captured one guy with a set, they could access the whole ship. I also ordered every seaman to lock every door behind them. On an earlier trip with Mike, the chief engineer, I'd complained about the pirate cage bars on the engine room, which the crew liked because they allowed air to pass into the hot interior. But that meant the heavy watertight door was often left open, and I wanted it secured at all times, as the engine room led directly into the house and intruders could race straight up to the bridge. Mike agreed to get the pirate bars off and to have the big steel door secured at all times. And we'd previously agreed that deadbolts needed to be installed on the inside of the watertight doors, in case the pirates were able to shoot off the locks. We'd already done that on the superstructure, but there were a few doors elsewhere that still needed the deadbolts. Mike ordered his guys to get on it.

"Good," I said. "I know these precautions are a pain in the ass, but they might save our lives. We need to do better next time."

With that, I let the guys get back to their work. The drill had taken fifteen minutes, the critique thirty.

Another captain might have taken that moment to pull some crew aside and chew them out. But over the years I'd learned a different way of command. I didn't want to be a screamer like my father or some captains I'd sailed with. I knew how completely that had turned me off to what he was saying. I didn't want to aim for perfection when some guys weren't capable of it. We had to crawl before we could walk. Then we could think about running.

That instinct also went back to my initiation into the merchant marine — my first trip on my license.

When I left the academy, I had a third mate's license, which allowed me to work at the bottom of the officer ladder on any ship. But you have to wait for the call. I went home and started painting houses, waiting for the right job to come along. I'd passed on Florida and Bahamas runs — too boring for my taste. I was at a girlfriend's swimming pool when a personnel guy for a shipping company called me and said, "I've got a ship and I need a third mate."

"Where you going?"

"Alaska."

Alaska sounded different, alluring even. I was on a plane to Seattle three hours later.

After half a day in the air, I pulled up to the dock in a taxi. The driver stopped in front of what looked like a floating junk pile. "Wrong place, buddy," I said. "I'm working on a ship. This is a barge." And he looked at me like I was slow or something and said, "You're the third guy I dropped here today. This is your ship."

When I walked onboard, the second mate said to me, "You'll never be on another ship like this one." He was right.

The *Aleut Provider* was heading up from Seattle to Alaska and back. We were scheduled to go through the Inland Passage up through Charlottetown over to Kodiak, through the Aleutian Islands, and then up to the Pribilof Islands in the Arctic Circle, hitting a bunch of tiny fishing villages where they process the salmon and king crab that the trawlers bring in. We would also be bringing supplies up to the Indian villages on a contract with the U.S. Government, but anything we hauled back at a price was pure profit. So the ship was loaded down with every kind of frontier product you can imagine: seal skins heaped in the cargo hold, salmon meat stuffed in the refrigerated holds. And piled on the deck, high above the gunwales, were trucks, empty beer kegs for refilling in Seattle, motorcycles, telephone poles, snowmobiles, and fire hydrants.

It looked like the Beverly Hillbillies' Cruise to Nowhere.

I was a third mate on his first trip. I rarely spoke to the captain, that's how low on the totem pole I was. My room was a tiny space with a wooden door, which would later be ripped off its hinges by a storm and be replaced by a wool blanket, my only protection against the arctic winds. I would wake up in the morning and there would be water flowing under my feet. I wondered what the hell I'd gotten myself into.

My third week on the water, there was trouble. The captain had logged (that is, reported) myself and the second mate for a minor infraction — not doing the tide report for our next port. We'd actually written the tides down, but then the chief mate had mislaid them, thinking our report was scrap paper. The chief mate went to the captain to argue our case, but the guy refused to hear him out. So the chief mate quit. The second mate quit in solidarity, followed by his wife, who was working as the steward utility. The bosun quit. The able-bodied seamen quit.

Everyone quit working and left the ship. Suddenly I, a glorified taxi driver, was the chief mate on a ship headed toward the Arctic Circle. We were so short of men we had to hire a couple of teenagers, one fourteen and the other sixteen, as able-bodied seamen. The captain didn't care. All that mattered was that he believed everyone onboard was sober. The captain was an ex-alcoholic who'd banned any kind of liquor from the ship. But after hours some of the crew would get buzzed on Everclear grain alcohol. It's very, very strong stuff and something about it and the weird light up there kind of made everyone a little crazy. So the captain would come out of his quarters once a day and shout at me, "Are those guys drinking, Phillips? I think I smell alcohol on this boat." And I would say, "I'll watch 'em, Cap, I'll watch 'em." Meanwhile I'd been drinking with the crew most nights.

I managed to coax everyone back on the ship. But after a couple weeks we pulled in to Pelican Cove, Alaska, which has a fish pro cessing plant, six or seven houses, one bar, and that's it. The captain ordered some extra work and the entire crew marched off the ship again. Everyone walked down the gangplank and headed to Rosie's Bottom-less Bar.

We walked in and the bartender said, "Hey, did you guys see any bears?"

"No, why?"

"Well, two guys coming from a ship the last time around were eaten by bears."

So not only did I have to persuade the guys to return to the ship again, I also had to watch my back for black bears while I did it. It took me until the early hours of the morning, but I finally shepherded all the deserters back to the *Provider.*

The captain was standing on the bridge

wing as I marched the crew back.

"I brought 'em back, Cap," I said.

He just glared at us. Everyone went to bed, including the captain. We got up the next day, had breakfast, and got back to work. No one said a word. It seemed like creative chaos was the order of the day in the merchant marine.

But the trip also had its glorious moments. From the deck of the boat, gliding along those beautiful waters, we'd see moose, bears, foxes. Orcas breached the surface twenty yards away and then swam alongside us for miles. We rescued two fishermen, a father and son, who were floating along in a rowboat in the middle of the Gulf of Alaska. Their boat had gone up in flames and even though they were in their exposure suits, the cold was so intense that they were near death from exposure. So the fishermen were debating who was going to shoot the other with a shotgun when we spotted them from the deck. They were so cold they couldn't talk for hours; they just sat there shivering. For a day, they'd watched ships sail by, so close they'd been able to read the names off the bows, but no one heard their cries for help. And later in the trip, I saw an island with trees and snow on it growing out of the middle of the ocean where the charts said there was nothing at all. When the sun rose, the bottom of the island slowly melted away and then the whole thing disappeared. It turns out it was a phenomenon called super-refraction where at high latitudes you can see around the curvature of the earth. I was actually staring at a mountaintop three hundred miles away, but it seemed like we were going to glide right up to it.

This was a world few people get to see. The wild characters, the heart-stopping scenery, the outrageous behavior. It was everything I'd become a merchant mariner to be a part of.

I was hooked.

That trip began my education in how to command men. (Lesson number one: Learn how to talk to your guys.) It also taught me that, on the sea, nothing goes like you expect it to. You have to be prepared for a staggering amount of possibilities, from mutiny to hungry bears to optical illusions at sea. And you have to improvise. Captains who become fixated on one thing — like the crew having a beer or two — quickly lose the trust of their men.

That was doubly true in the waters off the Somali coast. To survive in Apache country, you have to think like an Apache.

■ ■ ■ ■

The next day dawned sunny and hot. The Office of Naval Intelligence in Maryland e-mailed its latest Worldwide Threats to Shipping Report. I opened it immediately. Pirate attacks and other threats were broken down by region. For the North Atlantic, the Mediterranean, and the entire Atlantic, there wasn't a single incident reported.

I skipped ahead to the East Africa section. There were thirty-nine attacks reported. *For a single week.* I sucked in my breath. The bulletin was like a police blotter for mariners, and it told me that East Africa was the last place in the world you wanted to be right now.

I flicked my eye over some of the entries:

1. Vessel reported suspicious approach 20 Mar 09 at 0600 UTC while underway, Bab-el-Mandeb.
2. Five men in two speed boats armed with guns approached vessel from the port bow, Bab-el-Mandeb.
3. Chemical tanker reported attempted boarding 29 Mar 09, Gulf of Aden.
4. German navy tanker (FGS

SPESSART) fired upon 29 Mar 09. Seven pirates in a skiff opened fire on the naval ship, mistaking it for a merchant vessel, Gulf of Aden.

5. Vessel fired upon, approached by one skiff with seven men onboard armed with AK-47s, Gulf of Aden.

6. Bulk carrier (TITAN) hijacked 19 Mar 09. Six men in a speed boat armed with AK47s and pistols boarded and hijacked the vessel, Gulf of Aden.

7. Cargo vessel (DIAMOND FALCON) fired upon 14 Mar 09. Two skiffs with men onboard armed with automatic weapons and RPGs fired upon the vessel.

8. Vessel reported attempted hijacking 1 Jan 09 at 1730 local time, Gulf of Aden.

9. Bulk carrier fired upon 30 Mar 09. A speed boat approached the vessel while a mother ship was sighted further back, Indian Ocean.

10. Container ship reported suspicious approach 28 Mar 09, Tanzania.

The pirates were approaching and attacking each and every kind of vessel that ventured around the Horn of Africa: tankers, fishing schooners, even luxury cruise ships. Nothing was safe out there. There were so many ships flying down the coast of East Africa, you had to hope you weren't one of the unlucky ones to see a few pirate boats pop up on your radar. Once you saw them, you had very few ways of preventing an attack: speed, fire hoses, and deception were pretty much your only tools. The Somalis had automatic weapons, speedboats, rocket-propelled grenades, and a reputation for complete ruthlessness.

It was like a lion and a herd of wildebeest on the African plain. You just hoped there was safety in numbers, because if the lion chose you, you were going to have a very, very bad day. And just as the lion looks for weakness — the slow, the lame, the young — pirates zeroed in on ships that looked defenseless.

But Americans seemed out of the reach of pirates. The last time seamen on a U.S. ship were taken hostage by pirates was two hundred years ago, during the days of the Barbary corsairs, Muslim bandits who'd operated out of North African ports like Tripoli and Algiers, on the other side of the continent. Back then, piracy was near the top of Thomas Jefferson's priority list. In 1801, 20 percent of the U.S. federal budget was spent paying ransoms to the African buccaneers. Crewmen from the ships lived and worked as slaves in the luxurious homes of the Algerian pirate chiefs. America even fought two bloody wars with the Barbary states, giving the Marines' Hymn its famous second line — "to the shores of Tripoli."

That was a long time ago. Piracy had faded from the nation's memory. And if you did get in trouble, it was assumed you were on your own. The U.S. Navy hadn't been in the pirate-hunting business for two centuries. But by the end of that second day, I felt the crew was ready for an attack. Things could always improve, but we'd made a good start. Little did I know that the men who were going to test us to our limits were already on the water.

FOUR:
-6 DAYS

The situation in this region is extremely serious. We have not seen such a surge in pirate activity in this area previously. These pirates are not afraid to use significant firepower in attempts to bring vessels under their control. Over 260 seafarers have been taken hostage in Somalia this year. Unless further action is taken, seafarers remain in serious danger.

— Statement by Pottengal Mukundan, director of the International Maritime Bureau, August 21, 2008

I'd never been approached by a pirate ship in my entire career, but I'd come close. On a run through the Gulf of Aden the previous September, I'd been standing on the bridge when Shane, my chief mate, pulled me aside.

"Cap, you know I mentioned to you that ship we passed earlier?"

I nodded. On the more well-traveled routes around the world, you'd see the same ships again and again, running the same legs of the trip you're on and stopping in the same ports. Their names pop up on the AIS, the Automatic Identification System. We'd passed a container ship the night before. Shane had been monitoring the radio and heard its name mentioned.

"Six hours ago, it was taken by pirates."

"Where?" I said.

"Just north of the Kenya-Somalia border."

It had been a roll of the dice. The pirates had turned north and gotten them, instead of turning south and attacking us.

Piracy has seasons, just like the weather. The Indian Ocean is usually as smooth as glass, a dazzling tropical blue, what sailors call "pretty water," but from late June through early September, the *khareef* season arrives, bringing southwest monsoons sweeping across the ocean, making it dangerous for small craft. That means pirate season runs from October through May. By April, the bandits are looking to make a few rich hauls before the stormy season puts them out of business.

Most of the pirates, I knew, came from a northeastern region of Somalia known as Puntland, named after the mythical Land of

Punt, known to the ancient Egyptians as the source of gold, ebony, and African blackwood. But from a place that exported riches to the Pharaohs, it had become a place where famine, bandits, and chaos were the order of the day. The government's collapse in 1991 brought on mass starvation and the arrival of a U.N. peacekeeping force led by the U.S. Army. That all ended on October 3 and 4, 1993, when the infamous "Black Hawk Down" incident occurred and eighteen American soldiers and one Malaysian lost their lives in a horrific gunfight.

The pirates claimed they were former fishermen who'd been forced into banditry when their livelihoods disappeared. According to them, foreign trawlers had arrived off their coastline and taken hundreds of millions of dollars of tuna, sardines, mackerel, and swordfish out of the ocean. Other ships dumped hazardous waste in the water to make a quick buck. The local fishermen couldn't hope to compete with the advanced fleets from Spain and Japan and found that the intruders shot at them when they tried to work the same coastline. Soon they were reduced to begging, and even starvation.

But I'd seen schools of mackerel, tuna, and other fish every time I'd gone down the coast of Somalia. There was a living to be made out there. I believed the Somalis had simply found easier work: piracy.

In the 1990s, boats began leaving Somali ports like Eyl with armed young men aboard to seize the foreign crews and hold them for a small ransom. They were ruthless, professional bandits who'd seen a chance to make it big and took it. They made $120 million in 2008, in a country where most people make around $600 a year. These guys had left any thoughts of sardines and swordfish far behind. To me, there was no difference between them and a bunch of Mafia extortionists, or armed robbers sticking up a gas station. Sure, they're poor, but stealing is stealing.

When the pirates began, in the early 1990s, they would shoot out of their local ports in beaten-up wooden skiffs with a single outboard engine, so they could only prowl along the coastline, covering a few thousand square miles of ocean. Their boats weren't equipped to go out any farther. But ships did what they always do when faced with a pirate threat along known shipping routes. They altered their routes. The big ships started sailing farther offshore and the bandits found they were out of luck.

That's when the Somalis changed the game. Instead of capturing trawlers and freighters and holding them for ransom, they stole the vessels and used them as mother ships. These trawlers can travel hundreds of miles offshore in rough weather, and the Somalis simply tied their skiffs to the back and went searching for bigger game. When they spotted a ship, they'd offload teams of three or four pirates into the skiffs and go hunting. It didn't matter if they failed. The mother ship gave them the ability to stay at sea for weeks at a time, searching for the right victim. By 2005 or so, there was nowhere to run off the coast of East Africa. Anywhere you could sail, the pirates could follow.

The standard operating procedure for a pirate attack goes this way: three or more quick boats would approach a ship just before sunset or just after sunrise, moving fast. There would be a mother ship lurking behind, shadowing the target from over the horizon. The pirates would come up to the hull of the target ship, throw grappling hooks up to the deck, secure them, then shimmy up to the deck. From then on, it's a game of ransoms and threats.

If you are targeted, you can't call 911. There is no such thing as a Somali coast guard and the Europeans and the Americans can't guarantee anyone's safety. There is a twenty-nation task force with warships in the region to combat piracy, but they are concentrated in a corridor in the Gulf of Aden, along the southern coast of Yemen, leaving the coast of Somalia practically unguarded. And the entire area represents millions of square miles of ocean. The pirates could have control of your ship and your crew in a matter of minutes. The best you could do would be to make a fast call to the UKMTO, or United Kingdom Maritime Trade Operations, which is a security clearinghouse for mariners in the Persian Gulf and Indian Ocean. They would get the word out.

Ship owners desperate to get their cargo moving — let's face it, their real motivation for ending these hostage situations — would hire helicopters and drop ransom money in burlap sacks onto the decks of the ships. Or they would send it in waterproof suitcases in tiny boats with outboard engines. One company even used a James Bond–style parachute to get the money to the criminals, dropping $3 million on the deck of the MV *Sirius Star*. Everyone made money. The professional security companies were paid handsomely to negotiate the deals with the Somalis. The guys who delivered the ransoms were paid $1 million to risk their lives.

The shippers got their vessels back and their insurance companies paid them for the lost time and doubled the premiums for everyone else. Their statisticians would tell them, "Well, only .04 of all shipping in the Gulf of Aden is taken by pirates." So the vessels kept sailing through it. And the pirates walked away with a king's ransom.

But the crew members? They usually went home to a hot meal, a few tears from their family, and then they were back on the water again as soon as possible. There was no such thing as combat pay for a merchant mariner.

The pirates always claimed to treat their hostages with care, and from what I heard through the grapevine that was usually true. But I knew they killed when their backs were against the wall. When a group of Somalis hijacked a Taiwanese fishing boat, the *Ching Fong Hwa 168,* in April 2007, one crew member was shot in the back during the attack. When the owner refused to pay the Somalis' demands for $1.5 million in ransom, they chose another Chinese sailor at random and shot him six times, executing him in cold blood. The pirates wanted to throw the body to the sharks that swarm in the Indian Ocean but the captain convinced them to store it in the ship's freezer. Then the bandits put a gun to the head of the captain's twenty-two-year-old son and threatened to pull the trigger unless the man called Taiwan and got the ransom negotiations on track. For seven months, the crew went through pure hell: they were pulled out of their beds for mock executions, beaten when they couldn't understand the Somalis, and fell victim to the oldest killer on the ocean — scurvy — when their vegetables ran out. The Somalis even forced the men to call home and beg their families for their lives.

If they don't get their money, the pirates get brutal. They flogged Russian sailors whose bulk carrier was being held for $10 million and forced them to lie down on boiling hot decks when the temperature was above 100 degrees. Captured Nigerian crewmen were held in their cabins for three months straight without being allowed to see the sun or breathe fresh air. Indian seamen were tortured and threatened with execution. And as the *Maersk Alabama* entered the Gulf of Aden, there were more than two hundred crew members of different nationalities being held hostage by pirates on twenty different ships, most of them captured in or near the Indian Ocean.

There were four main groups who were causing most of the havoc, including the National Volunteer Coast Guard, which mostly stuck to raiding small commercial boats and fishing vessels. There was the Marka Group, which operated out of a town by the same name, and the Puntland Group, who were actually former fishermen turned bandits. The last was the Somali Marines, and these guys thought of themselves as a kind of national navy: they had an admiral of the fleet, a vice admiral, and a director of finances. They launched speedboats from mother ships and then directed their members to their targets by satellite phone. And they specialized in the big targets: tankers, container ships.

Us.

The most disturbing news about the pirates actually came from my brother, who's a Middle East analyst with a conservative think tank down in D.C. He told me that he'd seen reports about Al Qaeda fighters from Pakistan making their way into Somalia and Yemen. That worried me to the nth degree. Al Qaeda is just a whole other ball game. There was actually one bizarre incident I'd heard of where a group of pirates approached a ship in the Strait of Malacca off western Malaysia, threw hooks over the side, and boarded it. They rounded up the crew and stuck them in a room. You would think the next stop would be to demand ransom, but they didn't. What they wanted to do was learn how to sail the ship. They went down to the engine room and inspected it. They went up to the bridge and practiced steering the ship. They got on the radio and practiced using the VTS (Vessel Traffic Service), utilizing calling-in points for monitoring a ship's route. When they'd learned everything they could, they left, taking the manuals from the engine room and the bridge manuals and a list of checkpoints that captains use when they're maneuvering through heavy traffic.

It seemed like a dry run for an Al Qaeda operation, a seaborne 9/11.

After I'd read through the security bulletins, I wrote a short e-mail to Andrea. I guess I was feeling a little lonely, because I started with our ongoing search for a dog to replace the dear, departed Frannie.

Hey Ange —
No word on the dogs? I actually was thinking of Frannie last night, a tear came to my soul. That dang dog is still bugging me! I need a dog!

En route to Mombasa, will call around the 11th or 12th of April. Weather is very nice, until the monsoon sets in. The pirates are getting more active lately. They are attacking even naval military ships. I guess a lack of recognition on their parts.

Love, R.

I didn't want her to worry, but I couldn't pretend the Somalis weren't out there. Andrea and I were in this thing together. We always had been. Before I left, I'd told her that it was getting more dangerous with the pirates. "Eventually they're going to take an American ship," I said.

"They're not that stupid," Andrea said. "They wouldn't attack one of ours."

Deep down in her heart, though, she knew that sort of thing could happen. It's part of being a merchant mariner's wife. But somehow she was counting on that American flag to keep me and the crew safe. Who would dare to attack the Stars and Stripes?

Andrea never lost sleep over my being out there. Maybe it was wishful thinking, but she's always been good at keeping her mind away from that idea. We've always been lucky. We've worked hard for everything we've had and we consider ourselves blessed. I guess she thought that would continue.

Andrea's friends always marveled at her, saying, "I don't know how you do it, being a merchant mariner's wife." Her joking response always was "Are you kidding me? Your husband's away half the time, you get a check every two weeks, what's not to like?" That always got a lot of laughs. But it's true that most seamen's wives are strong, independent women capable of picking up a shovel or a hammer or grabbing a flashlight when the water heater stops working. When I left for sea, I often gave Andrea what she called the "honey-do list": "Honey, can you make sure to get the oil changed in the car, see that the taxes are paid, get the dryer fixed, et cetera." In the early days of our marriage, when she was home with two kids in diapers, in the dead of a Vermont winter, Andrea really had to be strong. "There were many times when I felt like the proverbial woman standing on the side of the road with a flat tire," she's fond of saying. "You either learned to survive on your own or you got a divorce and went back to a normal way of life." Thank God we have terrific neighbors and family who would always be there if Andrea needed anything at all. If a tree fell down on our property, our neighbors would show up with a chain-saw and a tractor.

Maybe her strength came in her DNA. Andrea's mom had her own load to carry. Andrea was a teenager when her parents divorced and her mother was left with six kids to support. Andrea's mom worked full time and then came home to a houseful of rowdy children. Andrea knew how hard it was because a lot of the responsibility for the kids fell on her. She learned to be pretty resourceful: how to cook, mend clothes, and keep the house clean. When he was young and fell and skinned a knee, Andrea's younger brother Tommy would run to her. Her mother was hurt by that, but later she realized she'd raised a pretty capable woman. One thing that meant a lot to Andrea is when her mom pulled her aside and said, "I'll never have to worry about you or any of my daughters." I often felt the same way. Andrea can handle almost anything.

As a merchant mariner's wife, you know it's not a matter of "if" but "when" your husband will face a dangerous situation. We both just hoped the *most* dangerous — a pirate attack — wouldn't happen to us.

On April 5, Andrea e-mailed me with some family news about her stepmother Tina and her husband, Frank:

Hey there —

So it's 0700, Mariah had to wake me up to tell me it was snowing. She was heading to the barn. . . . Tina's reception [memorial celebration] was really nice, in spite of the cold wet weather. . . . Perhaps we should get my mom and Frank together? I laughed.

So I must be missing you. I find myself waking up on your side of the bed. Hope things are OK with you. Miss your voice.

LOVE
Andrea

FIVE:
-3 DAYS

"You only die once."
— *Somali pirate onboard a hijacked Ukrainian vessel, phone interview with* The New York Times, *September 30, 2008*

The trip to Djibouti went smoothly. There was chatter on the radio about pirate boats being spotted, but we didn't see anything on the radar or on the watch. We sailed southwest along the coast of Yemen and arrived on April 5. We spent an exhausting day off-loading cargo in the port there, and the next day, April 6, we left port and steamed due northeast. We were halfway through our Gulf of Aden run. We'd made it in. Now we had to get out alive, and around the Horn of Africa.

Every port in the world has a reputation. Sailors judge ports by a strict set of criteria that hasn't changed for three hundred years: Is it cheap? Are there girls nearby? Is there beer? And is there something to do? That's it. If the answer to all four is yes, sailors all over the world will be brawling in their union halls to get there. Alexandria, Egypt, is a great port because it's inexpensive and you can jump on a train for an hour and see the pyramids. Subic Bay in the Philippines has dirt-cheap beer and scads of pretty women with questionable morals. On the other hand, Chongjin, North Korea, is a god-awful port because you're restricted to the ship and even if you got off it, the people there are terrified and poor. There are harbors in Colombia and Ecuador where you hear automatic gunfire at night, where you can watch stowaways shimmy up your ropes, and where you stand a fair chance of getting rolled or chopped up in the waterfront bars. But any sailor will take those little inconveniences over Kim Jong-il's hellhole.

African ports have a mixed reputation. Mombasa, where we were headed next, was fairly secure, with armed guards patrolling the fences and very basic security measures in place. Locals would slip in under the cover of night and load their skiffs with twist locks, then sell them back to you for $25 apiece. No harbor in the third world is entirely safe.

I'd been to Sierra Leone during the civil war and watched people waving from the shoreline. You could see that their right hands had been chopped off by the rebels, because they'd voted. I was in Monrovia, Liberia, a week before they had the revolution and Charles Taylor took over the country. It was another world: as we glided into the port, we could see there was no electricity except for those places that had generators. The West African peacekeepers came onboard and immediately started shaking us down for bribes. There was no security at all, just hundreds of people on the pier waiting to hand us letters, some of them written on the backs of matchbooks. They would say, *Leave me, but take my family to America.* I spoke to one guy who told me: "I'm a college professor, I can't get any work, my family is starving. Can you give me something to do?" I felt just awful knowing there was so little I could offer people like him.

One time in Monrovia, there was a guy who desperately needed to work, so I said, "Okay, I need four workers. You pick out four guys, you'll be the boss, and I'll take care of you. If they don't do a good job, I'll get rid of you." The standard pay at the port was $1 a day, which was actually a good wage in Monrovia. And this guy earned it, working hard for seven or eight days straight, no messing around, which I liked. On payday, he came to me and said, "I don't want cash, I want plywood." The country had been so devastated that there was no building material there, and plywood was like gold. I tried to talk him out of it, telling him cash was safer, but he insisted. I gave him a truckload, packed it down to the springs, and he was ecstatic. The next day he came to me and he was beaten to a pulp. The man could barely walk. As he'd left the port the day before, the peacekeepers started to steal the plywood from the truck, and he just lay across it and took a vicious beating so that he could keep a third of the stuff. I gave him money and clothes and we took care of him, but they'd nearly killed the poor bastard over some flimsy wood.

In Monrovia, Liberia, every day at one o'clock would be the Show. We would off-load the first pallet of peas and wheat and then, when it hit the deck, this huge crowd would converge. Hundreds of people milling around the pier would just pounce on it and policemen would lash them with heavy wooden clubs. Guys would heave these sixty-pound sacks of wheat through holes in the pier and then dive in after them. And the security forces would come up behind them and stick their guns in the holes and blast away.

Any captain who sailed East or West Africa saw the desperation of the people there.

By 1 p.m., we were safely away from Djibouti without any incidents. As we made our way around the Horn of Africa and mirrored the Somali coastline, I knew we were still in the middle of the most dangerous part of the trip.

I scheduled a "fire and boat drill" for 1300 hours. We were training the new guys, checking out the lifeboat and going through how to launch it. Then we went over to the MOB (the "Man Over Board" or rescue boat) on the starboard side and showed the new guys how to adjust the safety harnesses. Each man is assigned a position on the lifeboat, so we also practiced taking our places on it. Shane was running the drill, asking each sailor what he'd do in a particular situation and then correcting the answers. It was a blazingly hot day, with a little bit of swell on the water, caused by the first of the monsoon winds. The bridge was baking in 95-degree heat and visibility was seven miles.

I was up on the bridge alone, scanning

the horizon and keeping an eye on the radar. About 1340, three blips came up on the screen, seven miles behind us on our port quarter and moving fast, at least twenty-one knots. I looked up and caught sight of a bow wave. At seven miles, you can never see the boat, just the wake it kicks up as it slices through the water.

My training kicked in and I steadied the 7 × 50 binoculars on the tiny white blip. I turned the little wheel at the top of the binoculars and saw the wake again. Another look at the radar. Now there were two other fast boats back there, plus a larger blip following eight to nine miles behind us, over the horizon and out of sight but visible on the screen. The mother ship. I checked his vectors; he was trailing us. Every move we made, he shadowed.

I thought I'd spotted a mother ship once before during my career, but now I was seeing a pirate outfit in full array. My heart pounded.

I radioed down to Shane.

"Possible pirate boats approaching, seven miles, port quarter," I said.

"You want us to end the drill?" he called back.

I thought about it.

"Not yet. We may have to call it off, but

119

right now I'm just keeping you apprised."

I still wasn't convinced it was pirates. Their normal time to attack was just after sunrise (5 a.m.) and just before sunset (7:45 p.m.). Those are the times when it gets hazy in the Gulf of Aden and visibility falls from seven miles to four or so. At 1 p.m., there was maximum visibility. It was a strange time for the Somalis to mount a sortie against a ship.

But they were closing fast. I called down to Shane to send up an AB named Andy. He was an old salt who had the best eyes on the boat. I'd been with him on the bridge previously and he'd called out, "I got a ship coming up on port side." I'd looked at the horizon, saw nothing, then checked with the binoculars and sure enough, there was a ship fifteen miles away. I couldn't believe he'd caught it. So now I wanted his eyes on watch with me.

I moved the stick on the EOT — the engine order telegraph — sending the new speed down to the engine room. The RPMs began to pick up and the ship surged forward. I was pushing the speed up to 122 revs.

As I nudged the throttle higher, I called down to the chief engineer. "Chief, I need you in the engine room now, I'm increasing the speed." I was bringing the revs up as fast as I ever had on this ship, eventually reaching 124. I wanted Mike down there to watch the engine computer and let me know if any of the indicators — engine load, exhaust temperatures, cylinder temperatures — veered into the red. The last thing you want to do is kill your power plant when the bad guys are on your tail. If anything looked like it was going to blow, the chief would let me know.

I ran over to the satellite phone and dialed up UKMTO. A voice with a British accent answered.

"This is the *Maersk Alabama*," I said, and I rattled off our coordinates: position, course, speed. "We have three ships approaching at five to six miles, with a possible mother ship trailing one mile behind them. Potential piracy situation."

The voice at the other end didn't seem impressed. I'm sure they were getting calls from every ship off the Somali coast who spotted a fishing skiff or a floating barrel.

"We have a lot of captains who are nervous out there," he said.

I'm not the nervous type, I wanted to say.

"It's probably just fishermen," he continued. "But you should get your crew together, get the fire hoses ready, and you may

121

want to get the ship locked up."

I couldn't believe what I was hearing. First, he told me it was probably just a bunch of local guys chasing mackerel, and now he's telling me to go to DEFCON 1.

"If I was that far behind the eight-ball, I wouldn't be talking to you now," I said, a little heated. "I'm just letting you know the situation."

"Keep us posted," he said.

"Will do," and the phone was already down before he could answer.

There's a U.S. emergency line for piracy and I dialed that next. If you're going to be taken hostage, you want your own government to know. I watched the blips on the radar coming closer and closer. The phone was just ringing.

After ten rings, I slammed it down. Nobody home. Just unbelievable. The Brits were condescending as hell but at least they picked up the damn phone.

The ships were still closing. I could see them in my binoculars. The crew was going through its drills, but everyone was looking at our port quarter. They'd spotted the ships and any thoughts of fire had gone out of their heads. I could tell they were getting nervous.

Five miles away. Then four. I could see

the lead boat now, not just the wake. It was a typical Somali pirate skiff: white, thin across the bow, and fast.

The seas began to pick up. As we got farther out into the gulf, the swells rose from two feet to four and five. I could tell that the fast boats were having trouble. They'd run flat out for a while and then slam into a swell, which would twist them sideways and kill their speed. They'd have to turn, gun the engine, and start building up momentum again. The ocean was helping us. If we could get into heavy enough seas, we could outrun them.

The minutes ticked by. They were gaining, then falling back, gaining and retreating.

By 3 p.m., the fire drill was over. I realized with a start that we'd been racing with the pirates for over an hour. They were down to three miles now and gaining again. I spotted four men in the lead boat, with long black objects in their hands — automatic rifles, for sure.

I looked around and realized there were five or six guys on the bridge. They'd materialized there without my noticing and they were staring out at the port quarter, dead quiet. Usually, I would have ordered them off the bridge, but in a situation like this, the more eyes, the better. They weren't panicked, yet, but the atmosphere on the bridge was electric.

An idea came to me. "Hey," I shouted to the second mate. "Go ahead and talk on the radio to me. I'm going to pretend to be a navy ship." If the pirates were monitoring our frequencies, which they often did, I wanted them to believe that we were in contact with a navy destroyer.

"What, Cap?"

I didn't have time to explain.

"Forget about it," I said. "Just watch me."

I got on the radio and hit the mike. "Warship 237, Coalition Warship 237, 237, *Maersk Alabama,* come in."

I deepened my voice and tried to cut out my Boston accent. "*Maersk Alabama,* come in, this is Coalition Warship 237," I said. I was pretending to be a navy ship within radio range.

I switched back to my natural voice. "This is the *Maersk Alabama.* We're under attack by pirates. Position is two degrees two north by forty-nine degrees nineteen east. Course is one hundred and eighty and speed at eighteen knots. Request immediate assistance."

"Roger that, *Maersk Alabama.* How many people aboard?"

"Twenty aboard. No injuries at this time."

"Roger that. We have a helicopter in the air. Repeat, we have a helicopter en route and he'll be at your position at approximately fifteen hundred hours. Repeat, helicopter's ETA to your position is five minutes."

I was almost laughing. What we were doing was probably illegal, and the navy guys would have rolled their eyes. They had their own codes, but any Somali bandit would have been damn impressed to know that a helicopter gunship was on its way to blow him to smithereens.

Then I noticed the mother ship had dropped off our radar. What was going on? Had they given up on the attack?

One of the fast boats peeled off and headed away from us. I felt a tiny jolt of adrenaline. *It was working.* Then another. The swells were just too much for them. They were being tossed around like shoes in a washing machine. We were down to one pirate skiff. But he was coming hard.

I looked at the readout on the side of the radar: 0.9 miles away. *Holy shit, that was fast.* This bastard was really not giving up. And I knew that it took only one skiff to take a ship.

I saw the boat slam into a wave with a big

sheet of spray. It stopped him dead in the water. The swells were getting even bigger, up to six feet, and even the *Maersk Alabama* was pitching through the waves. I could feel a slight thud in my feet when we hit, but after thirty years at sea, it was barely noticeable to me.

The last boat started up again and pointed his boat at our stern.

Finally, at 0.9 miles away, he peeled off. Then he was at 1.1, 1.5, 1.7. It was like being chased by a car full of thugs on the highway and watching them run out of gas.

The guys gathered on the deck let out a collective breath. "Hell, yeah!" someone yelled and laughter bounced off the bridge windows. I smiled, too. Our detection procedures had worked well. We'd dodged a bullet. But the pirates were still out there.

I brought the engine down to 120 revs. The chief called up and told me there was no problem pushing it to that speed. Now I knew we could do 124 without blowing the engine up. And the chief and I agreed once we went over 122, he'd head down to the engine room. We had a speed procedure for the next pirate attack.

The pirates had made a classic mistake. The mother ship had dropped the fast boats into the water too far away, and the flimsy little craft had been unable to negotiate the high seas. I didn't want to think what would have happened if the water had been smooth.

As well as we'd performed, we'd gotten lucky. There was no other way to look at it.

Six:
-2 Days

"It's that old saying: where the cops aren't, the criminals are going to go. We patrol an area of more than one million square miles. The simple fact of the matter is that we can't be everywhere at one time."
— *Lieutenant Nathan Christensen, spokesman for the Fifth Fleet,* New York Times, *April 8, 2009*

What was it that Winston Churchill said about there being nothing more exhilarating than being shot at and escaping unhurt? The same goes for beating a pirate attack.

I felt elated. I felt I had done my job as a captain. We'd been vigilant, spotting the pirates at the edge of our visibility range, and we'd ramped up our speed in time to outrun them. The toughest part of defeating a pirate team is detecting them, seeing them while there's still time to react. We'd passed that key test.

It's a tricky thing to be in charge of a ship with nineteen other guys, most of whom you hardly know. The merchant marine is different from the navy or the army or the marines in that you don't have a crew or a battalion that's grown to know you over several months or even years. You walk on a ship and you have to earn instant respect, instant faith in your leadership, or the whole thing falls apart. You need to do on-the-spot appraisals of what every man is capable of and bring them up to their potential in a matter of hours or days.

Coming up, I'd made a study of how that was done. And how it wasn't.

The first lesson I learned came from a merchant marine legend named Dewey Boland. Exhibit number one in how not to command a ship.

Dewey was a tall thin guy in his sixties, an Idaho horse farmer who'd taken to the sea for what reason, only God knows. He was well known and dreaded throughout the merchant marine. I've been in union halls where a sweet assignment has come up on a ship and a guy throws down his ticket to get a job on a ship. "Looks good. Who's the cap?" "Dewey Boland." And the guy would snatch up his card. "No thank you."

Dewey never called you by your name,

only by your job on the ship. "Hey, Third," he'd yell, for "third mate." It was a way to put you down. I was the third mate on one of his ships. Dewey really had it in for me because I graduated from the Massachusetts Maritime Academy and his son had just been thrown out of the federal academy, probably for being a carbon copy of his father.

Every day at 12 p.m. sharp, we'd do what is known as the "noontime slips," where you chart your position, your average speed, your fuel consumption. Depending on how you did the calculations, there was a variance of a few miles or so on the number you'd come up with. So I'd get out my books and tables and calculator and I'd get the number. And here would come Dewey at 1300, climbing up to the bridge to compare notes. He did his own calculations by taking a divider — the two-legged compass used in geometry class — and sending it skittering across the map. In three seconds, he had a number. Who cared if it was completely inaccurate?

"Hey, Third, what do you say? What number did you get?"

"Cap, I got three hundred and ninety-four miles." Meaning 394 miles from our last position.

Invariably, Dewey would blow a gasket. *Invariably.*

"Jesus Christ, what the hell are you talking about? I got three hundred and ninety-six."

Two miles difference means absolutely nothing in nautical terms. But Dewey specialized in exploding over nothing. His aim was to make your life miserable, not for endangering the ship or steering it into a jetty, but for the most mundane stuff possible. I was ready to go back to driving a cab. You might be able to get away with being Captain Queeg in the navy, but not on a merchant ship.

Dewey taught me not to put the energy into screaming. I actually had a chief mate once tell me that I was too soft-spoken. "You need to yell more," he said. I told him what I tell everyone: "It's when I get quiet that you need to get worried." That's the truth.

I've learned as much from terrible captains as I have from good ones. I've had captains who stayed in their rooms all day and watched *The Big Chill* over and over. I've found captains hiding in the bowels of the ship, crying because they didn't feel like the crew loved them. I've had captains who nearly capsized the boat by sailing straight into a typhoon because they didn't want to get in trouble with the company by being a day late into port.

That happened to me coming out of Yokohama on a steamer. We hit thirty-five-foot swells going forty miles an hour and they put us into a synchronous roll, which happens when your natural motion is accentuated by the seas themselves. It's a good way to flip a ship over. The captain's reaction? He sidled up to me and, nervously chewing on the end of a cigarette, mumbled under his breath: "I better call New York and see what the weather is like."

"We know what the weather is like, Cap," I said. "It's a *typhoon.*"

But this captain was such a company man that he was terrified, not of sinking, but of pissing off some bureaucrat back at headquarters. He was willing to endanger the lives of twenty men so that he could make his schedule. Meanwhile, I was holding on to the bulkhead for dear life and hearing chains snap down below and watching equipment fly off one bulkhead, shoot straight across the ship, and crash into the other bulkhead forty feet away, without once touching the deck.

That's what you call a roll. And that's what you call a failure in leadership.

Another time, I was on a tanker taking heating oil from the refineries in the Gulf of Mexico up the East Coast. We ran smack dab into a hurricane. In three days, we went minus twelve miles. We were just trying to keep the bow of the ship pointed into the wind while the ocean was exploding around us. I would stand in the bridge and watch this gigantic wave of black water come over the bow and roll straight toward me until it smashed against the windows ten feet in front of my face. The bridge would go dark, like you were underwater for a few seconds, which in fact you were, and then it would be past you and you'd see the next one cresting over the bow. I thought, *Jesus Christ, I'm standing seven stories above the ocean and I just got buried by a wave. That was a seventy-footer.* Those are the kinds of waves that eat tankers.

The captain was a short Greek guy named Jimmy Kosturas. He was like a statue on the bridge. As the storm tried to rip his tanker apart, he stood there and lit one of these little cigarillos that he liked and then he calmly watched the waves come at him. Jimmy was grace under pressure personified.

"Course?" he'd say.

I'd give him the course.

"Speed?"

I'd give him the speed.

He'd nod and take a puff on the cigarillo.

Then *CRAAAAASSSHHH!* The wave would hit and the water would slither down the bridge windows, black against the green glass.

Jimmy stood calmly, a curl of smoke wafting up from his cigarillo.

I watched as the captain barely ate and barely slept and yet kept his crew focused like a laser beam. By showing no fear. If that hurricane had turned us lengthwise, we would have broken up. But he was as calm and cool as if he were sailing a little dinghy across Boston Harbor on a calm summer day. He barely said a word, but he inspired such confidence that I never doubted we'd make it through.

Deeds, not words. I'd always remember Jimmy, standing there like Gary Cooper as the ocean tried to kill him. I liked that.

By the time I got my captain's license in 1990, I'd seen the good, the bad, and the really bad. I wanted to be the kind of captain I'd loved serving under.

I can still remember taking charge of my first ship, the *Green Wave,* a container ship out of Tacoma, Washington. I'd been serving as chief mate on it and a good friend of mine, Peter, was captain, and we were carrying military supplies — planes, helicopters, M16 ammunition, you name it — from base to base all over the West Coast. It came time for the captain to leave and I had to take over. We did our handover of the ship all day and then went out to dinner. We rolled back to the port around 10 p.m. and Peter pulled up in front of the gangway. We got out, and I was standing there looking up at this immense ship in the darkness, and he turned to me and said, "Okay, you've got it." We shook hands and he laughed and said, "Good luck, Cap." It was the first time anyone had ever called me that in my life.

I was nervous. I didn't *feel* ready. But I had to do the job, so it didn't matter how I felt.

I'm sure I made a thousand mistakes that first trip. I was just holding on, trying to learn as I went. But I didn't try to whip the guys under me into my idea of a perfect crew. I didn't want to be the Coach Marshall of the high seas. I felt that if you did the job right, if you let people be themselves and cracked down only when they blew an assignment, then morale would take care of itself. You have to show people that you deserve the respect that goes along with the title Captain. You can't browbeat them into looking up to you.

My motto became "We are all here for the ship. The ship isn't here for us." That really served me, because it's true. When you're out of port, the ship is your mother, your temporary country, your tribe. And there was an unspoken part of that saying that I kept to myself: "The captain is here for the crew."

Coming up, I got a reputation of being a tough guy to work for. When I'm working, I'm working. I become a little obsessed with making sure things are done right. So if you're lazy or just plain bad at your job, I'm going to be a nightmare for you. But if you're on top of your duties, I'll leave you alone. I'll never give a good man make-work just to feel like I'm in charge. My attitude is "You hope for the best, but you train for the worst." Because one day, the worst will find you.

A bosun, one of the hardest workers I ever had, gave me the best compliment from a crew member. He'd worked with me on more than one ship. "You know, you are a pain in the ass, but I know what you're going to say before you say it," he told me. Meaning: You're consistent. And I am.

When I got off the ship, as captain, I asked myself the same question: Was the ship better than when I came on? Is it run better, is it safer, is its crew more motivated or smarter about what they're doing? That's how I judged myself as a captain. Did I make a difference? There were times the answer wasn't what I was looking for, and then I analyzed why I hadn't succeeded.

In some ways, I'm an accidental leader. I was just an ordinary guy who wanted more for his family. I wasn't driven to wear the stripes and have power over a group of men. When you walk onto a ship as the captain, you get the good room, the good hours, the good pay. But you have to accept everything that goes with them. And that includes putting your crew's lives before your own.

"The captain is always the last off a ship" isn't just a line in the movies. It's your duty.

When you enter the merchant marine, you're walking into a different world. Danger is your frequent companion. There are any number of things that can kill you: there are people who want to steal what you're hauling, or the ship itself. It's not rare to lose a man. Containers drop, wires part, a heavy piece of cargo shifts and turns into a man-killer. A fire onboard can be a death sentence, because there's nowhere to run and no one to come to your aid. And the loneliness is a fatal part of our lives, too. Men simply lose the desire to return to their lives on land and just disappear in the middle of the night.

I've had my brushes with the grim reaper. In 1988, I was unloading a fire truck in Greenland, trying to get it off the deck onto a barge, and having to do it with a bunch of army guys who'd never been on a ship before. We were sitting at anchor and I was between a heavy spreader bar and a metal hatch combing. The ship took a little roll and suddenly four tons of metal came swinging toward me. I went to hold it off but it kept coming at me and I thought, *I can duck down and this steel may crush my head or I can take the hit.* So the bar swung in and crushed up against my body and then swung back out as the ship corrected its roll. I broke four ribs in two places each, snapped my collarbone, collapsed a lung, and separated my shoulder. Another three inches and the load would have crushed my chest cavity and I would have been dead.

The army guys and the crew left on the ship thought I'd been flattened. When we all recovered from the shock, they put me onto a metal stretcher, tied my arms down so I wouldn't hurt myself any further, and lowered me to the barge about twenty-five feet away so I could be loaded on a landing craft and taken to the base clinic. I knew if they dropped me, I'd be dead — I'd drop straight into the water and to the bottom of the fjord. The soldiers hot-wired a bus and rushed me to the local clinic over a rutted, rock-strewn road, sending jolts of pain through me with every bump.

And the first thing that ran through my mind, even though I was in constant agony, was "Andrea is going to kill me for getting hurt." Just out of the clear blue. Maybe it took getting that close to death to know what I would miss about life.

Then I said to myself, "What the hell do I care what *she* thinks? I'm the one who's hurting."

I knew I loved her then, if I hadn't before. I wanted nothing more than to see her again.

Andrea was in Boston when she got the phone call from Greenland. It was the captain on my ship. Even back then, she knew they never call with good news.

"What happened?" she said. "Tell me he's alive." The captain described the accident and said they were airlifting me down to Fort Dix. Andrea flew down immediately.

Soon after I arrived, she was sitting on the corner of my hospital bed. My company, Central Gulf Lines, had flown her down and even found her a room at a local hotel.

She kept a close watch over me. One of the Fort Dix doctors kept inserting chest tubes — which was excruciatingly painful — without any narcotics. Being a nurse, Andrea knew things are done differently at different hospitals, but I was suffering so badly she couldn't stand it. She went and chewed the guy out, really giving him hell. To this day, when I'm having trouble with a mechanic or something like that, I'll look at him and say, "Listen, do I need to bring my wife in here?" And I'm only half-joking.

Andrea wanted me moved to Brigham and Women's Hospital, where she was working, and my company had me air-lifted there, since I needed special care on the way. Once I was installed in my bed, I jokingly told everyone Andrea was my wife: "Oh, don't worry about cleaning that up, my wife's coming in and she'll do it." On her dinner break Andrea would come to my room and sit on the edge of my bed. On one of those breaks, I told her about being in that stretcher and how she was the only thing I could think of. Finally, I said, "Well, I suppose I should ask you to marry me."

"Yeah," she said. "I guess you should."
And I did.

But I never did get down on one knee.

As different as we were, we had a lot in common. We both came from big families, and we were comfortable in that crazy atmosphere. I'm very Irish and steady-nerved and Andrea is Italian and emotional. When she's flipping out over something like not being able to find her keys, I'll sit there and say, "Okay, let me know when you're done."

"Rich grounded me," she says. "He laughs at me when I should be laughed at and he pays attention when I need him to pay attention."

Andrea likes to say that I became her rock. "I know it's right out of a movie," she tells people, "but he does complete me."

Sailors are superstitious by nature. Seeing dolphins at sunrise, for example, means you're going to have a good day. Redheads, priests, fresh flowers, and stepping onto a boat with your left foot first are bad luck. Your life is controlled by the weather, by the pull of the moon, by storms that are brewing in some corner of Africa. And every sailor has his unlucky places. Until I started sailing the Gulf of Aden, mine had always been the Bay of Biscay, a hellacious gulf that lies between France and Spain. The continental shelf runs out under the bay, which makes for shallow water all across it, and shallow water means one thing: rough seas. I was cursed in that damn patch of ocean. Nearly every time I sailed through it, I hit a storm that gave me something to remember.

One time, I was making my way from Nordheim, Germany, to Sunny Point, North Carolina, with a load of ammo for the U.S. Army. Down below I had millions of rounds of bullets and five-hundred-pound bombs and crates of ammo and who knows what other kinds of explosives. The ship itself was a wreck; the sheathing that prevents the cargo from slamming into the steel hull during rough weather was shredded and useless, the starboard anchor was out of commission, and every other damn thing on that boat was either falling apart or broken. The owner had slashed wages on the ship and the crew was bitter and underpaid. It was a bad situation, but that's when you learn how to handle disaster.

So we were making the run out of the bay and a storm whipped up and at the same time we lost power. Our engine stopped dead. I couldn't steer the ship. We were being thrown around the bay like a cork and down below I could hear these enormous thuds. I could actually feel the vibrations all the way up at the top of the bridge. Something was loose in the hold.

The storm intensified by the minute. The ship began to pitch until I looked down at the inclinometer, a pendulum that tells you the degree of roll, and saw that we were at 40 degrees. I'd never seen that number before. Never. We were close to turning turtle and going over completely and sinking to the bottom of the bay. The loose cargo was shifting the center of gravity on the ship. A couple more degrees of tilt and the entire load could shift port or starboard and send us to our eternal rest.

I started for the engine room. Running down the central passageway, I spotted something odd to my right. I stopped, turned around, and went back. It was part of my crew, seven guys in life jackets huddled together, looking like they were the last men onboard the *Titanic.* They were staring at me from the darkness, their lips quivering, all of them scared out of their minds.

I was, too, but I couldn't show it.

"What are you doing?" I said, incredulous.

The sailors looked at each other. The din was even louder down there.

"Well, Cap," one sailor finally said. "We're preparing to abandon ship."

I looked at them.

"You're telling me," I said, "that you're getting ready to get off this big ship to get into a tiny boat, in this weather? Is that what you're telling me?"

They looked at one another. I don't think that had occurred to them.

"It doesn't seem like a smart bet to me," I said. "This is what we're going to do. Anyone who can work, come with me. Anyone who can't, go to your rooms. You're scaring the rest of the crew."

Four of the guys came with me and the others scattered to their quarters.

I raced to the engine room. Our chief engineer was working furiously on the power plant.

"Get me a status report," I said. He nodded. He was what we call "fully tasked," that is, working like hell on six different things that needed doing immediately.

I hurried down to the cargo holds. Opening the door, I shone my flashlight in to the enormous half-lit space. What I saw wasn't encouraging. Six inches of viscous motor oil was slopping around the floor. Fifty-five-gallon drums were reduced to the size of footballs by the constant pounding on the hulls. Five-hundred-pound bombs, stacked twenty to a pallet and two pallets high, were tipping back and forth and slamming against one another and the hull.

I called the chief mate. "You need to get some guys in the hold and secure that cargo," I yelled. If one of those bombs blew, pieces of the ship the size of a quarter would be raining down on the Spanish coast for half an hour. He rounded up two ABs — the only ones out of twenty men not too sick or scared to go into the holds — and they went and wrestled the bombs and the barrels back into place.

Twelve hours later, the engine was back up and running and the bombs were on their way to being secured. Disaster averted.

There are a thousand ways to die on a ship. But when you run into one face-to-face and survive it, it teaches you how to think your way through the next one.

SEVEN:
-1 DAY

From here down to Mombasa, potential is high for a piracy incident. Keep a wary eye.
— *Captain's night orders,* Maersk Alabama,
April 7, 2000 hours

That night the crew gathered over the dinner table. You could feel the electricity in the air.

"Was that your first piracy situation, Cap?"

"Sure was," I said, as I sat down to the meal. "Hope it's my last, too."

This wasn't the first time the subject had come up. Just the other day Colin, the third mate, had asked, "You know what I was thinking?"

"What's that?"

"What do we do if we're taken hostage?"

I had stared at Colin then.

"You're worried about that?"

Colin nodded. He seemed nervous.

"If you're scared, Colin, you should never have gotten on this ship," I said. "You didn't know where it was heading?"

I didn't want a crewman injecting a note of panic into our run. I needed the crew to be confident and to project confidence. If Colin was terrified of ending up in a Somali boat, he should have worked that out with me before we sailed.

Being taken hostage was sort of a taboo subject among sailors. Anything — even shipwreck — is better.

"Look, we've got to crawl before we can walk," I said finally. "I want to make sure we master the antipiracy drills first."

But I could sense his unease. Suddenly the problem of piracy wasn't abstract anymore, it wasn't a headline or a rumor they heard in the union hall. They'd seen the Somali ships with their own eyes and they'd felt pretty damn defenseless against them.

"I can give you the short version right now," I said.

Colin nodded.

"That'd be good," he said.

"It's pretty simple," I said. "First off, do not mention religion. It's kryptonite. Don't antagonize them by trying to talk about Allah or Jesus and whatever you do don't try to convince them that your faith is better than theirs. Politics is out, too, especially the Middle East. They may try to antagonize you by saying America is the worst country in the world. You're not there to defend the nation's honor. You're trying to survive. So let that pass."

It was all we had time for at that moment. Later, Colin came up to me, still seeming nervous about the possibility of being intercepted by Somalis. There were other crew members around, so I continued my tutorial.

"Do whatever they tell you," I said. "Give them as little information as possible. You've got giveaways, things that aren't important that you offer up to build rapport, and hold-backs, which are things you keep to yourself unless you're under severe threat."

"What would constitute a giveaway?" someone asked.

I shrugged. "Showing them how to get fresh water. Getting them familiar with the safety equipment. You've got to make them feel they're in control while all the time you're guiding them away from the really important stuff, like radar or the engine controls. Not to mention the other crew."

"Got it," Colin said.

"And, last of all, humor helps."

I looked at an AB.

"Unfortunately," I said, "none of you guys are funny. So rule number one: don't get taken hostage by pirates."

I'd always felt if pirates got onboard, it was all over. We had to stop them before they got on the ship.

We were paralleling the coast of Somalia by now. I went back to my room and wrote up my night orders. Every captain has standing orders for the entire trip. They're posted on the first day and never change. But night orders cover any special messages or duties that need to be addressed during each overnight shift. "We're still in Apache country," I wrote that evening. "We're on our own, so we need to make sure we stay vigilant. All we have is each other out here." You have to come at the crew in new ways to keep them interested. I knew the pirates had their attention now, so I kept it short.

I went to my room. At about 3:30 a.m., I was asleep on my bunk when the phone rang.

It was the second mate, Ken, who was on the 12 a.m. to 4 a.m., the "dog watch."

"Cap, I think you better get up here."

"What is it?" I said.

"Somali pirates," he said.

"Where?"

"On the radio," he said. "They're talking

on the radio."

"I'll be right there."

I hurried out to the passageway and climbed the internal ladder up to the bridge level. Clouds scudded past a full moon as I emerged into the fresh air.

I pulled open the door on the bridge and there was Ken with an AB standing watch with him. I was about to say something when I heard a voice.

"This is Somali pirate," it said. "Somali pirate."

I looked at Ken. His eyes were wide as saucers. I looked down. The radio was tuned to Channel 16, the international hail and distress channel.

"Somali pirate, Somali pirate, I'm coming to get you."

It was spooky. The voice was recognizably African. I hadn't spent enough time on the continent to tell a Somali accent from a Kenyan one, but it sounded authentic. More than that, it sounded like the guy was serious.

"What happened?"

"I saw a ship go by about seven miles away. It was very well lit up." I nodded. Fishing boats are always lit up like Christmas trees, to get some illumination on the men working the nets, and to avoid being run down by some tanker doing fifteen knots. A pirate ship would rarely have all those lights going. It burned up too much precious fuel and allowed them to be seen on the horizon, which they never wanted to happen.

"And then a few minutes later, I heard this," Ken said, pointing at the radio.

I picked up the binoculars. There was a boat about seven miles away, astern, on our starboard quarter, its lights blazing like a typical fishing boat. But I looked closer and could see that it had a second boat tied to its stern.

"Somali pirate, Somali pirate," the voice came over the radio again, filling up the dead silence of the bridge. The guy was almost chanting. *What the hell was he playing at?* The Somalis were known for their stealth; the last thing they would do is alert you that they were on the way. It didn't make sense.

It could have just been a couple of fishermen having fun with us. Or it could have been pirates who'd swept past for a look at our security profile. They could be sitting up ahead, trying to unnerve us before gunning their engines and heading back to intercept our ship. Like I said, these guys were constantly innovating, constantly probing for weak points.

I studied the ship in the glasses. It wasn't under way. It was drifting, which is a typical thing for a fishing boat to do.

"Let's go to a hundred and twenty revs," I said. We were doing our normal RPMs of 118.

"One hundred twenty revs," the second mate called. He was on the EOT, the Engine Order Telegraph, controlling our speed.

"What's our course?" I said.

"Two hundred thirty," the helmsman said. Meaning a heading of 230 degrees.

"Bring it over to one eighty," I said. I wanted to make a drastic course correction that the pirate — if that's what he was — would recognize, to show him we knew he was up ahead waiting for us. And I wanted him as far astern as possible.

"Left five to one hundred and eighty," Ken called out. The quartermaster called it back and swung the wheel over.

The ship began to turn and thirty seconds later we were on the new heading. When you're going fast, it takes only a flicker of the rudder to turn fifty degrees.

I watched the mystery ship through the glasses. He was drifting still astern us. But the boat behind him didn't move out and head toward us. If they were going to mount an attack, it would be from that fast boat. As long as that skiff didn't leave the fishing boat, we'd be all right.

I swung the glasses around the quadrants of the horizon: north, south, east, west. Sometimes what pirate gangs do is put a vessel in plain sight and trick you into focusing on it exclusively. While you're fixated on that ship, they'll come at you in three skiffs from the opposite direction, racing in from your blind spot. But the water was clear. No other boats were within range of the *Maersk Alabama.*

For thirty minutes, I kept an eye on the mystery ship. It didn't attempt to follow us, and it didn't launch the fast boat. Strange. But without any other partners within seven miles of us, he wasn't going to try an attack.

"I think we're good," I told Ken. "If anything else comes up, call me right away. Make sure you tell the next watch about this. And stay on one hundred and twenty revs until I'm back up here in the morning."

Pirates had never attacked at night, as far as I knew. (Since that time, pirate crews have attacked under the cover of darkness at least once.) But if I was a Somali bandit, that's exactly what I'd do. Sneak up stealthily in the darkness and take the ship over before the crew had time to react. I had no idea why they hadn't tried it yet — boarding would be more difficult, getting those grappling hooks up, but the payoff would be huge.

I didn't want to be the first.

I went back to my room and collapsed into bed. I'd never had a confirmed pirate incident before and had just had two possible threats in the last twenty-four hours. It told me that the sea around us was swarming with these guys and that we were in an entirely new world. Forget that .04 percent that the statisticians threw around. It seemed like every other ship going through the gulf was being targeted.

As I lay in my bunk unable to sleep, I thought of an old merchant marine term. During World War II, convoys of one hundred or more ships would make their way across the Atlantic to bring desperately needed supplies to the GIs in Europe. The ocean was infested with German submarines and these cargo ships were sitting ducks out there on the water.

Not all of them, though. If you were in the middle of the formation, you were rarely attacked. But if you were on one of the four corners, you were exposed. Vulnerable. Bait.

They called them the "coffin corners." I felt like the *Maersk Alabama* was sailing on one right now. And there wasn't a destroyer in sight to keep the enemy at bay.

EIGHT:
DAY 1, 0600 HOURS

"Once you have a ship, it's a win-win situation. We attack many ships every day, but only a few are ever profitable. No one will come to the rescue of a third-world ship with an Indian or African crew, so we release them immediately. But if the ship is from a Western country . . . then it's like winning a lottery jackpot."
— *Somali pirate, Wired.com, July 28, 2009*

In the merchant marine, we have a saying — "sleep fast." Sailors can drop off in ten seconds and be ready to work again in two hours. You either learn to do it or you don't survive.

I slept like a dead man and awoke at 6 a.m. the next morning when the sun crept under the hem of my blackout curtains. Wednesday, April 8. We'd made it to another day.

I took a shower, the freshwater pumping

up from our tanks down below. I toweled off, dressed, and looked at the weather update. Sunny again. Perfect sailing weather. I checked the incoming messages — more chatter about pirates. *Tell me something I don't know,* I thought.

I went up to the bridge. The sun was like a red-hot poker suspended above your face. I grabbed a cup of coffee and joined Shane, who was on watch. Immediately we started planning out what we needed to do that day. We were getting ready for Mombasa and that was going to be a very busy time. Pirates or no pirates, we had cargo to unload and supplies to take on and the million other things a merchant crew deals with as it approaches port: laundry, paying off, taking on new crew. Plus there's all the unanticipated stuff that inevitably hits you: some government official decides to inspect your ship (that is, until you pay him a bribe) or a stowaway comes crawling up your line.

I was in the middle of this housekeeping when ATM, the Pakistani-born AB, interrupted us.

"Boat approaching, three point one miles out, astern."

Shane and I swiveled to look out. There it was, a white skiff, approaching at twenty knots, at least. It looked like one of the boats that had chased us yesterday, maybe twelve meters long, with a powerful outboard engine. I could see his wake, white in the turquoise water. With the haze, visibility was down to three to four miles so ATM had gotten on it as quickly as I could have hoped.

I looked at the water. The winds had dropped down since yesterday, and the seas were calm. We weren't going to get lucky again. We were in a race with a much faster boat and the waves weren't going to stop them today.

"Mate, find out where the bosun has his people."

Most of the crew would have been in their beds or just getting up and beginning their morning routine. But I knew that the bosun was working somewhere on the ship with a team and I wanted everyone accounted for.

"He's on the bow," Shane said.

"Make sure he knows what's going on in case he has to pull his men in," I said.

"Got it."

"Course?" I called out.

"Two hundred thirty."

"Set a course for one hundred eighty," I said.

"One hundred eighty."

The quartermaster turned the wheel and

I looked through the glasses. The fast boat was closing at 2.5 miles. It shifted into our new course.

There was no question now. These guys weren't out for tuna. They were coming after us.

"Call UKMTO right now," I called.

I didn't have time to mess with the Brits. Shane made the call.

I could hear him answering a barrage of questions: How many people in the boat? How many guns do they have? What color is the boat? What color is the *inside* of the boat?

Finally, he hung up.

"What did they say?"

"Call back when they're within a mile."

I didn't have time to ask why. I grabbed a portable radio — it would be in my hand for the coming hours — and checked the radar.

"Where's the goddamn mother boat?" We were over three hundred miles off the coast of Somalia. There was no way these guys had made it this far alone. There had to be a trawler out there with a leader calling the shots. But I couldn't see it and nothing was showing on the radar. I thought, *What if these guys are herding us straight toward the mother ship?*

Shane had gone to the pyrotechnic box and taken out eighteen flares as soon as we spotted the Somalis. He started breaking out flares before heading down toward the main deck to get eyes on the crew. "I'm going down to get ready, I'll send the third up," he called out as he dashed off the bridge.

I knew the chief was up. Mike was an early riser, and right now he'd be sitting on his bunk reading the Good Book. I rang his room and he answered. "We're in a piracy situation, I need you in the engine room," I said and jammed the phone back down. I needed his eyes on the engine console as we ramped up speed.

The boat was two miles away. We were doing 16.8 knots, and they were doing 21. They were chasing us down.

At one nautical mile, I called to Colin, "Sound the intruder alarm." He hit the ship's whistle, long short, long short, long short. Then he ran to the wall and hit the general alarm, same code. That told every man on the ship to head to his muster point immediately. I looked down over the stern and saw the spray from the pirate hoses shooting out water. At one hundred pounds of pressure per square inch, that stream would knock a man down. I called into the radio, "Switch to Channel One." That was our emergency band. Colin started issuing a succession of orders. "Get the fire pump going, hit the lights, tell the bosun to bring his men in."

I pointed to the pyrotechnic box. "Get ready to start shooting those flares," I called to Colin. "When they get within a mile, fire your first one. Aim directly at them." He nodded.

It was 7 a.m. ATM, Colin, and I had the bridge. The crew was mustering to the safe room. The engineers were locking themselves in the engine room. The first and third engineer were making their way to the after steering room. The chief engineer was already in the engine room. With him installed there, he could shut down the engines if he needed to, and the first engineer could take over the ship's steering if the bridge was breached. They had a full set of controls down there, a way of bypassing the bridge.

Now I could see the top half of the men standing in the pirate boat. They were leaning forward, rocking with the bouncing of the vessel.

"Call back UKMTO," I called to Colin. "Tell them this is real. And leave the phone line open when you finish so they can monitor what's happening. Got it?"

"On it," he called back. Colin made the call, then grabbed half a dozen flares and headed out to the starboard bridge wing.

I ran over to the SSA, the secret security alarm, and pressed it. That would alert the rescue center that we'd been hijacked. Colin also pressed the SSA.

All of a sudden I heard automatic fire. I could see the muzzle flashes from the pirate boat. They were strafing the ship from a quarter mile away. I heard the *slap, slam, slap, slam* of bullets hitting the metal house. Bullets were ricocheting off the smokestack.

I sat ATM down on the floor near the wheel and told him to steer the boat to my commands.

"Get in here, Colin," I called out. He was out on the bridge wing. He ducked behind the pyrotechnic locker.

"I will in a minute," he shouted back. "As soon as they stop shooting."

We're in it now, I thought. It had happened so fast. *But where was the goddamn mother ship?* If the bigger vessel got alongside, they would be able to put twenty-five armed men onboard. Game over.

I wanted the crewman sitting on the deck. The pirates were firing up at an angle. The only way to get hit by a ricocheting bullet

162

was to be standing up. When there was a break in the gunfire, Colin came hustling onto the bridge.

"Quarter mile away," I called into the handheld radio. "Shots fired, shots fired."

The bullets were making a huge racket as they slammed into different parts of the house and ricocheted off: *splat, whooom, pat.* I looked down at the pirate ship. They were now about 150 feet away. Suddenly they revved the motor and came around behind us to our port side. They were still shooting, semiautomatic mixed with automatic. The AK-47 makes a distinctive sound, a fast, deep *tat-tat-tat-tat.* I'd never heard one shot before except on TV. Bullets were pinging off the superstructure a split second after the AK-47 spat them out.

I had to do something. I grabbed a few flares and ran out to the port bridge wing and started shooting down at the pirate boat. I could see they were coming alongside at the point of our number two crane. Bullets were flying everywhere, but the Somalis' aim had gotten better — the bridge wing was getting raked with fire and they were stitching their way across the wing where I was, *ping ping ping.* I ducked down and then popped right back up, spotting one Somali sitting in the boat cross-legged, firing up at me. I could actually see his face, concentrating hard on drawing a bead on me.

I started popping up, firing a flare, and then ducking down behind the wind dodger, which is a metal hood that deflects the wind over the bridge. I was like a jack-in-the-box, hiding and then standing to fire. Those flares were our only chance of stopping them at this point — putting a flare in the boat, hitting a gas can . . . a one in a million shot — and the best way to draw fire away from my guys on the bridge.

Out of flares, I dashed back onto the bridge. "Fifteen degrees left," I called to ATM, who was now manning the wheel. I looked down at the GPS and we were doing 18.3 knots. I was putting us into what's called "racing maneuvers," a zigzagging technique that makes it hard for another boat to come alongside. The deck of the *Maersk Alabama* was only twenty feet above the water's surface. All the pirates needed to do was put their skiff parallel to our ship, toss a rope with grappling hooks on our deck, then shimmy up. "Now fifteen degrees right," I called. You don't want to turn too hard or you'll kill your speed. You get it swinging and then take it back the other way.

I looked down at the water and couldn't

believe what I saw. The pirates were lifting this beautiful long white ladder into the air. I thought, *Where the hell did they get that thing?* It looked like something you'd get at the Home Depot, a pool ladder with rungs that hook on top. Usually, the Somalis used grappling hooks or a pole or a line, but this damn thing seemed custom-designed to take our ship. It had two vertical pieces that connected nice and tight to our fishplate, a piece of solid metal that comes six inches high off the deck.

I saw the hooks fasten onto my ship. Within five seconds, a head popped up over the side, followed by a body jumping quickly to the deck. He was a little aft of the number two crane, so he was about seventy feet away from me. It was the guy I would come to know as the Leader.

Goddamn it, I thought. *They're onboard.*

"One pirate aboard," I called into the radio. "We've been boarded." The Somali didn't have a weapon in his hand. I leaned over and saw he was bringing up a white bucket on a yellow line. That's where his gun would be. And right behind the bucket was a second pirate.

"One pirate aboard, one pirate climbing," I called into the radio.

We were sliding down a slippery slope

toward disaster. The pirates had guns and we didn't. All that we had to fight them were our brains and our willpower. Most guys would take the guns in that contest, but we had to play the hand we'd been dealt.

I ran back onto the bridge wing with fresh flares in my hand. The Somali on the deck turned and raised his hand and I heard *pow, pow, pow.* He had his gun now and he was shooting. I shot back a flare and it bounced off the deck and tumbled into the water. I ducked down just as the guy blasted off a few rounds and *BAMMMMM,* a bullet slammed into the wind dodger directly in front of my face. I looked up and saw the dent in the metal.

"Oh, shit!" I said. If it had gone through the steel, that bullet would have caught me squarely in the face.

I hopped up. The first pirate was gone. *He must be hiding behind the containers on deck,* I thought. I knew his ultimate target had to be the bridge, but it would be a while before he could reach it.

The second pirate came over the top of the ladder and landed on the deck.

"Two pirates aboard," I radioed.

I faced a decision: Give up the bridge now, lock it up tight, fall back to the safe room, and wait it out. Or I could hold the bridge and pray the pirates couldn't make it through the piracy cages and up seven stories.

I didn't want to give up my ship. *Hell, no,* I thought. *I'm not giving up the bridge to anyone.* There's something about the bridge that's special to a captain: It symbolizes your control of the ship. It's like a pilot in the cockpit of a 747. You've been trusted with this thing. You don't want to hand it over unless you absolutely have to.

It was what I call my first mistake. I should have begun the retreat right then. But I thought I still had time. I wanted to be in control for as long as I could. It was hubris, I guess. *Come and take it from me.*

I fired a couple of flares at the second guy. I could see the pirates were very thin and dressed in dirty T-shirts and shorts with rubber sandals. The second guy immediately sat cross-legged on the deck and began firing up at me with his AK-47.

From down below, I heard three shots that sounded like a rifle. I later realized it was the first pirate shooting off the locks on the chains that secured the outside ladder. But I still thought he was tucked behind those containers on deck, waiting for the other guys to join him. The pirates had time on their side. They knew we weren't armed.

There was nothing to stop them except the piracy cages. If they got through those, we were hostages. But until the Leader started coming aft, I still felt secure on the bridge.

I dashed back onto the bridge, ready to lock up and start our pullback into the depths of the ship. ATM was crouched on the floor, looking up at me anxiously, waiting for the next order while Colin was moving around the bridge. I opened my mouth to talk when I thought I saw a shadow in the corner of my eye. I turned. It was the first pirate, and he was outside the bridge door pointing a battered AK-47 at me through the window.

NINE:
DAY 1, 0735 HOURS

"The key to our success is that we are willing to die, and the crews are not."
— *Somali pirate, Wired.com, July 28, 2009*

Just as I turned, the Somali shot off two rounds into the air. *POWWW. POWWW.* Up close, that weapon sounded a hell of a lot louder than from down below.

"We're fucked," I heard one of my crew say behind me.

"Relax, Captain, relax," the pirate yelled at me. He was short, thin, and wiry. His face was tense. "Business, just business. Stop the ship, stop the ship."

I was so shocked I couldn't answer. I couldn't believe he'd gotten up so fast. He'd gone through the piracy cages like they were child's play.

It was 7:35 a.m. The pirates had taken about five minutes to board my ship and take the bridge.

I still had the portable radio in my hand. I turned my back to the pirate, pressed the key, and, in a low voice, said, "Bridge is compromised, bridge is compromised. Pirates on the bridge." This would let the first engineer in the after steering room know the pirates were in control. "Take the steering," I half-whispered.

"No Al Qaeda, no Al Qaeda, no problem, no problem," the pirate yelled, the AK-47 pointed at my chest. "This is business. We want money only. *Stop the ship.*" He was twelve feet away.

"Okay, okay," I said. "It takes time, just relax." When you stop a ship, you have to shift down gradually through a program. I pulled the ship back from our sea speed of 124 revs down to full ahead, which is the maneuvering speed we use in ports.

Different alarms were going off all around me, *brrrrrrrtt, brrrrrrttt, brrrrrrrtt, whoo, whoo, whoo.* The noise was incredible. I started dancing around the console, silencing them. I looked over at the phone. It was lying sideways on the desk where Colin had left it. I hoped to God UKMTO was on the other end listening to all this go down.

I realized the rescue center alerted by the security alarm hadn't called and asked for the nonduress word. Did anyone know this was a hijacking and not just a malfunction?

I walked over to the stick and jiggled it. Nothing. The chief engineer had switched control over to his instruments in the engine control room. The first and third had control of the steering. They were now in control of the ship. They were on their own.

It was a small victory. Whatever happened, the *Maersk Alabama* wasn't going to head to the Somali coast, unless the pirates hunted down my entire crew.

"Stop the ship, stop the ship," I called into the radio. I left my finger on the key button so everyone could hear what the pirate was saying. I could feel the engineer kill the engines. That thrum that you grow so used to died away. We were now gliding through the water, going in circles.

That annoyed the pirate. "Stop this circling," he called to me, and the muzzle of the AK-47 circled around as he talked. "Straighten the ship out."

"Okay, no problem," I said. I started working the stick and the wheel. Nothing happened, of course, because the first assistant engineer, Matt, was steering the ship down below. I gaped in astonishment and then looked over at the pirate.

"Ship broken, ship broken," I said. I showed him how moving the wheel had no effect on the direction we were moving.

"What?!" he yelled. "Straighten out the ship."

I shrugged my shoulders. "I'd love to, but you broke the ship. You wanted me to slow down, and we did it too fast."

I pointed to the console and tapped on the bow thruster reading. The bow thruster is another screw at the front of the ship that enables us to maneuver. The indicator read "0." Then I pointed to the rudder angle indicator. It was dead, too.

"Ship broken," I said.

The pirate didn't like that. "Shut off the water, shut off the water, stop the ship."

ATM went out to help the other pirates get up the ladder. I was going around the consoles, shutting off alarms. I killed the fire pump and the spray from the piracy hoses died away.

As I was moving around the consoles, I came to the radar set. I looked up. The Leader was distracted, barking orders to ATM. The radar set has three knobs on it. The first is the gain, which controls the sensitivity of the radar to incoming data. I turned that all the way down. Then there were the anti-rain and the anti-sea-clutter knobs, which screen out things like ocean waves, swells, and precipitation. I turned those two all the way up. By doing so, I'd degraded the radar completely. You could have parked a battleship two miles away and the radar would have looked as clean as an empty dinner plate. I wanted to rob the pirates of an extra pair of eyes, in case the navy came calling.

I walked away, strolled to the VHF radio, and switched the channel from 16 to 72. No one used 72. If the pirates tried using the VHF, they might as well try calling the surface of the moon.

I looked up. ATM came through the bridge door followed by three pirates. One of them was the tall guy who'd been shooting up at me, the other was the one I would come to know as Musso. He had an AK-47 slung around his shoulder and a bandolier of ammunition. He looked like he was ready to face down Rambo. He was limping; apparently, he'd injured his foot climbing up the ladder. There was the other bandit I came to know as Young Guy, just because he looked like he was a college student. But with his Charles Manson eyes, he would turn out to be one of the more sadistic of the pirates. And there was the other Tall Guy, who never made much of an impression on me. There was no question who was in charge — the first pirate onboard, the

Leader, gave the orders and the others obeyed them.

The three older pirates were probably between twenty-two and twenty-eight. Young Guy was no older than twenty-two, I would say. Between them, they had two AKs and several bandoliers of bullets. They also had what looked like a 9mm pistol, with a rope or lanyard hanging from the butt, and as I looked at it, I thought I saw a U.S. Navy insignia on the gun. *What the hell were they doing with a navy sidearm?*

That question would come back to haunt me later.

The pirates took up positions on the bridge. I could tell they had some experience. The Leader stayed with us. Tall Guy went to the starboard bridge wing, Young Guy went to the flying bridge, and Musso went to the port bridge wing. They told ATM and the third mate to sit on the deck, starboard side. Meanwhile, I was at the console, silencing alarms, because they were still going off continuously, *whoop whoop whoop* and *ding ding ding.* It sounded like a war had broken out and it just added to the stress.

The Leader gestured to me. "These guys are crazy," he said. "They're Somali pirates. I'm just interpreter."

I looked at him, like, *You can't be serious. The good cop, bad cop routine? Really?*

"Dangerous guys," the Leader shouted. "They will kill you. They're crazy!"

No shit, I thought. They looked dangerous. My heart was racing with adrenaline and fear.

But the Leader's approach was very smart, I thought. He wanted us to trust him, and what better way of doing that than making himself our only salvation against the rampaging pirates?

"Call the crew," the Leader said. I knew this was coming. The more hostages, the more leverage the pirates would have with Maersk. They wanted all hands on the bridge to prevent anyone from braining them with a wrench or garroting them while they slept. But I'd be damned if I was going to give them any of my men. In fact, my plan was to get Colin and ATM out of harm's way as quickly as I could.

"Okay," I said, and I picked up the mike on the PA system and the handheld radio. "All crew, all crew, report to the bridge. Pirates want the crew on the bridge, repeat, *pirates* want the crew on the bridge."

Nothing. I prayed that everyone stayed where they were.

The Leader was yelling at his men, so I

keyed my handheld radio. "Four pirates aboard. Two on bridge wings, one on flying bridge, one inside the bridge. Two AKs on the wings, one nine-millimeter in the bridge."

The Leader turned and snapped at me.

"Call them again," he barked. I repeated the "come to the bridge" message.

Not a sound from below.

The bridge was getting uncomfortable. The crew down below hadn't secured the secondary power supply yet, so most of the emergency lights were on — every third bulb was lit. And the air-conditioning was shut down, so we were beginning to broil up there. A deck is like a greenhouse. It traps heat. I felt the sweat just running down my back.

I wanted to open some kind of communication with the pirates, besides them barking out orders and me following (or pretending to follow) them. Any hostage training will tell you: don't appear too confrontational or too meek. *Maintain your dignity* was a phrase I remembered. If you're screaming at the boss or whimpering in the corner, you give your captors an extra, personal reason to put a bullet in your head.

I decided I was just going to be myself. It had worked for me so far in life. I decided to trust my instincts and forget about trying to be the perfect hostage.

I needed to start a rapport with the pirates. They were very on edge, not wanting us to get close to them. Whenever you approached one, their eyes would get wide and they'd wave at you with the gun.

I looked over at the Leader. "Can we get these guys some water?"

He nodded. I motioned to ATM, and he stood up and walked to the water fountain by the port door, watched carefully by the pirates.

As I worked the console, I sidled over to where the Leader was standing. "Hey," I said. "You guys got cigarettes? We have some if you're out."

He nodded. I went to the GMDSS table and grabbed a few cartons that I always kept there to give the harbor pilots and problematic port officials. I distributed them around. From being in places like Mombasa and Monrovia, I knew how popular tobacco was in Africa, and the last thing I wanted was some gunman with a nicotine shake pointing a gun at my guys.

They lit up and a bit of the tension went out of the room. I grabbed some sodas and handed them over, too.

The Leader took a puff and pointed to me.

"What nationality?" he said.

"Me?" I said. "Or the ship? What do you mean?"

"The ship, the ship, what nationality?"

"U.S.," I said.

His eyes lit up. I heard the other pirates whoop. Obviously, they'd hit the mother lode.

"What about crew? Nationality?"

"All different," I said. "American, Canadian, African."

Now that I had them in a good mood, smoking and laughing, I wanted to slow things down. I needed time to think.

The UKMTO knew we'd been taken by pirates. I was calculating in my mind how long it would be before help arrived, and I wanted to put the brakes on as much as possible. Any delay would give me time to strategize. I wanted to think out my moves a few steps ahead.

The Leader wanted me to stop the ship and he was getting agitated. I was going through my rigamarole — "Ship's broken, you must have done something to it" — when he finally barked at me, "STOP NOW!"

I raised my eyebrows and, pretending I

was trying to understand, dragged my index finger across my throat. *You mean, kill the engine?*

I heard a voice behind me. "Will you *please*," said Colin, "stop giving 'em the international sign for murder?"

I smiled. "Okay, okay."

The next thing they wanted was a cell phone. "We want to make phone call."

"Sell?" I said. "You want to do what?"

"They're saying they want to make a phone call!" shouted Colin. He didn't understand what I was doing, and he thought I was going to get myself — and him — shot.

"I got it," I said out of the side of my mouth. "Relax. I know what they're saying. Just let me talk to them. Just relax." I was trying to slow every conversation down.

Finally the Leader pointed to the satellite phone on the bridge and gave me a number to dial. It was a Somali country code.

The mother ship, I thought. *They want to get further instructions.*

The Leader watched me closely as I walked over to the phone. I dialed the number and waited. The numbers appear as you punch the buttons, so I couldn't misdial, but I didn't complete the final step. On most sat phones, there's a last key you have to hit to send the call when you're done.

I didn't do that. I showed the Leader the phone.

"No work," I said. "Phone broken."

He came over, glaring at me. "Let me see," he barked.

I showed him the LED display. There was his number, but the call wasn't going through.

I shrugged sympathetically.

"No cell coverage," I said. "Bad phone."

They gave me another number. Maybe it was their warlord or their backer in Somalia. Obviously they wanted to report they'd taken the ship and maybe get the ransom process started or get supplies or reinforcements out to the *Maersk Alabama.*

That wasn't going to happen. I kept dialing and the Leader kept glaring at me.

"Radar," he called out.

I went through my usual "What? Excuse me?" routine before pointing him to the console. He waved the gun that I should go first. I walked over and he stood by me and peered down at the screen. It was blank.

"Seventy-two," he said. "Seventy-two mile scale." He wanted to increase the range of the radar. So he knew something about navigation and onboard technology. More and more I was coming to believe that the Leader wasn't a simple fisherman. This guy had a little training.

I did him one better. I turned the knob to ninety-six miles. He stared down.

"Nothing there," I said.

He was perplexed.

"Where is that?" he said. "What is this showing?"

I knew by how surprised he was that the mother ship wasn't out there. He was stunned that the radar didn't show a nice comforting blip within a few miles of us. It was like his getaway car had disappeared off the face of the earth. By now he must have been convinced that he'd stumbled on the most broken-down, ramshackle ship in the U.S. Merchant Marine. *Nothing* on the entire ship seemed to work.

"There's nothing there," I said.

The three pirates started speaking in Somali. I turned my back and brought my handheld radio up. For some reason, they'd let me keep it. Maybe they thought I needed it to call the crew to the bridge or to run the ship. I intentionally kept it in my hand by my waist constantly so they'd get used to the sight of it. But I used it only when they were distracted or looking away, and then I would key the button and talk without raising the radio to my lips.

"Four on the bridge," I said. "No mother ship yet." I rattled off the Somalis' positions on the bridge again and their weapons.

"Cap," someone said. I looked over. Colin was motioning to me.

I walked over to him. He was sweating and his face was pasty, from the heat or nerves I couldn't tell.

"Cap, just give them the money," he said.

I looked around. I hoped the pirates hadn't heard.

Every captain carries cash in his safe, for supplies and for emergencies. I had $30,000 stowed in mine, in large and small denominations.

"Colin, they're going to want more than thirty grand."

"Just give it to 'em," he said.

I wanted to keep him calm. After his questions about being taken hostage earlier in the trip, I didn't want Colin freaking out. We were all scared, but it was crucial we didn't show it. Fear meant weakness, and weakness meant sloppy thinking. We couldn't afford that.

"It's an option," I said. "We've already given them cigarettes. We'll hold the money in reserve in case we need it." I couldn't care less about the money, but I wanted to slow things down and give myself a chance to strategize.

"I think you should just hand it over," he said.

I walked away.

The Leader went over to the VHF radio, very high frequency, which basically lets you talk to anyone from horizon to horizon, a range of fifteen to twenty miles. It had originally been set to Channel 16, which is the international hailing and distress frequency. Everyone monitored that channel — it's how you call other ships and report an accident onboard. But I'd flicked it to Channel 72 when no one was looking. Nobody ever monitored 72. The Leader might as well try calling the moon.

He rattled off a hailing call in Somali. He had to be trying to raise the mother ship. But he was getting no answer.

I watched the Leader. I knew I had to monitor his mood very closely. All the other pirates were taking their cues from him: when he got angry, they got angry. When he was cool, they were cool. He was like the detonator wires on a bomb. I'd have to watch him very carefully.

I was beginning to wonder just how far I could push the Leader. I wanted to get inside his head. What would he want to do next? How could I get there before he did?

But it's a fine line between deceiving your captors and getting a bullet in the forehead.

TEN:
DAY 1, 0900 HOURS

"We are like hungry wolves running after meat."
— *Somali pirate leader Shamun Indhabur, Newsweek.com, December 18, 2008*

The bridge was getting steamy. The temperature on the water in the Gulf of Aden can reach 100 and above. I knew we were going to get dehydrated quickly in that glass cage. The pirates had the bridge door, which was usually left open to let in a breeze, shut tight.

"Where are the crew?" the Leader asked again.

"I have no idea where they are, I'm here with —"

"Bring up crew NOW!" he screamed. "You have two minutes. If not, these guys are going to kill you."

Suddenly the two pirates at the wings rushed in and raised their AK-47s and pointed them over the console at ATM and Colin cowering on the floor. They jabbed the barrels down toward their faces, screaming.

"You want to die?!" they shouted. "Two minutes, we kill you."

"Calm down, calm down," I said. "I'm doing my best."

"Now minute thirty," Tall Guy yelled, his eyes bulging. He pointed the gun at my belly.

"They're serious," the Leader said. "I told you this. Bad guys, bad guys."

I got back on the PA system. "All crew, all crew," I called. "Report to bridge immediately. Pirates want you on bridge *now.*"

The Leader looked at me, his eyes cold.

"Can you do something with these guys?" I said. "Before someone gets shot?"

He just looked at me and shrugged.

"I'm just a poor Somali," he said. "But I tell you this. You better get somebody up here right now."

"One minute!" said Tall Guy. "We kill everyone."

I gestured with my hands, *Easy, easy.* My heart was racing, my hands felt like they were covered with porcupine quills. Was I going to watch my two crewmen die? If they shot one, I knew, they would go through the ship and shoot us all.

"Pirates threatening to shoot us," I called on the PA and radio. "They want people on the bridge now."

"Thirty seconds!" Musso shouted. "YOU HEAR ME? Thirty seconds and you die."

Tall Guy and Musso rushed toward Colin and ATM and jabbed their AKs violently down, as if they were daggers and they were going to impale my crewmen. The look on Colin's and ATM's faces was pure terror. The Leader ran over and put his hands on Tall Guy's chest and pushed him back.

"Dangerous pirates," he said to me. "Bring someone now!"

"What else can I do?" I yelled at the Leader.

He shrugged his shoulders.

I keyed the radio. "If you don't hear from us in one minute, we'll be gone. You'll get no quarter from them." I wanted the crew to know they'd have to kill these guys if the shooting started. There would be no other way out of this. No surrender.

"Bring the crew up now," the Leader said. "Bring them up to the bridge now or we'll blow the ship up."

I stared at him. Did he just say "blow the ship up?"

"Yes, we have a bomb. We will blow up

the ship in thirty seconds."

I didn't believe them. I'd seen the bucket come up and there was nothing that looked like explosives in it. I began to sense they were bluffing for a quick end to the crew's standoff.

Young Guy, watching me from the bridge wing, smiled at me. There was something odd in his face, as if he were enjoying what the Somalis were putting us through. As if he were watching this all on TV.

The deadline passed. I took a deep breath. It was our first hurdle — they weren't willing to kill us just yet.

I was running around shutting off the alarms, which kept tripping and restarting. I would occasionally key my radio and send off a quick update on what was happening on the bridge. Or I would strategize.

I had an idea where the crew was — the aft steering — but I couldn't be sure. Maybe there were guys still sleeping, maybe wandering the hallways. They were keeping their positions secret, so that the pirates wouldn't storm down and take them hostage. Later I found out that at that moment, Shane was up in the forward crane, spying on us. And the chief engineer was walking around the ship. The other guys were in after steering, the backup safe room we'd discussed during the drill when the chief engineer brought up the idea of having one. I knew they must be suffering down there; it would be 100 degrees or above. And there were guys in their sixties and seventies on the crew. If I left them there too long, hyperthermia — heat stress — would set in. They would get dehydrated, then the symptoms would hit them: confusion, hostility, intense headache, reddening skin, dropping blood pressure. Then chills and convulsions as the condition progressed. And, finally, coma.

There were really three clocks ticking on us: how long before the arrival of the mother ship; how long before my crew was affected by heat stroke; and how long before the cavalry arrived. I tried to calculate all three in my head at once.

But I knew I had to get the pirates off the ship as soon as possible.

The minutes clicked by.

Musso and Tall Guy charged back onto the bridge.

"Two minutes!" Musso shouted. He stood above Colin and pointed the AK at his face from five feet away.

"Captain, bring up the crew," the Leader said from behind them. "Pirates angry now."

"I'm here with you!" I half-shouted. "What do you want me to do? I don't know where these guys are."

"Crew NOW!" yelled Tall Guy. "Or we shoot everyone."

You can't pull the same trick twice and expect it to have the same impact. As menacing as those automatic rifles were, I felt the Somalis were bluffing. If they wanted to kill us, they would have executed one of my men already. The sight of the guns still made my heart race, but I didn't quite believe they were going to start shooting.

The Somalis counted down again, *minute thirty, minute, thirty seconds, twenty. . . .* ATM and Colin had their heads bowed. I felt the sweat roll down my forehead and sting my eyes.

Again, the deadline came and went. Tall Guy and Musso stared angrily at me before saying something to the Leader and walking off to the bridge wings. I felt my spirits lift. These guys were just businessmen, after all. Crooked, violent, thuggish businessmen, but they weren't going to waste precious resources like human lives unless they had to.

All of a sudden I heard a knock. I couldn't believe my ears. Someone was knocking on the bridge door looking to get in with the pirates. I thought to myself, *I bet I know who that is.*

The pirates didn't hear a thing. They were too fixated on terrifying us. I prayed, *Let him just go away.*

Knock, knock. Louder this time.

The Leader looked at me.

"Do you want me to get that?" I said.

He nodded.

I walked over to the bridge door and swung it open.

It was one of my sailors. I pointed toward Colin and ATM. "Come on in," I said. "You're dead."

The newcomer looked at me.

"Go sit over there with the rest of them," I said.

"Okay, Cap," he said, and walked toward his mates.

The sailor's appearance seemed to give the pirates an idea. Instead of waiting for the crew to come to them, they would go track them down. After all, if this sailor was just wandering around the ship, knocking on doors, how hard could it be to find the rest of the sailors?

The Leader pointed at me.

"We want to walk around," the Leader said. "You come with me."

I keyed my radio and started talking.

"You want to go search the ship? Okay, fine. Let's go. Let's start on E deck. That's a good place to look for the crew."

I walked through the bridge door and the Leader backed off. He didn't want me too close to him. I pointed to the door to the chimney and he nodded. I led the way down the stairs to E deck.

A ship that's dead in the water on emergency power has a spooky feel. It's just drifting, ghostly and very, very quiet.

A container ship like the *Maersk Alabama* can be compared to a skyscraper laid flat on the ocean. It has multiple rooms, thousands of square feet of space, passageways and service corridors to hide in. My knowledge of the ship itself was really the only tactical advantage I had over the Somalis. I began to think of how to keep the sixteen men hiding below me away from the pirates and how to get the three remaining men on the bridge into one of those rooms and to safety.

It was like a three-dimensional game of chess. I move my man here, you counter. I protect one player, you make a move on another. I just had to figure out the pirates' strategy before they figured out mine.

The Leader had left his gun with Tall Guy, so he was unarmed. He was maybe five foot nine, 135 pounds. Even though he was young and spry, I could have tackled him and stuffed him in a room somewhere. But what would I have done then? I still had three crew on the bridge. My getting away solved nothing.

"Open up this room," the Leader barked.

E deck held my room and the chief engineer's. There should have been no one in any of the quarters up here. I took my key out and inserted it in the lock of the first door and swung it wide open.

The Leader stepped in. There was a TV and a bed with the bedspread tossed aside and some clothes and a desk with a chair. The place was quiet as a tomb.

We went down the corridor and inspected the chief's room. I was chatting up a storm, in case one of the crew had somehow decided to lock himself in his quarters. My voice would act as a locator beacon, telling the men we were on the way. I also had the radio by my side with the key pressed down so anyone with a handheld set would know where we were.

I was scared. Really scared. But I had to maintain that appearance of control. Without it, I had nothing.

We went down, deck by deck. I unlocked another door and let the Leader pass by me to check it out. He let out a gasp. I thought, *He's found someone.* I turned the corner quickly and rushed into the room.

The Leader was pointing down. There was a prayer rug on the floor. Above it, swinging from a desk lamp, was a pointer that read "Mecca" with an arrow.

"Muslim? Muslim?" the Leader said. He seemed happy and confused at the same time.

"Sure," I said. The room was ATM's.

We went back out to the corridor.

"That's it for C deck," I said. "You want to go to B?"

He nodded.

"Okay, let's do it."

As we went lower, I started to worry. On the ring I was using to open all the doors were keys for the engine room and the after steering, where most of the crew were supposed to be. If the Leader demanded I open them, the jig was up. I had to get him to skip over some rooms, even though all the doors had signs on them with their functions written on them: CHIEF MATE CABIN, ENGINE CONTROL ROOM, whatever. I had to hope that the Leader's English wasn't that good, or that I could distract him with my banter.

We dropped down to B deck. The Leader

pointed out a door.

"Oh, that's just a locker, nobody in there," I said.

"Open!" he said, and jabbed his finger at the door.

I smiled. I wanted to build trust with him so that when we got to the really important rooms, I could skip them. I opened the door, and indeed it was a locker filled with wrenches and other tools. He nodded. The same thing happened a few minutes later. "This one's another locker, but I want you to be happy," I said. I opened the locker. Nothing but janitorial supplies.

After that he trusted me. When we came to the engine control room door, I used another key and it wouldn't work. I just waved at it and kept walking. "Locker," I said. "Waste of time."

We did seven decks and the main outer deck before walking back up through the chimney to the bridge. We walked in and the faces of Tall Guy and Musso registered shock. They started asking the Leader questions in Somali. He barked out short answers. They were clearly not happy.

I nodded to ATM, Colin, and the other sailor. I wanted them to know the crew was still hidden away.

"Captain, Captain come in."

I pressed the portable radio against my leg, hoping to mute the sound. Then I brought it up slowly and turned down the volume. I walked over to the radar and pretended to be looking down at it, while I lifted the radio up and spoke into it.

"Shane, go ahead."

I heard him breathe out. He sounded relieved.

"I'm down on E deck. Where are the pirates?"

I looked up. The four had moved back to their positions: one on each wing, the Leader with us on the bridge, and Young Guy on the flying bridge. I relayed that to Shane, while pretending I was working on the console.

"I think I can take them."

Shane was a take-charge kind of guy. That I liked. But attacking the pirates was not a good idea. "Negative, negative," I whispered, turning my back to the Leader. "Pirates all spread out. Automatic weapons. Do not attempt."

Musso yelled from the bridge wing. The Leader hurried over to the door and tilted his head down. It seemed like he was listening.

"Shane, I think they heard you. Stay quiet."

"Roger that."

Two hours had gone by.

The Leader tried the radio again, calling out in Somali. I turned and looked out the bridge windows.

I noticed something white in the water, about five hundred yards off our starboard beam, near where the pirates had come aboard. At first I couldn't make it out. It looked like a piece of flotsam that was half-submerged and drifting at the same rate we were. You see junk like that all the time, containers that get swept from ships during storms or floating piles of plastic. But something caused me to stare at this piece.

With a start, I realized it wasn't a piece of seaborne junk. It was the Somalis' boat. The skiff was floating upside down, most of the hull underwater, and the nice white ladder was next to it. They were slowly drifting along with us.

I turned to call to the Somalis, but I caught myself. *Did the Leader order them to scuttle the boat?* I thought. They could have just tied it off and let it float alongside the *Maersk Alabama.* Losing a boat like that doesn't happen by accident. They'd raised the stakes as they came onboard. Now I felt they were going to be even more desperate.

I wondered if the Leader had ordered the boat scuttled to intimidate his men. "Either we take the ship," he would have said, "or we die on it." Abandoning your only escape route meant the Somalis had to connect with the mother ship or take one of our lifeboats to make their getaway.

The elation I'd felt when the pirates' bluff had failed drained away. These guys were committed. There was no way they were going to leave empty-handed.

By noon, we'd settled into the beginnings of a routine. ATM and Colin were sipping water occasionally, sitting on the deck on the bridge on the starboard side aft. The third sailor was leaning against the wainscoting trying to keep cool. The Leader was alternating between the radar and the VHF, trying to find the mother ship, coughing and spitting every so often like he had TB. I was shutting off the occasional alarm and trying to think how to get my three crewmen down with their shipmates.

It wasn't going to be easy. If I gave the guys the signal to make a run for it, the pirates would cut them down before they'd taken four steps. No, we'd have to get the pirates to *take* the men off the bridge. I started to formulate a rough plan.

"Ah," the Leader said. I looked up. He was fiddling with the VHF radio.

Shit, I thought, *he's figured it out.* I walked over and looked at the readout. I'd tuned the set to Channel 72. He now had it on 16, the correct frequency for communications between the crew and the outside world.

"—*sk Alabama,* we've been attacked by pirates. Repeat, four pirates aboard."

The Leader stared at the set. So did I. It was Shane's voice, but what was he doing?

"Roger that, this is the guided missile cruiser USS *Virginia.* Helicopters are launching."

"Thank you, USS *Virginia.* When will the helicopters arrive?"

I smiled. There was no USS *Virginia* on the frequency. Both voices were Shane's. He must have made his way down to my room and taken the handheld VHF radio there. And he was doing the same routine I'd pulled yesterday, pretending to hail a navy warship and requesting help.

Now the Leader was truly perplexed. The entire crew had vanished into thin air but now one of them was talking to the U.S. Navy. Musso came over to investigate. His AK clanked against the console's side as he leaned over to listen.

"Who is that?" the Leader said.

I just raised my eyebrows.

"I have no idea, I'm here with you."

Shane's voice came over the radio.

"This is the chief mate. Repeat, Somali pirates aboard. They've taken over the ship."

"That's the chief mate?" the Leader said.

I listened. "It does sound like him."

Shane continued: "Four pirates aboard. All armed. All four stationed in and around the bridge . . ." And he continued his spiel with the phantom navy ship.

"Where is the other radio?" the Leader demanded. I saw real fear in his eyes. The last thing pirates want to do is negotiate with the U.S. Navy. They like to deal with ship owners only. Ship owners don't have laser-guided missiles and sharpshooters.

"There are only two radios I know of," I said. "The bridge has them both."

The Leader looked like his brain was going to explode. We were turning his plans inside out. The Somalis had taken over the ship, but we had taken over the Somalis. For now.

"We go around again," the Leader said.

I shrugged. "Whatever you say."

Again, it was him and me. We made our way down to E deck, then down all the way to the main deck.

I walked down the darkened corridor, the ship dead and silent as a bombed-out city. The chief had cut the emergency power. We had only flashlights. I saw the door to the AC room open ahead of me. I knew the Leader would want to check that out. I brought the radio up. "Okay, entering the AC room. Starboard side door is open. You guys need to get that locked up."

We stepped into the AC compartment. Its massive machinery cooled the entire ship. But the compressors were quiet now. Ahead was the engine room. I didn't want to go in there unless I absolutely had to. If, for some reason, the chief engineer hadn't gotten the message, we'd find him and his assistant waiting for us.

"Entering engine room," I said. I stepped in.

A dead engine room is an eerie, eerie place. There was a little smoke wafting from inside and a bulb burning off to the right, but the place was in almost total darkness. You could hear the *drip drip drip* of water from pipes. You could feel the bulk of the enormous diesel engine in front of you, but you couldn't actually see it. There are empty quiets and full quiets and this was the latter. I felt like we were going to be ambushed.

I led the way. Six steps in, the Leader

called to me.

"No, no, we're done. We go."

I turned, surprised. The Leader looked spooked. He turned and I followed him out.

We made our way around, poked our head in the dry storage room and everything was empty. Meanwhile, I was opening every external door I could. "Do you want to see out here?" I would say, and then I would just leave the door open. This would give the crew a chance to move around fast if they needed to. It would also give any rescuers a chance to get inside the ship quickly. *Hope for the best, but prepare for the worst,* I thought.

But I still didn't believe anyone was coming. What we were going through had never happened before in the modern age — a U.S. ship being taken by pirates. I had no idea if the navy would even be interested. I knew there were warships in the area, but there was no protocol for rescuing merchant mariners.

To me, the only one who was going to save us was us.

Again we found no one. I could tell the Leader was getting more and more unnerved. Every room we opened, there were clothes laid out as if someone was just about to get dressed, or a cup of orange juice sitting there as if someone had just poured it. We walked into the galley and on the cutting board were a knife and half a dozen slices of melon that looked like they'd been cut just a few minutes before. On the burner, a pot of coffee was sitting, steam coming out of its spout.

It reminded me of the famous case of the *Mary Celeste,* the ship found in the Atlantic Ocean back in 1872 with the crew's hairbrushes and boots and shirts all in their places, the cargo all accounted for, but no men aboard. It became the most famous maritime mystery of all time, the ghost ship that lost its eight-man crew on the way to the Strait of Gibraltar. (Piracy was originally suspected, but there hadn't been any reported in the area in decades and no valuables were touched or signs of violence found.) The *Maersk Alabama* had that same abandoned air as we walked through one silent room after another.

"Where is the chief engineer?" the Leader said.

"I don't know," I said. "These guys are crazy. They could be anywhere."

We entered the bosun's room. I'd noticed before that the Somalis were wearing cheap flip-flops. The bosun had some nice leather sandals by his bed and now the Leader was staring at them.

"Look at those shoes," he said.

It was like he was asking my permission.

"Go ahead!" I said. "The bosun doesn't care. Try 'em on."

The Leader kicked off his flip-flops and tried on the sandals. He nodded.

The next stop was the mess deck, which we'd been through on the first go-round. There was a long table with a blanket thrown across it. I stared at that blanket. I was sure it hadn't been there the first time we'd walked through. I didn't know it then, but Shane later told me he'd been roaming the ship when he heard us coming, and he'd dashed into this room just ahead of us. With him, he'd had the EPIRB (emergency position indicating radio beacon), which is a transmitter that can tell rescuers exactly where your distressed ship is. He'd taken it out of its housing, which activates the unit, before we came blundering down the hall. Panicking, he'd thrown the blanket over it, then turned and began searching for a hiding place. Right at that moment, Shane was in the next room, the hospital bay, crouched beneath the desk in the space where the chair usually slid in. We walked in and

Shane could see my shoes, only three feet away.

If the pirates had gotten him, we'd have lost one of our best leaders. But I didn't even hear him breathe.

We looked in a few more rooms and then headed back up to the bridge.

The crew and I were keeping one another safe at this point. I was alerting them to the pirates' movements, and they were keeping a wild card in our hands by staying hidden. Even if the pirates shot a couple of us, they gained no advantage. They still had sixteen guys secreted all over the ship, keeping the vessel out of their hands. And the ship was drifting, powerless. It was a standoff. But the Somalis had reinforcements a lot closer than I did.

The ship was becoming a gigantic oven. The AC was off, and the fans that sent fresh air funneling through the rooms weren't working. The heat was getting intense even when an occasional breeze moved through. I couldn't imagine how the guys in the after steering room were suffering. How long could they hold out before they needed to get some fresh air or water?

The fear I'd felt when I saw the first pirate board the ship hadn't faded. But I was just too busy to pay much attention to it. In some ways, ATM and Colin and the third sailor had it worse. They had to sit on the deck and imagine what could happen to them. I was constantly thinking of how to get us out of this mess alive.

We climbed back to the bridge, sweltering in the afternoon heat. The pirates were getting hinky. Why couldn't we find the crew? I just shrugged. "I don't know where they are," I told them again and again. "I'm here with you."

The Leader wanted another search. This time, Musso and Tall Guy came with me, both armed. Again, I entered the engine room, trying to keep them away from the half-hidden door to after steering, where I thought the crew was. Our flashlights were darting here and there, and we'd get flashes of equipment: lube tanks, dials, pipes. Musso and Tall Guy made it a few steps farther than the Leader before calling, "Enough!"

Even pirates are scared of the dark. It made me grin — they had the guns and they were frightened.

I took them to the mess deck and their eyes lit up when they saw the melons. "You want fruit?" I said. "It's all yours." I helped them load up their arms with juice boxes and melon slices. I headed back to the bridge and as I climbed the outside ladder on the house, I could see the Somalis two flights below, struggling with all their loot. I waited for them.

"You need some help?" I said to Musso. I held out my hands. "Here, let me carry the gun."

He laughed.

I took some of the juices and the fruit and went ahead.

Just as with the Leader, I could have escaped at any time. But the thought never really crossed my mind. Three of my men were in imminent danger. I couldn't leave them to the pirates. It didn't solve anything. Besides, it's just not possible to do something like that and remain the same person you were before. I wanted to be able to look myself — and the crew members' families — in the eye after all this was over and say, "I did my duty as a captain."

Like I said, you take the pay, you do the job.

Back up to the bridge. We filed in and the pirates took up their normal positions. It was past noon. The pirates were fidgety, agitated. Their jubilation at taking an American ship was souring. They were constantly chattering to each other in

Somali, and their conversations were becoming more abrupt. A note of panic had crept in.

I grabbed a drink of water, then wiped my forehead and took a few breaths.

The Leader handed me the phone. He barked out a number. It was like a broken record now, the pirates endlessly repeating the same tactics: search, call, threaten. But the threats were wearing thin. After the second ultimatum, when they told us they would start killing us in two minutes, they gave up that tactic.

The Leader had stopped looking at the LED on the phone, so I just entered random numbers and hit the pound button. The phone dialed, then buzzed.

"This phone is the worst. Seriously, I wish I could get it working for you."

One of the crew took this opportunity to start talking to the pirates. And despite my hostage advice the night before, the first thing he brought up was religion.

"Assalaamu 'alaykum," he said. He nodded at Musso.

Musso just stared at him.

"I'm African," he said. "We are Muslim brothers."

The pirates looked at one another. Musso began to laugh.

I tried to catch the sailor's eye. Next he'd be telling them to chop off the heads of the Christian infidels and take him back to Somalia.

But the pirates didn't care if he was directly descended from Mohammed himself. He was a pawn in their game.

The Leader looked at me. "We search again."

I'd been expecting this.

"No way," I said. "I'm tired of walking around."

I pointed at ATM. "Take him. He can show you whatever you need."

I knew if ATM could walk out, guarded by only one pirate, he might get away. One man knew the ship, the other didn't.

The Leader looked at ATM and seemed to be considering the offer.

"Okay," he said. "We go now."

ATM stood and came walking toward me. The Leader turned to give the other pirates some instructions in Somali.

As ATM passed me, I whispered to him, "He's not armed. Take him to the guys."

I couldn't catch his face as he slipped by. I don't know if he even nodded.

But I could feel the tables turn just a bit. It was our turn to take a hostage.

ELEVEN:
DAY 1, 1100 HOURS

"We are planning to reinforce our colleagues, who told us that a navy ship was
closing in on them."
— *Abdi Garad, a pirate commander, from
the Somali port of Eyl, Agence France
Presse, April 8, 2009*

ATM and the Leader left. I went back to
shutting off alarms, but in my mind I was
willing ATM to somehow ditch the pirate
and find a safe place to hide. The remaining
Somalis alternated scanning the horizon
with watching us.

My searches with the leader had taken
about twenty minutes. Fifteen minutes after
ATM and the Leader left, my radio sput-
tered to life. "Attention, pirates, atten—"

I grabbed it and turned the volume down.
I turned and looked aft. I could hear Mike
Perry talking on the radio. With the alarms
going off and their shouting at one another

and us, the pirates hadn't noticed anything. I brought the radio up closer to my ear.

"— one pirate. Repeat. We have your buddy. We will exchange him for the captain."

I gripped the radio and smiled. *Damn it, we'd done it.* But it was way too early to celebrate. I went back to shutting down alarms. I didn't want a confrontation yet. I wanted to keep things slow.

After thirty minutes, the pirates started getting fidgety.

Tall Guy came into the bridge and pointed his gun at me. "Hey. Where is he? Where is this guy?"

"I don't know," I said. "I'm here with you."

"Get the guy," he said.

I pointed to the radio. "Lot of interference. Too much metal in this ship."

He frowned, but he went back up to the bridge wing.

Fifteen minutes passed. Then another thirty. I could see the pirates shooting glances to one another and hear them asking questions in Somali. Tall Guy shouted over at me.

"Where are they?"

"I wish I knew," I said. "You have to send someone down to look."

Musso thought about that.

"Okay, you go."

"I'm tired of walking around. Why don't you send the big guy?" I said, pointing to Colin.

Musso nodded.

"Okay, big guy, you go down and find them."

I smiled. With two other sailors still under their command, the pirates apparently felt safe letting Colin search out the rest of the crew by himself. I was so close to my goal of clearing the bridge of everyone but pirates and myself.

The pirates were watching us closely, so I didn't have a chance to whisper to Colin as he walked off the bridge alone. I just hoped he had enough sense to lose himself in the ship.

With another man off the bridge, I felt a little lighter. It was like a weight was slowly being lifted off me.

I looked at the aft bulkhead, where we have something called the "watertight door indicator" that tells you which doors and hatches are open and which are closed. That way you can tell which parts of the ship are sealed off from onrushing water. But it also has another use. By watching the door indicators go from red (closed) to green (open) and then red again, I could chart which doors Colin was opening, walking through, and then locking behind him. Every time he opened a door, the indicator gave a little click and changed color.

Where's he going? I thought. There are places on a ship like the *Maersk Alabama* where you can hide and no one will ever find you. I've had stowaways onboard container ships for days and the crew never knew. I just hoped Colin would find the right hideaway. I thought he'd head to the after steering room, but then realized he didn't know about the secondary safe room — he'd been on the bridge during the drill critique.

Click. He was in the number one hole. *Click.* Now he was in the main passageway. Colin was heading down to the bowels of the ship, away from the crew's quarters. *Click.* He entered the emergency fire pump room. It was a little cubbyhole, rarely used and even harder to find.

I watched the screen. There were no more reds turning green. He'd found his hidey-hole.

I smiled. *Good man,* I thought. *Stay down there.*

Now it was down to me and one sailor. Not the first guy I would want to plot an escape with, but you work with what you're given.

I sidled over to him.

He looked up.

"We might have to make a break for the bridge door," I said. "Try and slide yourself closer."

He nodded. One of the pirates leaned over and glared at us, suspicious. The pirate's head disappeared.

"Just be ready," I said to the sailor, and walked back to the middle of the bridge.

I keyed the radio. "Three pirates on the bridge, all with weapons," I said. The radio beeped. I looked at the radio's power indicator. It was running low.

The Leader and ATM had vanished into thin air. It wasn't until days later that I found out what happened.

ATM had led the pirate down into the bowels of the ship, toward the engine room. Mike Perry, my chief engineer, was already down there — he'd headed toward the power plant at the first sign of the pirate attack. As ATM and the Leader made their way through the snaking corridors, Mike was checking on some equipment. "It was pitch black, not a photon of light," he recalled. The *Maersk Alabama* was sitting in the equatorial sun, the water reflecting the heat back onto the steel hull. The temperature inside was climbing toward 125 degrees. "We were starting to feel like we were dying," said one crew member. And Mike could hear the increasing desperation of the pirates — and how they were directing their rage and confusion at me. "I can tell [Rich] is in danger," he said, "just by the tone in people's voices."

Mike walked through the engine room, carrying a knife in his hand for safety, when suddenly a beam of light swept across his face — the Leader, just yards ahead in the darkened corridor, had spotted him. Mike turned and dashed down the passageway, with the Leader racing after him, screaming loudly, the words bouncing off the steel walls. Mike came to a spot where the passageway took a ninety-degree turn, and he quickly rounded the corner, then pressed his back up against the wall. Waiting in the darkness, with the crazy flickering of the Leader's flashlight drawing closer, Mike thought, *Is this sane, what I'm going to do?* His mind flashed back to the stories he'd heard of pirates forcing crew members to play Russian roulette in the bellies of their captured ships. "In my mind," he says, "right there, the question was answered."

Mike heard the footsteps approaching, the knife with its razor-sharp serrated blade gripped in his right hand. The screaming voice was coming closer and closer. When the Somali's face flashed around the corner, Mike snapped forward. "I lunged up at him," he said. Grabbing him around the neck, Mike brought the edge of his knife up to the pirate's throat. "All I had to do was move my hand sideways; it would have cut his throat wide open." Mike body-slammed the pirate to the floor and the Somali, feeling the blade on his jugular, immediately stopped resisting.

Mike didn't know the pirate was alone. He thought that the other pirates were going to come around that corner, AKs in hand, and light him up. "In my mind, I thought, 'Where's the gunfire? Why is there no gunfire?'" He looked down. The Somali's hand was cut badly in the struggle and blood dripped onto the metal deck.

ATM and Mike picked up the Leader and marched him to the after steering room. They knocked on the door and Mike hollered for the crew to open up. He shouted out the nonduress password and the door swung open.

Fifteen exhausted but grimly determined faces stared back at the Leader from the darkness. He'd finally found the missing crew. Just not the way he wanted to.

"I grabbed my radio and I called out to let the captain and everybody know," Mike said. "And I just said, 'One down.' "

The good news was that the giant life-and-death game of hide-and-seek we were playing with the Somalis was working. The bad news was they didn't like it one bit.

I could see Tall Guy's eyes bugging out as the minutes clicked by. Young Guy was up on the fly bridge, but Musso and Tall Guy kept checking on me and my seaman on the bridge. *One of these guys is going to go off,* I thought. It was like the ship was eating men, and it was starting to freak them out.

"Where is he?" Musso demanded.

"Listen, I don't know. My crew is crazy. I don't know what kind of game they're playing."

I wanted to play the dumb captain who couldn't control his own men. But I knew that had a limit.

"What about the big guy? Why hasn't he come back?"

I went back to the PA.

"All crew members, please report to the bridge. Colin, report back."

The Somalis' agitation increased by the minute.

"Why won't the boat go? Make the boat go!"

I held my hands out to them. Calm down. I got back on the PA.

"Chief engineer, please obey the pirates and come to the bridge."

Tall Guy and Musso were practically bouncing up and down with nerves. They'd found another handheld radio and were monitoring it. Mine was dying. I hadn't heard Mike Perry or Shane in at least thirty minutes.

The pirates started looking over the deck. They spotted something and Musso turned to me.

"What is that boat?"

"What boat? Where?"

"Right there." He pointed at the MOB, the Man Over Board rescue boat, secured on B Deck.

I told them what it was — a rescue vessel with its own engines and supplies.

"This boat, it works?"

"Sure it works," I said.

I wasn't trying to hide the fact that they could escape on the MOB. I *wanted* them to take the boat. Hell, I'd drive it for them. Getting them off the *Maersk Alabama* and getting my men in the clear would be like winning the Super Bowl for me.

"Show me," Musso said.

I walked out the bridge door and we made our way to the bright orange MOB. As I was walking around the vessel, I was talking loudly and keying the radio to let the crew know where I was. The MOB was about eighteen feet long, an open design with no canopy, made of fiberglass-reinforced resin with a single outboard engine and three rows for seating. To get it down to the water, you had to winch it off its cradle, get it out over the water, lower it down, and pull a release bar, freeing it from its falls.

I climbed into the MOB and hit the engine switch. I started it up briefly, then the pirates tried it. Each time the outboard roared to life.

"We can take this boat?" Tall Guy said. Some of the tension seemed to have left his face. Obviously, the pirates wanted to know they could get away if they had to.

"Sure," I said. "I'll even get it in the water for you."

He and Musso talked it over in Somali.

Their radio crackled.

"We have your buddy," Mike Perry said. "You there, pirates? We have your buddy and will trade him for the captain."

Tall Guy keyed the button.

"Who is this?"

"Chief engineer."

"You have our man?"

"Yeah. And we'll do a trade for our captain."

This sparked another round of intense dialogue in Somali. Tall Guy looked at me.

"We need money," Tall Guy said. "We can't leave without money."

I nodded.

"I understand that," I said. "I have plenty of money in my room. You can have it if you leave the ship."

"How much?"

"Thirty thousand dollars."

They weren't impressed. They were out on the Indian Ocean looking for a few million, not thirty grand. But I sensed it might be just enough to get them off my ship, if they still had hostages. Hostages would give them a shot at the big money.

A deal was coming into focus.

We climbed up to E deck and walked into my room. Little did I know that Shane had been monitoring our progress and had been caught in the passageway ahead of us. With nowhere else to go, he'd darted into my room and searched desperately for a place to hide. As I walked in with the two pirates, he was hiding in the closet not five feet away. "You don't know how many times you saved my life," he told me later. "I'd be walking around the ship and I'd hear you talking and I'd dive into the nearest opening."

Later, when I had time to reflect on these hours, I got a lot of satisfaction from the knowledge that I'd been able to keep Shane and the others safe. But I wasn't thinking about it then — I was so immersed in the details of getting the Somalis their money and getting them off my ship that I wasn't thinking of anything else, let alone whether a crew member was within arm's reach. I went right to my safe, spun the dial, hit the combination, and then opened the safe door. I pulled out the $30,000, which was arranged into stacks of different denominations, and handed it to Musso. He and Tall Guy counted the money and nodded.

All the while, the pirates were talking on the radio with Mike, the chief engineer. They agreed that the crew would give up the Leader, and the pirates would hand me over at the same time. I wasn't involved in the negotiations — I was too busy getting things ready for the Somalis to leave.

We went back to the MOB and I began to

raise it off its cradle with the davit, a small crane that lifts and lowers materials down to the water. I needed to lift the boat up, swing it over the side, and lower it to the water forty feet below.

But there was still no power. So I started to hand-crank the son of a bitch as Musso and Tall Guy watched over me with their AKs.

"Wait," Tall Guy said. "We need more fuel."

"More fuel?" I said. "You can make it to Somalia with what you have onboard."

You couldn't. With the two and a half gallons onboard the MOB, they'd make it halfway to the coastline and then be drifting. I knew that, but they didn't.

"More fuel," Musso said. "You listen to us."

"How much do you need?"

"Plenty, we need plenty."

Whatever it took. I went up to the deck to the Bosun locker and took out a hose, a pipe fitting, and a clamp. I cut the hose to the right length — the Somalis had never taken my three-inch jackknife off me — and brought it over to the tank for the emergency diesel generator. I knew there were a hundred gallons in there at the very least. I found some plastic five-gallon buckets, lined them up, attached the hose to the drain on the generator fuel tank, and let the diesel flow into the bucket.

Tall Guy came up next to me and looked at the panel on the emergency generator. He reached up and started flipping switches up and down. He probably thought he could get the damn ship running if he hit the right combination.

I yelled over to him. "Can you please leave those alone?"

He laughed and walked away. I went back to my fueling.

I'd chosen the buckets carefully. They were the dirtiest ones on that part of the ship, filled with grease and chemicals and the backwash that accumulates when you run a container ship. If that didn't gum up the MOB's engine, nothing would.

The buckets filled up quickly. The pirates helped me ferry them over to the deck near the MOB. Once we had the vessel in the water, we'd lower them down. With that much fuel, they could make it anywhere on the Somali coast.

As I was ferrying the buckets over, I passed the rope scuttle hatch sticking three feet above the deck. That particular hatch led down to the aft line locker, a little area where we kept all the rope for the *Maersk*

Alabama. And the hatch was standing wide open, with a line running down into it. There's only one reason that hatch would be open: the crew must have been down in the scuttle, lying on the ropes, trying to catch a breeze and escape the infernal heat of the ship.

I was hoping the pirates wouldn't notice. The hatch door had been shut the first time we passed it. Now it was gaping open. But, sure enough, instead of walking by they stopped right in front of it. And after a few seconds of confusion, Tall Guy and Musso leaned over and peered into the darkness.

I brought my radio up. "Guys, they see that hatch. Get away from it now. The pirates are right above you."

Musso brought out his flashlight and pointed it down. I held my breath. If they found the crew now, the deal was off.

Tall Guy unslung the AK-47 from his shoulder and pointed it down the scuttle. They must have heard the guys moving around down there. *Goddamn it,* I thought. *It's over.*

He pulled the gun back and handed it to Musso. Tall Guy ducked down and put his head into the hatch and tried to see if he could wriggle through the opening. They were going to go down there and hunt my men down. But not even he was skinny enough to get his shoulders through the hatch.

"Come on," I called to Musso from about fifteen feet away. "Do you want this fuel or not? I need some help here or we'll never get going."

Musso looked back at Tall Guy, who was wrenching his shoulders through the hatch opening.

"Get out of there," I whispered fiercely into the radio. "Pirates coming down."

Musso tapped Tall Guy on the side and said something in Somali. Tall Guy pulled his head out of the hatch and looked over at me.

"Grab those two buckets," I called out. "Quit fucking around already. Do you want to leave the ship or not?"

Tall Guy took another look down the hatch, peering with his flashlight darting up and down. Then he turned and started walking toward me.

I felt relief wash over me.

I got in the MOB. The pirates wanted me to teach them how to start and kill the engine. I was more than happy to do it.

Tall Guy and Musso were really warming up to the idea of sailing away. "We'll just get off your boat," Musso said to me, cracking a smile. "We'll be done here." Thirty thousand dollars wouldn't buy them a Mercedes SUV and a mansion, but it was a hell of a lot more than most Somalis would see in a lifetime of working. Not bad for a day's banditry. As far as I was concerned, they were welcome to it. It was a small price to pay for getting my ship and my crew back.

By now, it was late in the afternoon. I was rushing to get the Somalis off the *Maersk Alabama* before nightfall. I was winching the MOB off its cradle, but the progress was painfully slow.

"Where are the engineers?" Musso said. "Pains in the asses, those guys."

"I hear you," I said. I smiled to myself. I'd managed to create a little bit of reverse Stockholm syndrome with the Somalis. Tall Guy and Musso and myself were united in our disgust at the incompetence of my crew. *Shit,* they must have thought, *how does he sail with these idiots?* The two tall Somalis were competent sailors, I would find out later, and the Leader was as smart as they came. But I suspected they hadn't stormed enough ships to learn the basics of hostage-taking. Believing that the captain couldn't get his men on deck was an amateurs' mistake.

With $30,000 in their hands, the two

pirates were satisfied. Still, Shane's little trick of faking a distress call to the navy had clearly had its effect. They were continually sweeping the horizon for any sign of a destroyer. But their mood had improved.

As had mine. This nightmare was almost over. I wouldn't even allow myself to think we were nearly free. Too much Irish superstition, maybe — or my dad's insistence on finishing the job. But that threat of spending the rest of my life in a black hole in bandit country seemed further and further away.

"We can do this," Musso said to me. "But now we need our guy."

"You can't get your guy until we're in the water," I shot back. No way was I doing an exchange until these guys were off my ship.

"Okay, okay."

My radio was beeping but it still had a little juice left. I walked over to the fuel buckets and pretended to fuss with one of them. Meanwhile, I called the chief engineer on the radio.

"Chief, these guys are ready to get into the MOB. We'll make the exchange once we're in the water."

"Got it."

"As soon as they're off the ship, get it ready to go. I want you to get out of here

ASAP. When you see your chance, go. Don't worry about me."

There was no false bravado here. Victory to me was separating my men and my ship from these bandits. The rest I'd worry about later.

Now I saw Young Guy climbing down the ladders. I was ecstatic. That meant one seaman was up on the bridge, completely unguarded.

"Guys, someone proceed to the bridge immediately. Our shipmate is up there alone. All the pirates are with me now. Grab him and lock him up so he doesn't wander off again!"

I felt a surge of adrenaline. I'd won Round One. Now to survive the rest.

Twelve:
Day 1, 1530 Hours

THE PIRATES CHALLENGE OBAMA'S
PRE-9/11 MENTALITY.
> — Wall Street Journal

SOMALI PIRATES HAND OBAMA FOR-
EIGN POLICY EMERGENCY WITH NO
EASY SOLUTION.
> — FOX News

Things started to happen quickly. Young Guy joined the three of us near the MOB. I saw Shane and Mike three stories above on the bridge wing looking down. The crew still had the Leader down below — and there was plenty of steel between Shane and Mike and the pirates, so they weren't worried about being captured. But the Somalis were unpredictable. They might charge up the ladders shooting at anyone they saw. Shane and Mike began issuing orders over the radio to the crew, who were emerging out of the aft watertight door to the port side, where the emergency generator was.

I especially didn't want Shane or Mike to get nabbed. They were intelligent and they had balls and they were the vital cogs in getting the *Maersk Alabama* powered up and sailing away. The crew needed them to make good their escape.

"Hey, Cap, you okay?" Shane called down to me. On his face, I saw fear — not for himself, but for me.

I gave him a thumbs-up.

"Everything's good," I said. It was true. I felt the end of this ordeal coming into view. The adrenaline that had seeped into my veins in quarts now began to ebb.

But the MOB was still only a couple feet off its cradle. I had to get it moving faster and for that, I needed juice. I got on the radio.

"Chief, I got to get this davit powered up or we'll be here until the morning."

"Roger that."

The ship started to come alive above and below me. Men were scurrying out of their hiding places and running to get systems up and running: hydraulics, backup power, electricity, air. The pirates were a few feet away from me, watching the MOB lift and turning to check the horizon.

"Okay, the boat will be in the water soon," I said. I wanted to keep them cool and collected.

My radio was crackling with Mike giving orders to various crew members and status updates.

"Who's that?" Young Guy shouted.

I looked over. I saw a shadow on the aft deck and then it was gone.

"You got me," I said to the pirate.

I keyed my radio. "Chief," I said softly. "Tell these guys to keep close to the bulkhead. The pirates are going to see them."

He radioed a warning to the crew.

Shane called down on the radio. He could see that I was having trouble getting the davit to work. I was hand-cranking it up from its cradle, as the emergency power still hadn't clicked on.

"You want me to send the bosun down to help you launch the boat?"

"No, I do not," I said. "I don't want to give them any more hostages. I can launch the boat. You guys just keep out of sight and keep an eye on these pirates. I can't see them all the time and I don't want them showing up with a crew member in their clutches again."

"Roger," Shane said.

"What's taking the power so long?" I

called on the radio. "Tell the chief engineer there might be some switches flipped on the emergency generator panel. The Somalis were messing with them."

I heard the information passed down the line over the radio.

Then I started bossing the pirates a little bit. Once you're a captain, it's hard to let go of old habits. I also wanted to keep them busy, so they wouldn't notice what was happening with my men.

"Okay," I barked at Musso, "get over here. You work the motor mount. Make sure you don't damage the prop when we clear the cradle. You" — pointing at Young Guy — "get in the boat. You're the counterbalance. You're going to keep the prop up so the engine doesn't drop and snag. And you" — Tall Guy — "you can do something over there."

Tall Guy was on the radio with the chief engineer. They were like buddies now.

"Chief, what's the matter with the ship?"

"Ship is a no-go, pirate," Mike said.

"Chief, why you such a problem?" And the pirates started to laugh.

"Hello, my friend," I called. "Get off your ass and start doing some work or we'll never get out of here."

Shane must have heard this.

"That's my Cap," he said, loud enough so I could hear him, and laughing at the same time. "Now he's ordering the *pirates* around."

It was surreal. The mood had turned jovial. Suddenly we were just a bunch of guys trying to get a job done, and enjoying ourselves while we did it. For a few minutes, the pirates and the crew were no longer adversaries. That wouldn't last long.

Forty minutes in, we got power on the davit. I swung the boat out over the edge of the ship.

"Okay, everybody in," I said. "Jump in the boat and I'll follow."

Just then, a thought flashed across my mind. *The emergency release.* The MOB had a release system mid-ship that sits about shoulder high. It consisted of a trailer hitch pin and a lever. If you pulled the pin and dropped the lever, the boat released from its metal brace and dropped to the water forty feet below. The mechanism could come in handy when you needed to get off a ship fast, when a fire was raging on your deck or the vessel was about to turn turtle and take you down to the bottom of the Atlantic.

The thing was, I had to be on the boat to pull the pin. I couldn't do it from the *Maersk*

Alabama's deck. So I'd have to pull the pin, drop the lever, and in the same instant grab hold of the metal brace and let the boat fall to the water. *Boom, boom, boom.* I'd be left dangling off the side of the ship while the Somalis plunged toward the ocean. They'd probably break their backs at the very least. Water doesn't compress, which means it's no more forgiving than concrete when you're dropping onto it from a distance.

Once the boat was away, I could swing back onto the deck like Indiana Jones.

But if I didn't manage to catch the brace, I'd be dead. Or if my foot tangled in a rope as the MOB dropped, I'd be dead. Or if one of the pirates survived and fired off a few rounds at the bastard who'd nearly killed him, I'd be dead.

I was making the final preparations to lower the boat. The pirates were finding their seats and spreading out over the MOB's benches. I had maybe thirty seconds to decide.

Can I grab it quick enough? I thought. I just didn't know. My hands practiced the maneuver in the air. *Pull, release, grab. Pull, release, grab.* All in a split second. I tried to picture it in my mind. It was that last step that I fixated on. *Will my fingers slip off the metal? Will I have dropped too far to grab hold?*

Finally, I said the hell with it. Let me just get these guys in the water. The pirates lost their ladder when they boarded, so they had no way to get back aboard. Good enough for me.

That was what I call my second mistake. For the next four days, I came back to that moment over and over again. I kept thinking, *I should have dropped those suckers. If I ever get another shot, I'll drop them without a second thought.*

Back home in Vermont, they didn't know anything about the hijacking. Andrea had been sick all day Tuesday with a flu bug that had knocked her out. Her mother insisted that her sister Lea come over to take care of her. So that Wednesday morning, Lea was getting ready for work. It was sunny but cold, a typical Vermont March morning.

Around 7:30 a.m., Lea was heading out to her truck when the phone rang. It was 3:30 p.m. in Somalia, which is eight hours ahead. It was our neighbor, Mike Willard, who lives up the road and works as an engineer in the merchant marine.

Andrea remembers Mike's voice was a little odd. "What's the name of Rich's ship again?" he said.

"Why, what just happened?" Andrea said.

"Andrea, what's the ship's name?"

"The *Maersk Alabama.*"

"I think . . . I think they were just hijacked. I'm coming right up."

Andrea couldn't believe it. She didn't panic right away, because she knew that sailors get kidnapped regularly and they were all sent back home safe and sound once the ransom was paid. She ran outside to get her sister before she pulled away. Andrea was calling, "Lea, Lea, Rich has been hijacked. Don't go, don't go." Then they both ran into the house and turned on CNN.

Mike started making phone calls to the company, since he works for the same firm that I do. They were desperately trying to find out if the early reports were true. Meanwhile, Andrea ran to the computer and typed out a quick e-mail to me at 11:29 a.m.

Richard —
I am aware of what is going on. I am with you all the way. Keeping the faith . . . I love you with all my heart.

LOVE ANDREA.

236

I wouldn't get it until after the ordeal was over.

Andrea went back to the TV, which was her only source of news at that point. In a twist of fate, a Fox news crew had been up at the Massachusetts Maritime Academy shooting a feature on some totally unrelated subject. It turned out that Shane Murphy's dad, Joseph, was an instructor there, and when the news came out about the pirates, they rushed to talk to him. Shane had called Joseph Murphy from the *Maersk Alabama.* Joseph described the hijacking, saying, "My son, the captain . . ." Andrea was like, "What happened to Rich?" It was upsetting to her to constantly hear news of the hijacking but nothing about me.

As the morning went on, Andrea called our kids, Dan and Mariah, who were away at college. She wanted them to hear the news from their mother and not from some reporter or something. She left Mariah a message: "I want you to call me. It's about Dad — he's okay, as far as I know, but I want you to hear it from me."

Andrea ran back to the TV. Shane Murphy was still being called "the captain of the *Maersk Alabama*," and she didn't hear a single mention of me. For my wife, it was like I'd disappeared off the face of the earth.

THIRTEEN:
DAY 1, 1900 HOURS

The White House is closely monitoring the apparent hijacking of the U.S.-flagged ship in the Indian Ocean and assessing a course of action to resolve this issue. Our top priority is the personal safety of the crew members onboard.

— *White House statement, April 8, 2009*

I lowered the MOB to the water with myself and the three pirates in it. The davit put us down with a nice smooth touch. I looked up at my ship. Suddenly, it looked like an ocean liner. Just huge.

"They can still strafe the ship," I said into the radio. "Keep the guys out of harm's way."

The fuel was still on the deck. Shane's head popped over the side of the boat.

"Hey, Cap," he called.

"We're almost there, Shane," I said. "Start lowering the fuel."

The pirates really wanted that extra diesel. They were going to be anxious until it and the Leader were onboard. I turned to see Tall Guy and Musso sitting on the benches, their guns on their laps, the muzzles pointed toward me.

Shane disappeared. A minute later, the first bucket appeared over the side of the ship and Shane lowered it. When it was five feet above the water, he let it drop. The bucket plunged beneath the surface and then he pulled it back up, water streaming down the sides.

I laughed. Great minds think alike. Shane was trying to foul the gas so it would mess up the MOB's engine.

"Don't worry," I said, keying the radio. "I already got enough water in those things." The Somalis were going to find themselves two hundred miles from shore with a useless hunk of metal for an engine.

Bucket after bucket came down. When I grabbed the last one and set it down, Musso spoke up.

"Okay, we need more fuel and some food," he said.

I gave him a look.

"*More* fuel? Where are you headed — Disney World?"

He laughed. The pirates were back on

their element — the water — and they had an American captain as a hostage. In their minds, they hadn't lost a thing. So Musso could afford to crack up at my jokes.

I wanted to get the MOB away from my ship. I took the vessel about one hundred yards off the ship's port quarter and killed the engine. We drifted, waiting.

I called on the radio and ordered up the extra supplies. Shane went to the mess and rounded up some night lunch. Night lunch is what the cook puts out for the evening and early morning watches, or anyone who is clinically insane enough to want to eat it. I couldn't even begin to tell you what's in the night lunch. But we have another name for it: "horse cock." That's actually an insult to horse penis. I've had cooks who've put out the same stuff for a week straight, until there was so much mold growing on it you could make your own penicillin. The stuff is just unbelievable.

It also contains pork. I did know that. So it was Shane's final "fuck off" to the Somalis, who wouldn't be caught dead eating the stuff.

Everything was working fine. We were finally prepared for the exchange. I saw Shane running around, getting ready.

"Okay, we're ready," Shane said on the radio.

"Roger that," I said. I hit the ignition on the MOB.

Nothing.

I hit the ignition again. Nothing. *Don't do this to me,* I thought. Hit it again and it was silent — not even trying to turn over.

"Fuck," I said.

The pirates were looking at me.

"Something wrong, Captain?" Musso said.

"It's dead. Move over. I need to check the batteries."

The MOB was supposed to be on a constant charge. Both its batteries should have been topped up automatically from its connection to the ship's grid. But when I checked the charging switch, I saw it was set to one battery only. The right one had been getting all the juice, but now it was drained, too. When I switched from both batteries to the right one, the engine just went *woooo, woooo, woooo* and wouldn't catch.

"Shane, we got a problem," I said into the radio.

"What is it?" Shane called back.

"Batteries are dead."

I heard him breathe out.

"That's it. Ball game over."

"Not yet," I said.

I got some tools out and started working. I checked all the connections, praying there might be a loose wire. But everything looked good. It was the batteries for sure.

Now came mistake 2.5. I didn't want to get off the MOB. It was an open boat. If anyone did show up to help us, there was nowhere for the pirates to hide. True, we would have been broiling under a hot sun, but anyone with a rifle could have taken the Somalis out as easy as wooden ducks at the carnival.

I should have stayed right there. But I was in a problem-solving mode, eager to get things done. With the MOB dead, I moved to the only option left: The lifeboat.

The lifeboat is an enclosed craft about ten feet high and twenty-five feet long. It's bright orange, powered with a single outboard, with backward-facing rows of seats inside and a raised cockpit with windows, where you can steer the vessel. It drops from its mount, free-falling forty-five feet into the water with a big splash. And it was the last option left.

"Listen, we have to row back to the ship," I said. "This boat ain't taking us anywhere."

We rowed back and tied up alongside the *Maersk Alabama*. "Level your weapons," I said to the pirates as we moved in. I didn't want them pointing their AKs up at the crew as we approached.

The third engineer and the bosun got on the lifeboat up on the deck, after loading the extra fuel and the food. The lifeboat requires only one man aboard during launching, but the third engineer refused to get out. He wanted to be there in case I needed his help.

Shane wanted to be the one in the lifeboat, but I told him he was now the captain aboard the *Maersk Alabama* and he needed to stay where he was.

"But I'll be putting someone in danger," he said.

"Welcome to the job," I said.

When they were ready to go, Shane radioed me.

"Okay," I said, turning to the pirates. "Don't get crazy, this thing drops like a stone and it makes a lot of noise."

They nodded.

With a tremendous splash, the lifeboat dove into the water and then popped back up. My crew members came alongside the MOB and we began transferring food and fuel into our new vessel. We changed places with the bosun and third engineer and, thankfully, the pirates made no attempt to take them with us. What I didn't find out until later was that the third engineer and the bosun were both carrying concealed knives. They were ready to jump the Somalis at the first opportunity, but they didn't get a chance.

"Good luck," I said to the bosun as we were getting ready to shove off in the lifeboat. "Make sure they get you back up quick. And if something happens to me, don't worry about it. Just get the hell out of here. Don't worry about the MOB boat either. The pirates might swing around and try to take that, too."

I started the lifeboat up and the engine came to life. The third engineer and the bosun threw us our lines and we were free.

As I came around, I jammed the throttle down and rammed the stern of the lifeboat into the ship. We hit the hull of the *Maersk Alabama* with a jarring thud.

"What's that?" the pirates cried out.

"Oh, that's me getting used to this thing," I said.

I'd wanted to damage the prop on the lifeboat. I didn't want to go anywhere with the Somalis. But they build those things for survival and the prop was still pushing water.

My luck was turning. The wrong way.

■ ■ ■ ■

Back home, Andrea was walking around our farmhouse wearing my Polarfleece jacket, because it still smelled like me. She was mad at herself for doing the laundry after I left for Africa, because that jacket was the only thing in the house that still had my scent. "I wouldn't let go of it," she said. "I had it on from the moment I heard you were taken. And at night I'd lay it across the bed and my friend Amber and I would each take part of the jacket and sleep."

About noon on Wednesday, the media got hold of my name. Suddenly, local news crews started rolling up to our farmhouse and into our driveway. Andrea's sister, being a true Vermonter, invited them in for coffee. By early afternoon, they had a full house of local reporters and cameramen sitting on our couch and nibbling on cookies, watching Andrea watch the news. Shane Murphy's father was still calling his son the captain of the *Maersk Alabama* — which was technically correct, as the chief mate takes over when the captain leaves the boat — but it made Andrea feel like I'd been forgotten. There was still no mention of me on the national networks.

At this point, Andrea was thinking, *This is the scenario. A ship got hijacked. They'll demand ransom. The company will hold out for a little while. Then they'll pay the ransom. The crew will get set free and everybody will happy and safe.* A couple of merchant mariners who knew me called and said, "Andrea, you know the pirates' MO. They have a business plan. They just want the money. They don't want to hurt anybody."

"I know, I know," Andrea said.

"Knowing Rich, he's probably on the lifeboat telling bad jokes. And he's going to come home with a great story."

And that's what Andrea prayed for: just a normal, everyday hijacking. She didn't want heroics.

Our daughter, Mariah, called back. "Mom, what happened to Dad?" Andrea told her what she knew, managing to keep her composure. That set the tone for the kids. Mariah was strong — deeply worried but not hysterical. "I want to come home," she said. Andrea tried to convince her to stay, but Mariah was adamant. Dan called, too. Andrea gave him the choice to stay or come back and he chose to stay for the last couple days of exams week. "I want to finish," he said. "Oh, Mom, I just studied so hard for these things and I know Dad would tell me to stay. He'd say, 'Stay and finish the job.' "

"You're right, he would," she said.

They were right. Do you know how much I paid for that college? Dan stayed to finish his work. By holding it together, Andrea was hoping the kids would be able to handle the news.

When she knew our kids were okay, Andrea went right back to watching TV, flipping channels between all the major news networks. They were her only lifeline to what was happening thousands of miles away. No special arrangements had been made to keep her or the other families informed of unfolding events.

One thing did help her through that first day, she told me later. I never say good-bye when I leave for a job. I hate hellos and good-byes and want to hear only what Andrea calls "the plain living part" in between. So I always say, "I'll see you later" or "I'll be back." One of the two.

That helped sustain Andrea. "He told me, 'I'll be back,' " she kept telling herself. "And I believe him."

She went to bed having no idea what awaited her in the next few days.

I pulled up forward on the port side where

the pilot ladder was. Four or five crew members were standing at the top of the ladder. I could see them through one of the lifeboat's windows. The visibility was much more constricted than on the open MOB — you had to duck and weave to get a view of what you wanted through the foot-long windows.

"Okay, we're ready for the exchange," I said to Shane. "Look, make sure you start the Leader going down as we pull up. I don't want these guys hopping up on the ladder and retaking the ship. Got it?"

"Roger," said Shane.

"I'm coming in with the lifeboat," I said. I saw two crew men escorting the Leader along the deck. He had a white rag around his hand.

"Let him come down and when I get a chance I'll come back up," I said. We came alongside, bumped up along the *Maersk Alabama.* The end of the ladder was about four feet above the canopy of the lifeboat. I saw him descending and then he jumped the last bit and I felt the lifeboat rock.

"Pirate aboard," I radioed. The Leader came back to me. His hand was obviously hurting him, but he seemed to be in good spirits.

I was grinning, too. I'd done my duty as a

captain. Now all I had to do was save myself. If I saw a chance, I could take it. The oldest instinct — survival — kicked in.

"Show me how to run the boat," the Leader said.

I did. I killed the engine and restarted it a couple of times. I showed him how to steer it, start it, where the compass was. He had a course he wanted to steer — 340 degrees — and I showed him how to do that. Then I stepped down and let him up into the con — that is, the conning station, which is elevated above the rows of seats. He took the wheel and turned it away from the *Maersk Alabama* and pushed the speed up.

"What about the deal?" I said, shocked.

"No deal," the Leader said.

My mistake number three: Don't make deals with pirates. We should have never made the exchange.

I wasn't surprised by the double-cross. I still felt I was ahead of the game. I'd solved three of my four problems: my crew, ship, and cargo were safe. And I was depending on my luck and my tenacity to save myself.

The Somalis pushed me toward the front end of the boat. I spotted the hatch up there and I thought of trying to bust out through it and jump overboard. But it was a horizontal hatch door. I'd have had to pull myself up four feet and then dive into the water. I would probably have had a few slugs from one of the AK-47s in my back by then, so I abandoned the idea.

"We're taking off," I said into the radio. "No exchange."

The Leader was getting the hang of steering, sweeping one way and then the other. Once he got a feel for it, he set off in a straight line. *Next stop, Somalia,* I thought. I knew that's where the pirates would take me. That was their MO. That's where they would negotiate the price for my head. That's where their backers and their reinforcements were.

It was getting close to dusk. In the tropics, the twilight is extended because you're so close to the equator. And the moon was nearly full. We could still see the *Maersk Alabama* not too far away. Its running lights were lit and smoke was pumping from its stack, a wake churning behind it.

The pirates looked back in amazement as if to say, *Wow, the ship's running. Imagine that.* There it was, the ship that was broken beyond repair, working perfectly. There was the missing crew running back and forth doing their jobs. The pirates were incredulous.

I was just about to key the radio and tell

the ship to watch out for other pirate boats when I heard Mike on it, saying, "Make sure no other small boats are coming at us from astern." I nodded. I knew the ship was in good hands.

I was damned glad to see they were under way. We were still in bandit country, and there was nothing to prevent another pirate team from appearing out of nowhere and taking the *Maersk Alabama.* If the ship was dead in the water, the crew would have no chance.

The ship turned its bow toward us, and the smiles disappeared from the Somalis' faces. The *Maersk Alabama* was coming at us fast, and from that angle it looked like the *Queen Mary.* I wasn't worried. I knew if the ship rammed us, the lifeboat would just punch under the water's surface and then bounce back up. I didn't inform the Somalis of this amazing feature of the modern lifeboat, however.

"That chief mate is going to run us over," the Leader said.

"Damn right," I said. "He wants my job. He's been after it ever since we left Salalah."

Musso had his gun on me and his eyes went wide.

"You get up here!" the Leader shouted

251

and jumped down from the con.

"All right," I said.

"Tell them to stop getting close to us," the Leader said. "Tell them to let us back onboard."

I got into the cockpit and we moved around the *Maersk Alabama*. It would cut across our bow, and then swing around and do it again. I held the wheel for thirty minutes, and finally the *Maersk Alabama* went dead slow in the water and lay off about a hundred yards.

Night fell.

The pirates got on the radio and were talking back and forth with Shane.

"Hey, we'll come on back tomorrow," they said.

"Oh sure, we'll start afresh," Shane said. "It was just a misunderstanding."

"Yes, you let us on," the Leader said.

"Definitely," Shane joked. "Come back in the morning, we have food and water for you."

Strange, really, but everyone was relieved at how things had turned out.

The only thing that was bothering the pirates was the sky. The Somalis were sitting on the stern of the lifeboat, scanning the night sky, looking for planes and heli-

252

copters. They still had in the backs of their minds, I thought, the idea that people were coming for me. The sky was so clear you could even see satellites passing overhead. And we did spot two planes — a big one and then a smaller one that flew over and came back and circled.

The pirates seemed to be expecting a plane to come to my rescue. They didn't like that idea. They kept squatting down and listening for the buzz of a plane's engine. It was like they thought the air force was going to start dropping bombs on us or drop a magical ladder and rescue me.

I keyed the radio. "Four pirates, two by the stern hatch, one at the cockpit, one at forward hatch. Two AKs at stern hatch, one pistol at cockpit."

I heard Shane roger that. I continued: "I'm going to be coming out the rear door. If you see a splash back there, it's me. Bring the ship to the splash and I'll come to the other side of your ship." If I escaped — and that was a big if — I wanted to get the *Maersk Alabama* between me and the lifeboat.

The Somalis installed me in the third seat, port side. It gave me a good view of the cockpit and the rest of the ship and I wanted to stay there. And I wanted to stay in one place, so any allies that pulled up on the scene would know exactly where I was located. Friendly fire will kill you just as dead as enemy fire. I keyed the radio and let my crew know what seat I was in.

The pirates closed both hatches. I guess they feared frogmen coming up and climbing down into the boat. That's when the heat began: unbearable, unrelenting saunalike heat just permeated the entire vessel. It was pure hell.

I probably nodded off a couple of times. I came to at around 2 a.m., Thursday morning. I looked out and saw one of the most beautiful sights I've ever seen in my life: an American navy ship steaming toward us at thirty knots, bright lights shining from the deck, sirens wailing and loudspeaker blaring. The spotlight was so intense it lit up the inside of the lifeboat like it was a movie set.

"Shut off the light, shut off the light," the Leader was screaming into the radio. "No action, no military action."

My countrymen had arrived. I felt my spirits lift.

On Wednesday, the media was reporting that the pirates had taken me onto a lifeboat. Andrea said, *My God, how did that happen?*

The news channels had by this point reached my second mate on the *Maersk Alabama,* who told them, "They have one of our crew members. I have to go! I'm steering the boat!" Then he hung up. The second mate wasn't steering the boat. I guess everyone was going a little crazy by then.

Thursday morning Andrea's sister, Lea, did a brief interview for several national morning shows. That was the beginning of the national media descending on our house. By late morning, a whole stream of minivans with satellite dishes was pulling off the two-lane road that goes past our mailbox and setting up in our front yard. Any time Andrea walked outside, this huge pack of journalists would call out, "We want a picture, we want to talk to you, we want an interview." Andrea went out and said, "Guys, I work in a very public place, and I just don't want that kind of publicity." She was also trying to protect our kids from the media frenzy. Soon it came to the point where Andrea looked out the window and saw an electrical line going from one of the news vans into a socket in our house. I'm sure the culprits asked Andrea's brother or someone, and he was just like, "Sure, why not?" On any given day, we're good-natured people.

One thing that was emotionally taxing for Andrea and my family was the constant barrage of rumors. Journalists would call the house and say, "Did you just hear X?" Or "We have unconfirmed reports of Y." All kinds of gossip and speculation were flying around: other pirates were coming to help the hijackers, a ransom payment was in the works, the lifeboat was out of gas. Andrea and her friends were answering every phone call on the first ring, just praying it was good news. And when she was told things that turned out not to be true, she said, "Please don't do this to me. You'll drive me out of my mind." The press even got her cell phone number. Andrea was amazed at that until she realized it was on the outgoing message on our home voicemail. She quickly changed the message, but the damage was done.

The reporters got more and more insistent. On Thursday, everyone said, "Just do it." They naively believed that if Andrea spoke to the media, they'd go away. So Andrea arranged to do a very brief interview with the media. The only TV spot she did was on Wednesday. But it opened up a can of worms. The next day, all three networks were taking turns, competing to get her on the air. The phone was ringing constantly.

That's when Lea decided to speak to the press herself.

There was a constant flow of people through our house. Letters and postcards from strangers poured into our mailbox. The Boy Scouts came by and cleaned up our yard, without anyone asking them to. Vermont's two senators, Patrick Leahy and Bernie Sanders, called, along with our local representatives and town officials. Even Ted Kennedy left his number and asked if there was anything he could do. Everyone was extremely supportive, including a couple from the local Somali community who came by to hand-deliver a note saying they were praying for Andrea and our family.

By Thursday afternoon, all of the calls and the letters and the constant barrage of news had become overwhelming. Even Maersk's CEO, John Reinhart, called and was incredibly caring and attentive. "I need Richard," Andrea told him. "I want Richard. Please just get me my husband home." Andrea was scheduled to do a press conference and was freaking out. She hates public speaking and was hugely nervous about doing it. Finally, a friend from LMS ship management, Pete Johnston, called to see how she was doing and Andrea told him how stressed she was by the idea of speaking to the media. "You don't have to do anything, you don't have to say a word," he told her. She nearly collapsed with relief. But someone had to go out and make the announcement. Our poor neighbor, Mike, who'd first told Andrea about the hijacking, marched into the front yard and told everyone the news, even though he hates public speaking as much as Andrea does. In a crisis, a good neighbor is worth his weight in gold.

Help was on the way for my beleaguered wife. Two wonderful women from the victims' services department of the FBI, Jennifer and Jill, started phoning her the latest updates. The Defense Department also began giving her bulletins as they came in, so she didn't have to jump from channel to channel on the TV trying to see if her husband was still alive. "I remember talking to Jennifer or Jill, I'm not sure which," she remembers. "And I said, 'To you, Richard is just another guy, but to me he's my life, my future, my everything. I need him back.'"

Out there in the middle of the ocean, I could only imagine what Andrea was going through.

The American destroyer was playing cat and mouse with the pirates. They would come up real close to starboard, and then just drift away. Once they were half a mile away, they'd come charging at the lifeboat again and sweep by us and then drift. It was an aggressive way of saying, *Any time we want to, we can take your boat down.*

The *Maersk Alabama* was back in the distance, maybe three miles away. I knew they were out of danger now that the navy had arrived.

I heard a navy corpsman announce the destroyer's name over the radio: the USS *Bainbridge.* The name brought a smile to my lips. The *Bainbridge* had to be named after William Bainbridge, a merchant marine who'd gone to sea at fourteen and eventually rose to be a dashing, impetuous commodore in the U.S. Navy. In 1803, President Thomas Jefferson sent Bainbridge to Tripoli, at the height of the Barbary pirates' reign, to subdue the bandits. But instead, he'd run the USS *Philadelphia* aground on the Tripoli coast and was captured and imprisoned by the pirates. Now his namesake was here to help free me from the inheritors of the Barbary corsairs: the Somali pirates. It was a hell of a coincidence. But one detail disturbed me: Bainbridge had been held for nineteen months before gaining his freedom.

The Leader climbed up into the cockpit

and got the boat going. He resumed our course, doing no more than six knots. There was a magnetic compass up there, so he could steer a course to the Somali coast without too much trouble. And he obviously wanted to have the engine running in case the navy tried to raid the ship. The pirates' normal routine in the lifeboat was to have two guys in the stern with AKs pointed at me, the Leader in the cockpit with the 9mm pistol, and the fourth guy on the bow, usually sleeping. They rotated back and forth to keep everyone rested. I radioed the Somalis' positions to Shane. I'd been on the lifeboat for a little under twenty-four hours by now.

Thursday passed in a daze of heat. And I hate heat. I'm one of those people who looks forward to the first snow in Vermont. I like that feel of cold on my skin. If it's over 80 degrees, I'm miserable. And it was easily 105 in that boat at 0600. After that, it got really hot. The sweat was dripping off my forehead and stinging my eyes. The lifeboat's engine was underneath the floor and an exhaust pipe came underneath the boat, so with the engine constantly running, that pipe and the engine were warming up the floor. It got to where you couldn't even put your feet down because it was so hot.

On any ship I've ever been on, you look forward to the sunrise. You really return to a kind of ancient calendar, where your time is measured out by the angle of the sun. But onboard the lifeboat, I dreaded the mornings, the sun coming up and starting to heat the boat. I looked forward to twilight and darkness as a time when I might get some relief from the blistering temperatures.

The navy came on the radio. They wanted to drop some food and water to us. The pirates okayed it. I couldn't see how they got the stuff over, but they must have launched a Zodiac or something and as it approached — I could hear its engine — I thought, *Freedom is twenty feet away from me right now.* The navy dropped a box of food in the water. There was tension in the pirates' faces. We circled around to the box and one of the Somalis opened the rear door and brought it in.

The navy, in its infinite wisdom, had sent over handheld radios, batteries, water, and Pop-Tarts. Boxes of chocolate Pop-Tarts. And only Pop-Tarts. Andrea loves them but I'm not really a fan of the things and I couldn't figure out why in the hell the commander of the *Bainbridge* chose them. Did they have some special nutritional secret I didn't know about? Were they laced with sleeping powder?

It was so hot, I couldn't eat the stuff anyway. My stomach was growling and I was famished, but the thought of food didn't interest me. I drank some water and picked up one of the military radios the navy had sent. I would find out it had one feature I'd never seen before. When you keyed the "Talk" button, the unit would beep. In civilian radios, beeping meant you were running out of power, and I thought that's what was happening here. So I kept telling the pirates, "Change your batteries, they're dying." I was worried they'd lose power and my only link to the outside world would be cut off. My portable radio from the *Maersk Alabama* had died by now. Later, the navy told me that all their radios beep like that when the "Talk" button is pressed.

The pirates were feeling the heat, too. Every few hours, one would open the rear door and jump in the water to get cool. Or they'd take a piss from back there. They let me back to the door that day to do the same. They had at least two guns on me as I stood there. I could see the *Bainbridge* off in the distance, but the chance for escape was nil. I couldn't even take a leak. It was like being at the old Schaefer Stadium in Foxborough after having four beers in the first quarter of a football game and four hundred guys are standing behind you, waiting for their turn. Too much pressure. I said, "Forget it, this ain't going to happen."

The mood in the boat was light. The pirates were nonchalant. They felt they still had the upper hand. They had a hostage and they didn't have to deal with an enormous boat or watch their backs thinking a hidden member of the crew was going to come up and brain them. In fact, I'm sure that pirates will intentionally do this in the future — board a ship, drop the lifeboat, and take the captain and another seaman off the main vessel. It's an effective strategy, from their point of view. It's far more manageable to have one or two hostages instead of twenty. I believe it's only a matter of time before we see the lifeboat strategy put into action off the coast of Somalia.

I was happy the navy was there, but I didn't think it changed my situation that much. The pattern that other hostage-takings had followed was clear: pirates take ship, pirates take hostages, pirates bring them to shore, and pirates work out a ransom. Any ship from the French or British or whatever navy that trailed them to Somalia was there only to make sure that the hostages weren't unloaded and driven to a safe house. Other than that, they kept their distance. They weren't in the rescue business.

It didn't occur to me that the navy would try to intervene. In my mind, I was still alone in a lifeboat in the middle of nowhere and it was going to be up to me to rescue myself. The idea that CNN would be flashing updates on my situation and that the president would be tracking the progress of the negotiations was beyond my imagination.

The conversation in the boat was mostly banter. The pirates weren't threatening me — yet. The main topic of conversation was what a bunch of mule-headed sons of bitches I sailed with.

"That crazy engineer," one of them would say. "Chief mate, too. What a pain in the ass. What is the matter with them?"

It was like the engineer had broken some code of the sea that said you must assist pirates in taking over your ship. The other Somalis were cracking up about how the crew had deceived them, but the Leader was genuinely angry.

"Why did your crew attack me?" the Leader said, accusingly. "They stabbed me!"

I almost laughed. You take my ship with AK-47s and threaten to kill everyone and you're offended that someone gashed your hand?

"Well, you were shooting at them," I said. "You scared them! What did you expect?"

As time went on, I showed the pirates where everything was on the boat: the first-aid kit, water, survival equipment, flashlights, food. Eager to see what supplies we had onboard, they started opening plastic bags and tossing the contents out, ruining the stuff they wanted to use and that we might need later. As they tore through the bags, I noticed the Leader was holding his injured hand in his other palm and every so often I saw him grimace in pain.

"Hey," I said. "Did you clean that wound out?"

He shook his head.

"Better do it. If that thing gets infected, it's going to get nasty."

The pirates opened the first-aid kit and started passing bottles and packages around. Obviously, Somalia doesn't have a first-rate medical system, because they were looking at these medicines like they were Mayan artifacts.

"What is this? What do you do with this thing?"

I said, "Give me that." Musso piled everything back in the box and brought it over to me and I told him what I needed: eyewash, saline water, bandages, and tape. I rolled out a length of bandage and reached in my pocket for my knife. I pulled it out, unclasped the blade, and started cutting lengths and laying them on my knee.

It had gotten quiet in the boat. I looked up and found the pirates all staring at me.

"What?" I said.

"Where did you get that?"

"This?" I said, holding up the knife. I'd completely forgotten they didn't know I had it. "Oh, you want my knife?"

I laughed and Musso and Tall Guy joined in. I handed the knife to Musso. The Leader also demanded my watch, so I unstrapped it and gave it to him. He already had my flashlight.

The Leader was whining like my kids when they fell off their bikes. I unwrapped the dirty rag and saw some minor gashes across his palm. He sucked his breath in.

"Oh, it's not too bad," I said. The Leader was acting like the hand was nearly amputated. I couldn't believe how quickly this pirate had turned into a whimpering baby.

I dashed some saline eyewash on the wound, and cleaned all the grime and dirt out. Then I put some balm on the gashes, applied some antiseptic, wrapped the hand

266

up in fresh bandages, and taped it up nicely. Then I gave him some ibuprofen and told him to take two every eight hours.

"You need to do this every day," I said.

The Leader nodded.

I thought I'd built a little good will.

I began to get a better sense of the pirates' personalities. Tall Guy and Musso smiled the most. They were easy-going, eager to talk, and in charge when it came to any sailing questions. *Maybe these guys were sailors,* I thought. They sure knew their way around a boat.

The Leader rarely cracked a smile. He was smart, always staring at me and trying to figure out what I was up to. It was beyond him that my fellow Yanks had fouled up his plans. Frankly, he reminded me of a few captains I'd sailed with. The world revolved around him and nobody else. But I'll admit: he was a good leader. He ran a tight ship and his men followed his instructions to the letter.

One incident that first day confirmed my opinion of the Leader's priorities. After he'd gotten familiar with the controls, he came down from the cockpit and demanded to see the money. One of the other Somalis handed him the bag, and he took out the cash: two stacks of hundreds, one of fifties, then twenty, fives, and tens. He began dividing the money into piles, one for each of the pirates.

It was as if he were saying, "Here's one for you, one for you, one for you, and one for me." But he was putting most of the hundreds in his pile and the others were getting the tens and fives. I laughed to myself. *You son of a bitch. There really is no honor among thieves.* The other pirates didn't say a word. I never saw the money again. Later, when they gave me a sack to lean against, I felt the stacks of money inside, but I never spotted the cash out in the open again.

Young Guy was just that. Young. He seemed less hardened than the other three. I could see him giving up the piracy business and becoming a solid citizen in Mogadishu or wherever he was from. Either that, or he could become a Charlie Manson type. Every so often I caught him looking at me as if I were a turkey in a cage on Thanksgiving morning, and he was feeling the axe blade with his thumb. He had the potential to be a maniac. But he wasn't there yet.

At one point, while the other three pirates were occupied in the cockpit, I even started giving Young Guy advice. I don't know what came over me, but he seemed like an immature kid who was getting in over his head. "You've got to get away from these guys," I said. "They're going to lead you down a road to some very bad places. You can choose another way." He smiled and nodded, but I'm not sure the message got through.

By midday, the heat was so intense that the pirates decided to break the windows out on the lifeboat. Tall Guy went up to the cockpit and started swinging the AK-47 back and ramming the bayonet into the Plexiglas above the Leader's upturned face. Every time, the muzzle passed within a few inches of his face. And the clip was still in the gun.

Christ, I thought, *these guys are idiots. They're going to shoot someone by accident and then the navy will be charging in with guns blazing.*

"Hey, hey," I shouted up to the Leader. "Tell him to take the clip out before he puts a bullet in your head."

The Leader looked at me and said something to Tall Guy in Somali. Tall Guy took the clip out and started banging on the windows again. Eventually, he broke two of the panes out, but there was only a trickle of air coming through them. At night, we'd

269

get a nice breeze but during the day we were just going to have to sit there and bake.

The navy had somehow found a Somali interpreter in record time and gotten him on the *Bainbridge.* He was speaking on the radio with the pirates. The Leader would key the radio and say, "Get Abdullah, get Abdullah, get Abdullah." Once Abdullah got on, I couldn't make out what they were saying, as they switched to Somali, but I'm sure they were demanding ransom and the navy was demanding to know my condition. Every so often I would yell something — "I'm Richard Phillips of the *Maersk Alabama*" — when the Leader keyed the radio, just to let the navy know I was alive.

I was down to my khakis and socks. I'd left my shoes in the MOB and it was too damn hot to have a shirt on. I was constantly wet from sweat. And I was starting to get frustrated, because I hadn't had a chance to escape. I was getting mad and thinking to myself: *Don't be a wimp, if you see a chance to get out, you have to take it.*

I also prayed. "God, give me the strength and the patience to see my chance and to take it. I know I'm going to get only one shot. Give me the wisdom to know it." I never prayed to get away, I just prayed for strength and patience and knowledge to know when to make my move. I believe God helps those who help themselves. Asking for Him to do all the work is just not my style.

But nothing helped my chances of escape. There wasn't a single instant when I wasn't under the Somalis' watchful eyes. I began to wonder if I'd ever get my chance.

Back at home, Andrea wasn't sleeping very well. She would lie down on my side of the bed just to have that closeness, with the Polarfleece jacket shared between her and Amber, each of them holding on to one arm. "I just wanted to connect to you so badly," she told me later. "I would say to myself, 'Rich, if you can hear me, if you can feel me, I'm okay and we're going to get through this.' " That was what was so hard for her: every time I'd been sick or injured, she'd been right there beside me, always in full nurse mode. But now she couldn't be. She couldn't help me or comfort me or even know what I was going through. And that was the hardest thing of all. I really believe she had it tougher than I did.

Before dawn was hardest. That's when she was all alone with no one else to take care of. So she would pray to God. " 'Why am I asking you?' " she remembers saying. " 'You know I'm something of a heathen.' I have

271

my beliefs but I don't go to church regularly and when you see all the pain and misery that any ER nurse witnesses, it wears on your faith." But Andrea was still a believer and now she needed God more than at any other time in her life. And she let Him know that.

A couple of days later, Father Privé, the former pastor of St. Thomas Church near our house, now living in nearby Morrisville, was sitting at our dining room table holding Andrea's hand. We both had a special relationship with him. Father Privé had brought us back to attending church regularly after we'd fallen away from going to mass. Andrea turned to him and said, "Father, you know we're not the best Catholics. But I'm frightened, I really am. I just don't want to lose Rich. You have a lot of pull. . . ." He smiled. Andrea was serious, though. "Please pray that if there is anyone out there who can help my husband, for God to give them the strength to do it." He promised to do that. "I just couldn't imagine not having you by my side for the rest of my life," she told me.

At the same time Andrea was holding Father Privé's hand back in Underhill, I was thinking about him in that dark lifeboat. I'd always liked the guy. He had this way of tell-

272

ing a story about getting up early in the morning to make doughnuts and watching the cardinals arguing with each other at the bird feeder in the parish yard. "And that reminded me of Saint Thomas," he would say, and he'd be off into a Biblical parable. Plus, he had balls. When the Vatican announced that altar girls would no longer be allowed, he climbed up into his pulpit that Sunday and told our congregation that he would be ignoring the order and would be keeping the altar girls in the church's masses. He was a rebel, in his own way. Thinking about him and his homilies helped me through some bad moments as the hours dragged by.

Back in Vermont, my friends and family, even the agnostics, held a prayer circle for me with Father Danielson, our current pastor. They said a prayer to give me some strength. That's what drove Andrea — providing strength to me. She's always been attuned to other people's needs, not her own. It's the Italian mother in her.

But Andrea had her doubts. She would think, *Why do I think I'm so special? Other friends have gone through divorces, or watched loved ones die, or lost their homes. I've always been lucky.* Those were the questions she had for Father Privé, and for God.

Because the alternative was too dreadful to contemplate: "I thought to myself, 'What would I do if Rich died?' " she said. " 'How would I go on? How would my kids pull through losing their father?' " But deep in her heart, she still believed I was going to make it.

She didn't have answers for those questions. All she could think was *We were planning to grow old together.* And she tried to avoid thinking about being alone for the rest of her life.

Andrea was desperate for news. At one point, she checked her e-mail and there was a message from Shane Murphy, my chief mate:

Andrea —
This is Shane Murphy, the chief mate of the *Maersk Alabama.* The last update I had on your husband was that he was still in good spirits but still detained. He will beat these guys. I know how strong he is. His will is stronger than any captain I have ever sailed with. I mean that. And the 19 men on this ship owe him our lives, and are thankful for him for every free breath we take. His attention to training and preparation is the

very reason we had time to react the way we did. Additionally I was able to stay in contact with him over the radio and pass information secretly that led to us turning the tables. All I can say is to try and stay positive and have faith that we will get through this. The four men that have him are weak, and scared. There is no telling how long they will hold out, but I'm sure that Captain Phillips will outlast them.

I hope you are holding up well under these trying circumstances. . . . There were several more armed pirate ships converging on the area, and the navy felt it best to get our crew out of there. I know that's what your husband would have wanted, because that's what he told me before we left. He would not let me come help him, he was adamant that he be the only one to go, and we are forever grateful to him for his sacrifice. Good luck and be strong.

SHANE

Andrea really appreciated his thinking of me when he'd just escaped being captured himself. And later, Shane even called her from the ship. He told her that the navy was asking them to leave the scene and sail for

Kenya. "I want you to know that none of us want to leave Richard," he said. Andrea told me she could hear in Shane's voice how pained he was about that.

"I'm glad you guys are okay," she told him. "Just do what you need to do. If you have to go, just go." It's what I would have wanted, and Andrea knew that.

Meanwhile, reporters and journalists were standing around in our driveway, freezing and stomping their feet to keep warm. Finally, Andrea, being the caregiver that she is, went out there and said, "Do any girls need to use the bathroom? If so, come on in. The boys will have to go up into the woods." But the minute she stepped outside, people started rushing over, yelling, "I have a deadline. I have to get something in the paper." And Andrea told them, "I'm just here to see if anyone needs to use the facilities. When I have something good to say, I'll be more than happy to come out and tell everyone."

It was also happening at her mother's end. When the press realized Andrea wouldn't say anything, they looked for someone who would. Her good-natured mother, who lives in Richmond, Vermont, was inviting the TV journalists in out of the cold and telling them our whole life story over a cup of coffee, never imagining the details would appear in the newspaper. Andrea would see all these articles and reports that said, "After their first date, Andrea called her mother and said, 'Mom, I've just met the man I'm going to marry.' " She couldn't believe it — the night we met, Andrea didn't call anybody. She knew who the stories were coming from. She called her mother up and was like, "Mom!" And her mom said, "Well, they were cold, so I just invited them in. And they started asking questions!"

Matt Lauer called the house, his third try at an interview. Andrea took the phone. "Matt, this is totally off the record," Andrea told him, "but I've always liked your show, so I'll say hi." And he asked her what I would think about all the attention the story was getting. Andrea said I'd probably laugh and say, "Andrea's got it harder. I'm only dealing with four pirates. She's got the whole media." (True.) And Matt laughed and said, "We're that bad?" And she told him, "Yeah, you are!"

Andrea paced from room to room, completely numb. She told me later that, for moments at a time, she would feel like she was having an out-of-body experience. You never expect to be the person on the cover of *People* magazine. You think, *This can't be*

happening. This only happens to other people.
Not just the tragedy, but the media satura-
tion, the disembodied voice from the TV
talking about the most intimate details of
your life. Andrea would see a picture on TV
and say, "Oh my God, it's Richard." What
was happening was intensely personal, but
now everyone was watching it unfold like it
was a made-for-TV movie.

She began to notice odd things: that in
times of crisis, people sent enormous
amounts or food: lasagna, bars of chocolate,
tins of cookies, brownies. Friends she hadn't
heard from in twenty years called, but
people she spoke to just last week never did.
Some people around her resented not being
at the center of the story, even if that story
was a tragedy. And Andrea realized that
when you're under so much pressure, you
tend to lash out at people close to you.
"When I got frustrated, I would snap at a
family member," she said. "You had to be
stoic with everyone else, so my family took
the brunt of my anger."

It was hard for her just to get out of the
house. But Thursday afternoon she managed to sneak away and walk back across
our fields to visit an elderly neighbor who
lives alone. Andrea knew she'd be worried
about me and the kids and she wanted to

let her know that everyone was okay. That little walk was one of the few times she could clear her head and be alone — except when she was in the bathroom.

The press frenzy was growing more intense. Andrea could see reporters from every window in our house as she paced from room to room. They were blocking the two-lane road in front — the only road into town — and barricading our neighbor's driveway. So when the governor, Jim Douglas, called and asked, "What can we do for you, Mrs. Phillips?" she told him, "Send the state police and get these people off my front yard!" The town clerk offered to have everyone up in the parking lot of the town hall and finally the family asked the reporters to pack up and go there. That took an enormous weight off Andrea's mind.

Later in the week, a neighbor told Andrea she was talking with a female television reporter while this whole circus was under way. This journalist said, "You know, I saw Andrea sitting out on the back porch and I so wanted to run up there and get a scoop, but this woman just looked so serene. She had a moment of peace and I didn't want to take that away from her." Andrea was so thankful that the journalist let her have those few minutes alone. Some of the reporters showed real humanity.

She kept getting updates throughout the night from the company and the two FBI women: the navy was on the scene and they'd had a visual of me, which, she later learned, in a hostage situation, they refer to as "proof of life." "What's he doing, getting a suntan?" Andrea joked to her friends. They understood that Andrea's offbeat sense of humor was a coping mechanism. She was really thinking, *What the hell was Rich thinking, getting on that lifeboat?* But deep down she knew I was smart enough to do what was needed. There was also a report that the navy had had some communication with me and actually heard my voice. So she was getting some straight information and she was really grateful for that. And Thursday night, they gave her this cryptic message: "It's either going to be a very good Friday, or it's going to be a Happy Easter."

"I went to sleep dreaming of you," she told me.

FOURTEEN:
DAY 3, 0200 HOURS

More Warships Head to Scene of Hostage American Ship Captain: Somali pirates and their hostage American sea captain were adrift Friday in a lifeboat off the Horn of Africa shadowed by a U.S. destroyer, with more warships on the way in a U.S. show of force.
— *FOX News, April 10*

As we passed into the early hours of Friday, I was able to catch some sleep, just sitting up in the seat. Other times, I would pretend to be dozing and see what the pirates were up to. Would they let down their guard? No such luck. The Leader in the cockpit would snap on his flashlight and shine it on me, to see if I was making a move toward one of the hatches.

Finally, I saw Musso make his way up the aisle from the aft end to the front of the boat. He put down his AK and lay down on the deck. After a while I thought I heard him snoring up there. The boat got very, very quiet. Pretty soon, I could hear two people snoring, Musso and Young Guy. The Leader was dozing in the cockpit; his head kept drooping as if he were at a bad movie. I was leaning out into the aisle to try to see if they were faking. They weren't. That left Tall Guy.

After a while, he stood up and stepped through the hatch. I saw he was going to the rear hatch to take a piss. And I saw him put his AK down right next to the door, so that he could have both hands free.

Maybe this is it, I thought. My whole body was fully awake and I leaned forward and balanced on the balls of my feet. I felt my heart begin to race.

I watched Tall Guy, standing in the open door with the moonlit water beyond him. The boat was rocking slightly in the swells. He reached out a hand to get a grip on the door frame. Then both hands were in front of him. It was calm enough that he didn't have to hang on.

Now, I thought. *Quit stalling and take your chance. Do it!* I tried to feel my feet. Were they asleep? I carefully put one down underneath me, trying not to make any noise, to see if it would support my weight.

It seemed like hours, but I'm sure it was just a few seconds. I got up from my seat and moved toward the guy. In two strides, I was out of the hatch and at the same time I extended my arms and shoved Tall Guy. He turned halfway, falling, and I pushed him again, harder. He screamed — My God, it was so damn loud — and just as I was getting ready to dive into the water I looked down and saw the gun. For a split second, I thought of grabbing it and turning it on the pirates. I would have been just able to stop my momentum and grab it and turn and fire, but I thought, *You have no idea how to shoot an AK.* And with that thought, I swept forward and dove into the water.

My first thought wasn't *Freedom* or *Swim like hell,* it was just, *Good Lord, this water is so deliciously cool.* The pirates had never let me jump in and cool off and my body was so exhausted from the heat that I just had a sensation of pure refreshment. I almost wished I could lay back in the ocean and just relax and forget about the whole escape thing. The water felt that good on my skin. My second thought was: my glasses. I've lost them. They were mostly for reading, but I felt naked out there without them, exposed. I took a breath, dove under the water, and swam as far as I could. I did it again. I dove under the surface and swam, holding my breath for as long as I could. The water above me was surprisingly clear, with a greenish tinge to it, like swimming in a pool with a light above it. The moonlight actually shone through.

My lungs were burning and I had to surface. I came up, broke the surface, and gulped in lungfuls of air. I spotted the pirates immediately, one hundred feet away. They had started the boat and were going around in circles, hanging out the door of the lifeboat with their AK-47s pointing at the ocean's surface.

Tall Guy was screaming in Somali and I could hear and see movement inside the boat. And I said to myself, *Okay, what are you going to do now?* I saw that there were clouds skidding across the sky but the moon was out and the Somalis would be able to spot my head, a white blob, in the dark water.

The boat turned and now the bow was pointing straight at me. If I didn't do something, I'd end up as propellor chum.

I spotted the navy ship about half a mile away. I took a quick breath and began to swim with all I had in me, doing the Australian crawl. I kept an image in my mind of what I'd just seen, and it hit me: *Man, the pirates are pissed.* They were angrier than I'd ever seen them, swearing and yelling at the tops of their voices. Without me in that boat, the navy could strafe the vessel and they'd have more holes in them than Bonnie and Clyde.

I knew there were sharks off the coast of Somalia — great whites and tigers and even the ugliest of them all, the mega-mouth. Human smugglers had been known to toss their cargo off the sides of the boats in this area, and body parts would drift to shore with huge teeth marks on them. But I brushed aside any thoughts of getting eaten out there. If anything was going to kill me that night, it was the pirates.

I was caught in a bind, though. I wanted to make enough noise so that the navy would see me and put the *Bainbridge* between me and the Somalis, or just take them out. I knew they'd be on heightened alert. I knew there was some sailor watching the lifeboat through high-powered binoculars or a rifle scope and I wanted them to be able to see it was me in the water and not one of the pirates. But if I made too much noise, the Somalis would run me down.

I was gasping for breath as I swam. I was not in the best cardio shape. I could feel my heart pumping and I thought, *Jesus, just let me make it to the ship.*

I turned and looked back. The moonlight lay across the ocean like a white tablecloth and I could see the pirates as clear as day. They were headed straight toward me, with Tall Guy clinging to the side — they hadn't even bothered to pull him in. I didn't know if they'd spotted me or if they just assumed I'd be swimming toward the navy ship, but they were fifty feet away and closing fast.

I sucked in a breath and dove again, hearing the lifeboat approaching. Five feet down, paddling upward to keep from surfacing, I saw the wake of the boat above me, ghostly white. The pirates passed directly above my head, and then turned and did a full circle.

The lifeboat stopped and the pirates killed the engine. They were right above me. *They must have spotted me,* I thought. *No way they got that lucky.*

I started to drift up slowly. I surfaced near the stern of the lifeboat. I reached up and touched the side, then dove right back down. But there was nowhere to go. If I swam away, I'd surface and they'd be able to spot me in a second. I swam back toward the lifeboat and came up by the bow this time. I grabbed hold of the edge of the boat and just hung on for dear life, hoping the pirates wouldn't see me. I hung there for thirty seconds and I could hear them running and screaming around the boat. I was in the shadow of the boat itself. To see me, they'd have to lean out and catch sight of me below.

The lifeboat was rocking in the swell, and I had to hold on hard to avoid losing it and floating free. The Somalis started up the engine and began going around in slow circles. I grabbed the engine cooling pipes that come under the boat's keel and I held on to them as I moved along with the lifeboat.

The pirates stopped the boat and I came up on the other side of the bow. I heard footsteps and immediately dove back down into the water, swam under the hull, and came up on the other side. From playing hide-and-seek on the five-hundred-foot *Maersk Alabama,* I was now doing the same thing under a twenty-five-foot boat. I could feel my chances slipping away.

I'd lost any hope of getting to the navy ship. I had no idea if they were steaming right at us under full power, or if they were still sitting dead in the water, but I knew I wasn't going to make it. I made my way up to the forward port side. The pirates were running around the exterior of the boat, shouting at one another as they peered into the water.

I heard footsteps coming toward me and dove to the other side of the boat, my hands going one over the other on the cooling pipe. I dove down, pulled myself along the pipe, and came up midship on the starboard side. As I surfaced, I came face-to-face with Tall Guy. He screamed.

My heart stopped. I lunged at him, grabbing his neck and trying to force his head under the water. He was holding on with both hands to the safety rope that was tied to the boat and he had it in a death grip. I shoved his head under the water and his scream turned to a burble of air. He gasped and came up, his eyes and teeth bright white in the darkness. He kept screaming in Somali, spit and water flying out of his mouth. I was going to try to drown him but he had that safety rope so tight I couldn't get him down in the water. He was unexpectedly strong. There was a rush of footsteps toward the starboard side. I could tell the other pirates were running toward us, their feet drumming on the fiberglass.

I let go of Tall Guy's neck and dove back down. The bastards knew I was under the boat. *Will they shoot through the deck?* I thought. They were fucking cowboys with those guns and I wouldn't have put it past them.

Now I was like a rat caught in a tiny room. I had nowhere to go. I came up on the other side but I saw a shadow and heard voices coming close to me. I took a ragged breath and slipped under the water again. When I came up on the other side, I saw a pirate right above me with the muzzle of an AK-47 a foot in front of my head. It jerked up and fired two shots — *BOOM BOOM* — that slapped into the water just above my head.

"Okay," I cried out. "You got me. You got me."

The pirates kept the gun on me while they screamed, "We kill you! We kill you!" They pulled Tall Guy into the boat through the hatch and then they came for me. They were helping me into the boat at the same time they were beating me. They were so out of their minds with rage that they couldn't even wait until I'd collapsed into the lifeboat before they started whacking me with their fists and the butt of the 9 mm. As I raised my arms over my head, they whaled away at me.

After about a minute of kicking and punching, they brought me over the side of the boat and tied me to a horizontal bar on the canopy. Musso did the knots and he trussed me up good. I was on my knees and he took my hands and tied them to the bar and then pulled my arms up until my shoulders creaked. He tied my feet to the base of the seat in front of me.

And then they really went to work on me.

If I'd been captured by some burly guys, I'd probably still be getting plastic surgery, because the Somalis wanted to tear me apart. They were spitting mad, stomping on the deck, spittle flying as they abused me. But they were thin guys and they didn't have a huge amount of power behind their blows. Honestly, my sister Patty hits harder. I could feel my face and my ribs getting bruised up but I knew I could survive that. What really worried me was the gun. Young Guy was whacking me with it in the knee and every time he did, the muzzle would pass by my torso. *He's trying to beat me,* I thought, *but he's going to shoot me instead.*

"We kill you now! Kill you!" They were like angry bees.

They didn't let up. One would take a break and pace up and down the boat and then come up and start slapping and kicking me again. But there wasn't room enough for all four of them to get a shot at me. So they'd take turns.

Finally they wore themselves out pounding on me. They were gasping for breath and so was I. And I was back in that oven. That hurt almost as much as the beating.

"I'm losing sensation in my hands," I yelled at them. "You have to loosen the knots." I felt like the rope was going to sever my hands. The pain was excruciating, like pins and needles multiplied a thousand times.

Musso came over, untied the knots, and retied them looser.

They stopped beating me.

The Leader screamed at his guys in Somali, but I could tell what he was saying from his gestures: "There will be two guys on him always. And one by the door. *Always.*" From this point on, the guns were always on me, a few feet away, pointed at my torso.

That was the end of any joviality on their part. I'd killed the jolly mood but good. The mask had been torn off. They were shocked that I'd tried to escape. I wasn't playing by the rules and I'm sure they felt I was endangering them by trying to save myself.

Their attitudes toward me changed completely in that instant. I'd been their hostage before, but I'd been a human being. I'd joked with Musso and Tall Guy and I'd even had some fun with Young Guy. Now that was broken. They looked at me like I was an animal, a thing.

As I sat trying to catch my breath, I thought, *Either I'm getting out of here alive or they are. But not both.*

We were a few hours away from sunrise on Friday. It felt like the escape attempt had taken half an hour, but I'm sure it was just five minutes, if that. I thought, *Maybe I really am out here alone.* If the navy was here to rescue me, if they had sharpshooters laid out on the stern waiting for their chance, they would have blasted these sons of bitches out of the water.

Why hadn't they done anything? I thought. They must have seen me. They must have watched it all go down. But their ship had never budged.

Maybe they really are just here to observe, I thought. *Some kind of no-shoot orders.* I tried to think what the implications of taking down some Somali pirates would be on the world political stage, but my brain was too fogged from fatigue. Later, I learned that the crew on the *Bainbridge* had seen the incident unfold with their surveillance technology, but they thought it was the pirates taking a swim break. By the time they saw the white of my beard and realized it was me, it was too late to do anything.

Everyone was exhausted. I was trussed up like a pork roast, and the pirates were lying around, their guns pointed at me. The Leader had really thrown a scare into them. I couldn't move an inch without one of them popping up their heads and shining a flashlight at me to see what I was doing.

Young Guy had been just an afterthought up until then. He wasn't running anything. He was taking orders. Now he came and sat across the aisle from me. I was in the number-three port seat and he was in the number-three starboard. I watched him sit down and then I looked away.

Click.

I looked over. He had the AK in his lap and he was looking at me.

Click.

He was pointing the gun at me. I guessed there was no clip in it. Still, hearing a gun fired while it's pointed at your gut is a nervous feeling. I twitched the first few times.

Young Guy was looking at me like I was a laboratory rat. Just studying me with these cold, cold eyes. They were dead. I'd never seen eyes like that before. It was like a kid who doesn't really know what he's doing, who has no idea what life and death mean.

Young Guy wouldn't have done that before the escape attempt but now it was as if he had permission to treat me like a piece of garbage. Something had changed in him. Something had changed in me, too.

I'm a big John Wayne fan and I remembered a line from one of his movies, *The Searchers*. A cowboy has apologized for shooting a desperado. And John Wayne says something like, "That's all right. Some men need killing."

I'd never met a man who needed killing. But right then, Young Guy did. He was like an assassin toying with his victim before he put him out of his misery. He was enjoying it to all hell.

He went on that way for a good twenty minutes. I tried to ignore him, but every so often I'd look over at him. He loved that. But there was no emotion in his eyes. He was just prodding me, looking for a reaction, wanting to see terror up close.

The sun came up and the broiler switched back on. The pirates were talking with the interpreter on the radio and I heard a launch approach again.

Great, I thought. *More Pop-Tarts.* And it was. Pop-Tarts and fresh radio batteries and water. I couldn't believe it.

I looked out one of the hatches and saw that the *Maersk Alabama* wasn't in the same spot it had been yesterday. It had been behind the navy ship by a mile or two, but now it was gone. As we turned, I scanned the horizon and realized they'd sailed off. I was so relieved to see that the guys were on their way back to safety.

Later I found out that Shane had fought leaving me. He said he would have rather done anything than sail off without me aboard. But the navy insisted, as there were still pirates in the area and they didn't want another hostage situation on their hands. Eighteen armed servicemen went aboard the *Maersk Alabama* and they turned their bow for our original destination, Mombasa.

The Leader stayed up in the cockpit, occasionally hacking and spitting like an old man with TB. The pirates were smoking cigarettes continually. They were agitated as hell. The good times were over for good.

"That stuff will kill you," I said.

There was no banter back. Young Guy just stared at me with those dead eyes.

"Bad for your health."

Nothing.

And then the lighter they'd all been using broke. They'd either run out of fuel for it or it had just broken down from overuse, but the thing wouldn't light up. And that struck me as incredibly funny. Because the look in their eyes was one of panic.

"What's the matter?" I said. "Can't get it to light? Oh, that's too bad."

I was still trussed up and the ropes were painful. They'd stopped letting me urinate off the side of the boat. They'd given me a bottle to piss in. And they were rationing my water, even though we had gallons to spare. Sometimes they'd give me a bottle, other times they'd refuse.

In short, they were doing everything they could to make me miserable. So to see them suffer just a little bit was a bonus.

"Maybe you should break out the khat," I said. Khat is a narcotic leaf that everyone in Somalia uses. But it has to be chewed immediately after being harvested, so I guess it wasn't a good choice for extended hostage-takings.

The Somalis were going nuts. They searched high and low on the boat for another lighter but no luck. I didn't tell them about the spare matches that are kept in all lifeboats. Finally, they broke open one of the flashlights and took out the reflective cone.

"Oh, very smart," I said. Everything that happened on the boat became the subject of consuming interest to me. If I let my mind focus on the heat and the passing of time, I would have gone out of my mind. So the quest for fire became entertainment. These guys were getting the shakes and if they didn't get nicotine, they were going to die trying.

They placed the cone in direct sunlight and put some paper at the bottom of it as they chattered back and forth in Somali and English.

"Move it over here. Tilt, tilt."

They stared at the paper, just willing it to light.

"Got to get this going, oh yes."

I laughed, but I was leaning over to see what was happening too.

"Not working," I said after ten minutes. "Oh, that *is* a pity."

But they were committed. They just kept watching the paper at the bottom of the cone like it was going to reveal the secret of life itself. And after twenty minutes, smoke appeared. Musso and Tall Guy nearly pissed themselves with excitement.

"Yes! Yes!" they yelled. The paper caught on fire and the two pirates took it and lit their cigarettes. After that they would just light the next smoke off the old one and keep a constant source of fire on the boat.

But that was the only excitement. Everyone seemed to withdraw into themselves, myself included. I kept going over the escape in my mind, thinking, *Should I have grabbed the gun?* Or *Should I just have kept swimming?* And my other mistakes came back to haunt me: *I should have dropped the fuckers forty feet into the water when we were deploying the MOB.* Or *I should have never transferred to the lifeboat.* And, strangely, *Where did they get that white ladder?* That still mystified me.

What really hurt, though, was the failed escape. I didn't think I'd get another chance.

One of the pirates came over and felt my hands. They were getting puffy and sore from being tied up. They'd pinch my fingers to see if I reacted, but I barely felt it.

"Oh, that's good, that's good," they'd say. Maybe they wanted to incapacitate me, or maybe they just wanted to inflict pain. I didn't know. My mind was starting to drift. I was constantly moving my hands and trying to get some play in the rope. I even bent down and brought my hands up to my mouth and tried to chew through the strands. But it was high-quality stuff. It would take me a week to get through it.

Musso caught me gnawing on the rope.

"No, you can't do that," he said, springing up and rushing over to me. "That's halal. You can't put your mouth on it."

"Halal." They started to use that word. I gathered it meant clean in a religious sense.

"If you keep chewing that, we're going to put a stick in your mouth and gag you," he said. He was angry and kind of disgusted, too.

"Okay, I won't chew."

"Stop moving, too."

"I'm not going to stop moving," I spat back at him. I could barely move as it was. They wanted me to lie there like a corpse.

"No moving!"

"What are you going to do?" I said. "Tie me up?"

Musso hissed at me to shut up.

As I was arguing with the pirates, 7,500 miles away, Andrea was getting calls from everyone she'd ever known. She even heard from an old boyfriend she'd dated in her early twenties before we met. "He was my first real heartbreak," Andrea told me. "We hadn't really spoken since then, more than thirty years ago. When the person screening my calls said his name, I said 'I'll take it.' "

Andrea got on the phone. "Oh, I get a

phone call as soon as it appears I'm available . . . ," she said.

"I saw you on TV," the boyfriend said, laughing, "and I just had to call. I see you haven't lost your sense of humor."

"He told me I looked good, which was a little surreal," Andrea remembers. "He just wanted me to know he was pulling for me and my family. I knew it took a lot for him to call me out of the blue like that."

The support was overwhelming at times. There were people coming through the door crying hysterically and saying, "Oh my God, Andrea!" And she would say, "It's going to be all right." They were taken aback, of course. They'd say, "You're not supposed to be comforting me — I'm supposed to be comforting *you!*"

By Friday afternoon, our little farmhouse was full. My sisters came up and added their own special flavor to the mix. The Phillips are a wild bunch with our own brand of humor, which not everyone gets, including Andrea sometimes. One example: that night, my sisters were joking with Andrea about Hollywood making a film about the hostage-taking and began casting all the parts: "Hmm, maybe George Clooney for the lead role." Then my sister Dawn, God love her, for a reason known only to herself, brought out a framed prom picture from high school and placed it next to Andrea's pillow on our bed. Andrea came into the bedroom and saw it sitting there, and she said, "Dawn, what in the world . . ."

"Isn't that hilarious?"

"Isn't what hilarious?"

"My prom date, he looks just like Richard at that age."

It was true. The guy had the beard and everything. But what was his picture doing next to Andrea's pillow? "Everyone said I went to my prom with my own brother!" Dawn said, breaking into peals of laughter. "Oh, I just had to bring it."

Andrea's friends Amber and Paige, who'd volunteered to fly in early from her Colorado snowboarding trip, were also at the house. They knew not to treat her like a piece of broken china. At one point, Andrea told me, she was sitting at the dining room table next to the kitchen, and her friends were in there moving things around: her dishes and her tea kettle, just moving them a few feet from where she usually kept them. Paige and Amber had taken over Andrea's role of managing the house and knew she hated to lose control of her kitchen. Paige looked at Andrea and said, "It's just killing you, isn't it?" she said.

"What?"

"That we're in your kitchen."

They were rearranging things around just to get at her. Which is what Andrea needed. If you treat someone like her husband is going to die any minute, you're not doing her any favors. Humor helped.

Friday Andrea finally got some professional help. Maersk sent a couple of representatives, Jonathan and Alison, to deal with the media. It just about saved her life. But she was a little sarcastic when Jonathan walked through the door. Andrea looked at him and said in a half-joking way, "You got your ship back. What do you care what happens to my husband?" He must have thought, *Okaaaaay, here we go.* But Andrea was hurting.

Neither Jonathan nor Alison had any idea of what they were walking into before they arrived, whether it would be a house full of angry Vermont hicks or hysterical types. They were suprised by the warm, sympathetic atmosphere they found. Jonathan was a stable, no-nonsense guy, while Alison became my wife's new best friend. Alison instantly became part of the clan and she could empathize with what Andrea was going through. But what also helped was that Jonathan and Alison could see things as they were. They told the family, "Okay, this is what we're going to do: We're going to shut the TV off. We're going to put up a tripod and a big pad of paper and we're going to write on it any information that we can confirm. And we're going to have someone handle the phones and let Andrea take a call only if she really needs to." Alison always had a poster board and for every issue that came up, she would write down how the team was going to deal with it.

The constant pull of watching the news was hard to deal with emotionally. It was constantly the same news, over and over, without the breakthrough Andrea was hoping for. She kept seeing my picture on the screen and it would go right through her. So Alison turned off the TV and from then on, the family got their information from the State Department, from the Department of Defense, and from Maersk only, which got Andrea off the roller-coaster of waiting for the next bulletin to flash across the TV screen. Now she had people screening phone calls. She'd hear someone's name and say, "Oh, I'll take that" or "I just can't right now."

There was one thing that was kind of eerie that day back at my home. That afternoon, my optometrist called Andrea and said, "I heard Rich jumped off the boat. I'm sure he lost his glasses in the process. I've made up a new pair and I'm sending them over." Then, with all the people coming in and out of the house, the toilet stopped working. Finally, my neighbor Mike had to take it apart down to the seal and snake the thing. He discovered the thing causing the blockage was a pair of eyeglasses. My sister Nancy, who was at the house, said, "Oh my God, they're probably Richard's." Everyone laughed. Just hours earlier, I'd jumped off the lifeboat and had lost my glasses and it was as if they'd traveled around the world and ended up in our sewer line.

And Andrea was able to send me a message through the State Department: "Everybody in the 'hood is pulling for you. We love you." The 'hood was our nickname for our closest friends and family. Andrea knew that would put a smile on my face.

Fifteen:
Day 3, 1800 Hours

The FBI is confirming its hostage negotiators have been included in by the Navy to assist in negotiations with the Somali pirates. . . . What they'll tell you is, by all accounts, this is being done by remote communication. There are no FBI personnel on board U.S. Navy ships out in those waters at this time. So, it is most likely that what is happening is they are in some type of voice contact with the Navy, advising them on how to deal with this.
— *CNN Pentagon correspondent*

It's a very significant foreign policy challenge for the Obama administration. Their citizens are in the hands of criminals and people are waiting to see what happens.
— *Graeme Gibbon-Brooks, maritime intelligence expert*

The pirates were nervous. They avoided

sticking their heads up in the horizontal hatch or getting too close to the vertical ones. They didn't want to be picked off by a sharpshooter. They knew that if they were all visible at once, the navy could take them out. The doors were open but they didn't stand out there for a marksman to get a bead on. Damn smart of them.

But they knew the history, too. No one had tried to rescue hostages from Somali pirates. It just wasn't done. Negotiation and ransom-paying was the order of the day. At that point, no military had attacked pirates operating out of Somalia. And they clearly didn't want to be the first.

The Leader frequently got on the radio: "No military action, no military action." Whenever things got tight, he practically chanted it at the navy.

The engine was running constantly. And the pirates were tensed up, as if they were expecting something. I wanted to ask them, *What do you guys know that I don't?* But that wasn't possible. The only times they spoke to me were to call me a "stupid American" or to order me around. The arrival of the *Bainbridge* had clearly altered how the pirates saw me. In their eyes, a rescue attempt had to be imminent, and so I now represented not only a payday but a very real threat to their lives.

The navy demanded to speak to me on the radio. The Leader handed it to me.

"Are they treating you okay?" came an American voice.

"Well, they're acting pretty strange but they're taking care of me," I said.

"Okay, good. Let me talk to the Leader."

The hair on the back of my neck rose up. It was almost like he *knew* the pirates.

Later that night, I was sitting there, and the Leader started dry-firing the pistol. And then the chanting began. The electric charge in the boat changed. It was in their posture, in the way they looked at me. I think I'm able to read people pretty accurately — it's something you have to learn as a captain, when you're giving assignments to guys who have your life in their hands, so my sixth sense is pretty well honed. Something evil came on the boat that night.

The Leader was chanting. He gave the pistol to Tall Guy, said, "You do it," and whispered something to him in Somali. The others were answering, either with one word or with memorized stanzas that they chanted back together. The three pirates got up and approached me. Musso came back and held the ropes around my wrists, while Young Guy positioned himself at my legs.

Tall Guy was behind me with the gun.

"Stretch out your arms and your legs," Musso said.

I shook my head.

"Do it!"

Musso grabbed my wrists and Young Guy began pulling on my legs.

I was fighting them. "You'll never do it," I said to Musso through my teeth. "You're not strong enough." This went on for about fifteen minutes — taking a break, then grabbing my hands. Or trying to make me laugh so they could catch me off guard.

They rested. Musso looked at me like he was genuinely puzzled.

"What's your tribe?" he said.

"What? What do you mean, 'my tribe'?"

He laughed, like *How could someone not know what his tribe was?*

"Your tribe, your people."

I was still half-gasping for breath. *Now* you want to chat? But anything to keep his mind off murder.

"I told you I'm an American."

He shook his head.

"No, that's your nationality. What's your *tribe?*"

"I'm Irish."

"Ah, Irish," he said.

He shook his head.

308

"Irish, you trouble. You a pain in the ass, Irish."

I nodded. "You got that right."

He nodded. Then something changed in his eyes and he jerked up on the rope. I gasped, pulling my hands back down.

All of a sudden, *BOOOOM.* There was a white flash of stars in my eyes and my head drooped forward.

I thought I was dead. But I wasn't. Blood was trickling down my hands and onto the rope. Musso flinched.

"Don't do it!" he screamed.

Tall Guy emerged from behind me, the gun in his hand. His shoulders were slumping and his head was down. His whole body expressed total dejection. As Musso cursed me, Tall Guy went to the front of the lifeboat and just collapsed.

What just happened? I thought. *Did he shoot and miss? Or did he just whack me with the butt of the gun?* I couldn't figure it out. The sensation was so much more powerful than the taps he'd been giving me before. *He had to have fired.*

The Leader spoke up. "No action, no action. In three hours we will untie you."

I was happy to be alive. But I was pissed, too.

"What did you do?" I yelled up to the Leader.

"Shut up," he said.

"You tried to kill me?"

The Leader turned his head and spat.

"Shut up."

"Oh, you mean, 'Please be quiet, Captain.' "

I heard Musso snicker at that. Even the Leader cracked a smile. That was the first and last I'd get out of him.

"You trouble, Irish," said Musso. "Yeah. You a problem."

I didn't know if they'd tried to kill me or if it was a mock execution. If it was a mind game, it'd been pretty damn convincing. My head was still ringing and the blood was still trickling down my face. But why bluff with me when I had no control over the ransom? And why was Tall Guy looking like he'd failed at something very important? It didn't make sense.

I decided I had to get ready in case they tried again.

I started to stay my good-byes to my family. I called up Andrea's face in my mind and I spoke to her like we were sitting at the dining room table at our farmhouse in Vermont. I could see everything — the view of the yard through the dining room window, which runs to a field of tall grass and then backs up to a hill covered with pine.

I said, "Ange, I'm sorry for the call you're going to get. The one that wakes you up at four in the morning and you already know what they're going to tell you before they say a word." I saw her answering the phone, afraid, and tears came to my eyes. I wanted to spare her that pain but I couldn't. I said, "I love you. I know you'll cry for a few days but you'll be all right." I knew Andrea was a strong person, and I thought, *She'll be okay. Maybe in a month or three months, she'll be over the worst of it.*

Then I thought of Mariah. She is like her mother, emotional as an Italian opera but, deep down, independent and strong. "Be yourself," I said to her. "Stay strong, because I'll always love you." I knew she'd cry a lot longer, and be deeply affected by it, but eventually she'd come through.

I came to Dan. This was where I almost lost it completely. Dan is a lot like I was at his age, tough on the outside but still searching. He hides his pain. He's not as open as his mother or his sister. And I heard his voice saying, "Oh, I don't have a dad, my father's never home. He's always at sea. He doesn't love me." That just went through me like a sharp knife. Because I knew he said it to cover up the pain of my not being there. I worried about Dan more than anyone else.

"God," I said to myself, "please give him the strength to get through this." Because I didn't know if he could. I didn't want that thought — "My father doesn't love me" — to be his last thought of me before I died. I didn't want him passing down to his kids the belief that his father didn't care about him or mess up his relationship with his kids when he had them.

I bowed my head. I didn't want the pirates to see my face. I moved on to something more practical. "Ange, don't sell the house," I said. "Not until the kids finish college." It's amazing what goes through your mind as a dad. I thought of the unfinished repairs on the house. I wondered if there was enough money in my insurance policy for the kids to finish school. The basics.

I began to see all the people I was going to meet in heaven. My father and my uncle and Tina, Andrea's stepmother who had died just a few days earlier of cancer. I hadn't gotten to see her before she passed. I was going to see James, my brother's son, who'd died unexpectedly the previous October at too young an age. It was comforting. Each of their faces flashed in front of my eyes.

And I was going to see the best-looking dog and the worst-acting dog in the world. Frannie. The dog that never came when you called her name . . . a real nutcase. Just thinking about her made me grin.

I've always said that, when the time comes to die, if I can think back and laugh about what I've done and experienced, I've had a good life. It's not about the money or fame or fortune. It's how you live your life. And I'd had a lucky one.

But I wasn't giving up on it yet.

I stared up at the green strut on the bulkhead that formed what looked like a cross, and I closed my eyes.

Three hours later, the sun was just about to come up. The pirates started the chanting again. I started to think that they were on the Muslim schedule of praying five times a day, and that these death rituals were timed around that. Out of the corner of my eye, I caught Young Guy looking at me. He could see I was emotional and he was really enjoying my grief and the pain I was about to cause my loved ones. In my peripheral vision, I saw the others watching me, too.

That pissed me off.

I wouldn't let them see me cowering or

quaking in front of them. I wasn't going to give them the satisfaction. The anger washed away the faces of my loved ones. I had to deal with these bastards now.

I looked Young Guy full in the face and then I looked away. I steeled myself. I emptied my eyes of emotion and made my face as hard and cold as I could and tried to look as fanatical as possible. I looked back at Young Guy, really projecting that mad dog look into his face. I started to laugh. Then I looked away again, smiling.

"You think you're in charge," I said, "but none of us are getting out of this alive."

His face crumpled and he drew back. He looked at me as if I were some kind of lunatic.

I cackled. In my peripheral vision, I could see the others looking at me like I had two heads.

"You're mad, you're mad," Young Guy said.

"Me? Irate?" I looked at him. "No, I'm not mad. But I am crazy."

Well, fuck them. Both sides can play mind games.

That afternoon, the Leader was on the radio with the navy interpreter, speaking in Somali.

"How'd it go?" I said, after he'd finished. I wanted to get any information I could.

"With those guys?" the Leader said. "Oh, I work for them."

I was surprised he answered me but even more surprised by what he'd said.

"You work for the U. S. Navy?"

"Of course," he said nonchalantly. "This is a training mission. I do these all the time. We take ships and then see how the navy responds. Your company hired us. There are no pirates out here anymore."

"You're serious?"

He nodded.

"I know these navy guys a long time. We're friends!"

My brain seemed to go in two directions at once. My first thought was *That's ridiculous.* But then I thought, *Well, he does seem friendly with the navy guys. And there was what looked like a navy insignia on the butt of the 9 mm along with the kind of lanyard navy personnel use. How did they get that? And why hadn't the navy rescued me when they had the chance?*

Crazy thoughts were flying through my head. I could feel the beginning of paranoia creeping up on me.

"We told your chief mate," the Leader said. "He knew this was a test."

"Uh huh," I said.

"And your chief engineer. The navy and your company gave us this job."

I remembered the faces of Shane and Mike when we were getting the MOB ready. There had been real fear there. The Somalis had to be lying.

"Right. And was trying to kill me part of the job?"

He laughed. Then he coughed and spit.

"Kill you? When did we do that?"

"You almost killed me on the ship. And in the lifeboat you fired an AK about a foot above my head."

He waved the gun in front of him.

"Warning shot. Part of the training."

I was incredulous.

"And was what happened back there part of the training, too?"

"What you mean?"

"When your boy fired the pistol at my head."

He scoffed. "He didn't fire! He just hit you in the head." He snorted with laughter.

I thought about that. He could be right.

"Hey, Phillips, after this job, I'm going to work on a Greek ship," the Leader said.

"Oh yeah? How nice for you."

"Yeah, I'm going to be a sailor there. After that I go to work on U.S. ship."

"You on a U.S. ship?" I said, laughing. "You'd never cut it."

That got the whole boat riled.

"What! You think American sailors better than Somalis?" Musso cried out. "Ha! All Americans do is sit in their rooms and watch TV and drink beer. Lazy, lazy. We're Somalis, we're twenty-four/seven sailors. We can do anything."

He threw a length of rope at me.

"Here, tie the rope like I did."

I looked at the rope.

"Why would I want to do that?"

"To show you are real sailor."

"I don't need to tie a knot to show I can sail a ship. I've been doing it for thirty years. I can get by with three or four knots. "

Musso scoffed. "You baby, Phillips, you baby. Somalis the real sailors."

"American sailors are the worst," Tall Guy chimed in.

I ignored them and tried to get some rest. I was dozing off when, out of the corner of my eye, I saw the pirates do something that snapped me out of my stupor.

The navy was getting more aggressive, shooting water from fire hoses at us and sending helicopters (which I could hear but not see) to hover near our bow. They were trying to keep the pirates from heading to the Somali coast. Frustrated, the pirates opened up the caps on some of the spare fuel buckets. The fuel didn't spill out, but they lined them up ready to tip over on the deck, which was hot as hell, even with the engine off.

It looked to me like they were going to respond to an assault by burning down the boat.

The Leader looked up at me. "Ha, you see? You are going to die in Somalia and I am going to die in America."

"What the hell are you talking about?"

"You die here. I die in your home."

What he meant was they were going to kill me in Somali waters, so my soul would never be able to leave here. And the Americans were going to kill him. So our souls would switch places. He'd die by an American bullet and I'd die by a Somali one.

"But I fix them," he said. "If they try anything, we do suicide attack."

I looked at him and then back at the buckets of diesel. *Holy shit,* I thought. *Maybe they didn't want the fuel to get back to Somalia. Maybe they wanted it to blow up a navy warship, like Al Qaeda did the USS* Cole.

After that, any time they felt threatened, they would open up more gas cans.

The Leader fired up the engine and we

got back under way. After a couple of hours, sparks were flying from the outboard's exhaust. The thing was overheating. The pirates argued back and forth about what to do. Finally, they cut away some of the insulation that surrounded the exhaust and started to pour water on it.

If they get the fuel buckets near that, I said to myself, *I won't have to worry about a bullet in the head. This thing will go up in a fireball.*

"I kept going back to the moon," Andrea told me of this time in the ordeal. "It was the only thing I had that I knew you were looking at, too. I'd say, 'Richard, you're under that moon and I'm here with you.'" Friends in Florida called Andrea on videophone and all of them toasted the moon with glasses of champagne under the night sky, saying, "This is for Rich." Every night from the time I was captured, Andrea would search out that white shape in the night sky. From our bedroom window, she could look out and the moon was right there. "Richard, I'm here with you," she would say. It was the last thing she did at night.

Halfway around the world, I could catch only a glimpse of the moon through the lifeboat window.

Andrea's best friend, Amber, lay down

with her on the bed that night. Their joke was that it's hippy Vermont, so they could do that without any controversy. They spread my fleece jacket over them and were just talking back and forth about everything except the crisis around them: the fond memories they had of the days they'd roomed together in Boston, the cars I used to pick them up in when they were student nurses, the romantic boat rides Andrea and I would take on Lake Champlain, skinny-dipping at night. Then in the early morning before the sun came up, Amber would wake up with Andrea and they'd talk about her fears. "She became my rock, my Richard substitute," Andrea joked.

The one disagreement they had came when Amber wanted to sleep on my side of the bed. Andrea said, "Amber, there's no way! I'm not going to fight you over that. I'm his wife, I win." They laughed about it. But mostly they tried to imagine what I was going through at that exact moment on the other side of the world. Nobody had any clue, actually. I could hardly fathom it myself.

Predawn was always Andrea's lowest point. That's when she would have her "alone thoughts": What if he doesn't make it? What will I do? Saturday morning was no exception.

Amber woke up and they started talking: "What if he doesn't make it, Amber? What am I going to do? I don't know if I can live without him. He's my ground. And what about the kids? Could I keep the house? And, my God, I'd have to work full time!"

Amber laughed.

"He's got to be so tired, so hot," Andrea said. She knew how much I hated being hot. It just drained my strength and sent me right up the wall. "How much longer can he keep going?"

"Rich is stronger than you think," Amber said. "He'll never give up."

She did her best to reassure Andrea. Finally, they dropped off to sleep for another hour.

Later Jonathan and Alison told Andrea that the people at the Defense and State Departments told them around this time: "You need to prepare Andrea for the worst. You need to be ready to break it to her that her husband is dead. Because these things usually don't end well. They end up with a phone call to someone who can't bear to hear the news they're about to get." But by then, I think, Andrea had faced the facts. "I got it," she told me. "The ship was safe and the crew was safe. Rich was just one man. You can't expect to save everything."

Sixteen:
Day 3, 1900 Hours

The pirates on the lifeboat sounded desperate. "We are surrounded by warships and don't have time to talk," one said. "Please pray for us."
— *Reuters, April 9*

"The situation will end soon. Either the Americans take their man and sink the boat with my colleagues, or we will soon recover the captain and my colleagues in the coming hours. But if the Americans attempt to use any military operation I am sure that nobody will survive."
— *Da'ud, Somali pirate, Bloomberg.com, April 11*

All Friday, they kept trussing me up with these intricate series of knots. Musso explained to me how they worked. The white line you could touch only with the right hand. The red line you could touch with either hand. The white lines are the "halal ropes." You tie it on here. So you have to tie this knot and then this knot and you connect it over here. The ropes could never touch the deck. And if I was going to touch one of the halal ropes with my mouth, I'd have to clean it first. It was very important to them to keep those special knots clean and not to touch them with anything except my right hand. The purpose of all this knot-tying was to prove how superior the Somalis were as sailors, and also to be a pain in the ass.

Musso kept trying to get me to tie some. I played along for a while. Finally, I gave up. It would take months to get as good as Musso, and I wasn't planning on being with them that long. I stopped tying the knots.

"You baby, Phillips. Lazy American."

I thought about how different this was from the ship. That had been a battle of nerves and wits. Like chess. The crew and I had won because we'd prepared to win, because we'd been ready for the unimaginable. And because we knew the ship and its systems. We'd outsmarted the bastards.

But that wasn't going to work on this lifeboat. This was something rawer. It was a battle of wills. The pirates were constantly trying to wear me down, to confuse me, to humiliate me, to turn me into a child instead of a man. I was trying to persevere. To prevail.

This was making what happened onboard the *Maersk Alabama* look easy.

The sun sank down. It was Friday night. I dozed off to sleep and I must have been out a couple of hours when, suddenly, I snapped awake. It was dark in the boat. We were into Saturday morning now. The moonlight filtering in showed me that the four Somalis were in the lifeboat. The hatches were all closed. Then I heard voices outside. Up near the cockpit, the Leader was talking with someone. There were two people talking Somali from outside the cockpit window. Not on the radio. These voices were actually *outside* the boat. I could see the silhouette of two heads through the cockpit window. All the pirates were debating with these strangers on the deck.

Who the hell is that? I thought. The Leader and the strangers were arguing about something in Somali. I could hear the words "Sanaa" and "Palestinian" and "Fatah" mentioned again and again. A chill went through me. Sanaa is the capital of Yemen, a real Al Qaeda stronghold. Tourists and aid workers were being kidnapped left and right there. Some had been murdered.

Yemen was my ultimate nightmare.

I leaned forward and strained to hear what they were saying. All the pirates were talking, and each one seemed to be giving his opinion, like they were weighing in on what should happen next. The more I listened, the more I realized they weren't only saying "Fatah" — the Palestinian group — but "fatwa," a decree from an Islamic scholar. They were talking urgently, as if they were negotiating, and occasionally one of the pirates would say, "Oh, fuck" as if they weren't hearing what they wanted to hear.

But who were these Somali men talking to my kidnappers?

My first thought was *The Somalis have sent reinforcements.* That was a common tactic among pirates. They would call for fresh troops and boats would come out and relieve the original bandits. But how would they sneak a skiff past the navy and come right up to the lifeboat? I couldn't believe that had happened. The *Bainbridge* would intercept anyone trying to approach our vessel, of that I was sure.

Then it had to be the navy's Somali interpreter. But why were they talking about fatwas and Yemen? I thought again of the Leader's claim that he knew the navy guys, and it sure sounded like he was familiar with these two. The tone of their voices was intimate, as if they'd known one another for years. The guys on the outside of the boat were pleading with the Somalis, trying to get them to see reason. But the pirates were having none of it.

The debate raged on. I could tell from their posture and inflection that Musso and Tall Guy were gung ho. I got the feeling that they didn't want to give up for anything, that they wanted to fight to the death. Young Guy was just nodding, with an attitude that seemed to say, *Whatever you guys decide, count me in.* But he didn't seem to have an opinion of his own.

The Leader was conflicted. Of all of them, I think he had the best sense of how much danger they were in.

I could see it was a desperate time. They talked about death; in English they would say "death." And they would say "family." And "fatwa" again. And then, "Oh *fuck*."

I kept quiet. It seemed the interpreters were trying to negotiate for my release. When they left, I could hear them walk along the deck and get into a boat. I heard the engine start and then fade into the distance.

I knew that no compromise had been reached. It had been a tense debate and when the negotiators left, the mood on the lifeboat was even more tense, more expectant. *Something is going down,* I thought.

Later, the navy swore to me that none of their personnel had ever been on that lifeboat. But I wasn't dreaming. There had been an attempt to reason with the pirates and it had failed.

The sun came up. I'd been on the boat for two days and three nights. The heat began to rise. The pirates were down to their underwear.

That morning, they began by discussing — mainly in English, I'm sure for my benefit — when they should kill me. They went to get the Leader, who was dozing in the aft end of the boat. I could see his thin legs on the floor. But they couldn't wake the guy up. No matter how many times they prodded him, he kept snoring away. Finally, they gave up, saying, "Oh, we'll kill him later."

Man, I thought, *they can't even wake the guy up to execute me.*

Time passed slowly. I was tensed up, waiting for the next try at a ceremonial killing. The episode with the negotiators — at least I thought they were negotiators — was lingering in my brain.

I heard helicopters approaching, that *whap whap whap* of the rotor blades. I could feel them settle above us, because the wash from their propellers buffeted the lifeboat. Spray flew into the lifeboat through the windows. I thought, *Wow, they must be close, to kick up this much water.* But later I learned it was the *Bainbridge*'s hoses — they'd pulled up right next to us and were spraying us, trying to keep us from heading toward the coast of Somalia. I didn't care what the reason was. It was so refreshing, like being in a sprinkler on the hottest day of the year. I was like, *Oh, don't leave. This is heaven.*

The Leader got up. He was very nervous. "No action, no action," the Leader was calling into the radio. "No military action, no military action."

I looked out the aft window and saw a helicopter skid hovering there. It was surreal. It was maybe ten feet away and if I could have jumped and caught it, I would have been free.

"Okay, we're going to kill the hostage now."

I looked over at the Leader. He was on the radio. His face was taut.

The helicopters flew off. I could hear the noise of the rotors receding. I didn't really expect Navy SEALs to rappel down and take the ship. That would have been suicide for them and for me. I just missed the spray, and so did the pirates. It died off as the helicopters left.

The pirates started with the bullshit again.

"There are no pirates in Somalia," Tall Guy said. "That's just media. We were hired by the navy and your company's security officer and your chief mate and engineer knew about it."

Tall Guy even told me the pirates were bidding on a navy contract to do Raycon work — operating what is essentially an electronic lighthouse off Somalia. He asked me to sign up. "Sure," I joked, "I'll work six months with you in the Gulf of Aden."

As much as I knew it wasn't true, there was that tiny sliver that wanted to believe. I thought, *Maybe this heat is causing me to hallucinate. Maybe this* is *a drill.*

"Tell me something," I said. "The night before you came, there was someone on our radio saying 'Somali pirate, Somali pirate.' Was that you?"

The Leader nodded.

"Yeah. That was me."

"Somali pirate, Somali pirate, we are coming to get you," he said, and it was the voice from the radio. He laughed, and the other pirates joined in.

"Nice," I said.

"I love to see the ship speed up and run away. You guys scare so easy!"

"So you do this all the time?"

"Yeah, all the time. The ship goes into maneuvers, the hoses come on, the lights come on. We watch and laugh about it."

The other pirates found this hilarious.

"So how much is the ransom you're asking for?" I asked.

"What do you think?"

"I have no idea. But the Americans won't pay anything for me. Not a dime. You should know that. You're going to die on this boat with me. Unless you let me go."

The Leader stared at me for what must have been a full minute.

"Not true. Americans pay the most."

I shook my head. "They won't pay you, but they will let you go. Americans are stupid. We keep our word, unlike you guys. We'll let you go. If you release me, we'll even let you keep the boat."

The Leader just laughed at me.

"How much you worth, Phillips? Two million?" He literally spat. "I would as soon kill you for two million. That's not even worth my time."

"That's nothing? You stole my crew member's shoes!"

He shook his head.

"I hijacked a Greek ship. I killed the captain, because they only offered me two million."

The Leader started giving me his whole pirating history. "I took a Lauritzen," he said. Lauritzen is a French shipping company that specializes in refrigerated cargo. The Leader swore up and down that he'd hijacked one of their ships not too long ago. "I took six million off that."

"Six million?" I said. "So what are you still doing here?"

I laughed in his face. But he went back into his spiel about going to work on a Greek ship as an AB. He was trying to confuse me, I knew, trying to make me think he was legit so the next time an opening came up, I'd hesitate.

I looked out one of the hatches and saw an inflatable zooming by. It looked like a Zodiac with a few men inside. I thought, *We must be near land.*

"I see him," said Tall Guy. "Who is this guy?"

"I am going to lure him onto the boat," the Leader said. "And then we will kill him."

"Yes, that would be good," Musso said. "Get as many people here and kill them all."

I heard more outboards, zooming this way

and that around us. Musso ran over to one of the hatches with the glass broken out.

"Hey, navy man," he shouted. "American seaman, you want a beer? Come on, we have beer for you."

They laughed uproariously. The Somalis were convinced that beer was utterly irresistible to American sailors. They weren't wrong, come to think of it.

The lifeboat was constantly rocking up and down with the swells. It was hard to get a fix on anything outside of it. But suddenly the *Bainbridge* loomed into view out the aft hatch. I caught a quick glimpse of a sailor on a bow gun, a big .50-caliber monster. Next to him was a photographer shooting pictures, the lens of his camera pointed directly at me.

"Thanks a lot, guys," I said, waving to them. "Why don't you use that gun instead of that camera." Later, as one of the Zodiacs full of navy corpsmen passed by on one of their checks, I yelled out, "Take these fuckers out."

We were drifting, the engine turned off.

My head was hurting. What seemed so simple — a kidnapping for money — had turned weird. Yemen, suicide attacks, fatwas, Fatah, souls exchanging places. I had to fight to keep my mind right.

The real obstacle wasn't the Somalis, I told myself. It was fear. Every time I pushed through it, I found that I could persevere. *This isn't over until you say it's over,* I said to myself. *I'm not going to give up. I will outlast these guys.*

I looked out and saw the *Bainbridge* had been joined by two other navy ships, the USS *Boxer* and the USS *Arleigh Burke.* They were all coming broadside, perpendicular to us. It looked like they were maneuvering into a line. Now that is something ships do only when they're getting ready to lay out their anchors. Which you normally do only in port. *Where am I?* I thought. *Are we near land?* Maybe they were trying to hide something on the other side. A strike force.

Nothing was as it seemed. But at least I could see the ships. *Those things are real. Those ships exist. They are my countrymen. That is true.*

The mind games started again.

"There are no pirates," the Leader said. "That's all make-believe. I've been down to your ship. We've met before in Mombasa!"

I chuckled.

"I think I'd remember you."

"I'm not even from Somalia," he continued. "I live in Mombasa, in Kenya."

"Yeah, I know it," I said.

"Us three live in Mombasa," he said. The Leader pointed at Tall Guy. "And he lives in New York City."

"Really? What part?"

"Over near Times Square," the Leader said before Tall Guy could say anything.

"He must be rich. It's very expensive."

I was playing with them as they played with me.

"Yes, we work security. Very good money."

"But you nearly shot me when you took the ship! One of your bullets hit the ship six inches from my head. And when I tried to get away from the lifeboat, you were trying to shoot me."

The Leader shrugged, as if to say, *All part of the drill, my friend.*

They even tried their mind-blowing routine on the navy.

"We need a body bag," the Leader shouted into the radio. "Body bag now."

"Why do you need a body bag? Over." It was the navy.

"We had to kill a woman here. She was not halal. She went against the preaching."

Pause.

"Okay, we will throw over a body bag."

I thought I was hallucinating again.

"Put the body in the body bag and we will

pick it up. Over."

I'd had enough. "This is Richard Phillips of the *Maersk Alabama*!" I yelled.

The Leader put the radio down.

"Crazy navy guys," he said. "I've been working with them for years."

I ignored him.

"This guy is an idiot. This lieutenant commander. I'm going to kill him, he's such an idiot."

"That seems to be your solution to everything," I said.

He nodded.

"The Leader," said Tall Guy. "He would love to get a woman to kill."

Were they trying to impress me, the sensitive American, with how bloodthirsty they were? All they were doing was increasing my disgust.

"I can't help him with that," I said.

Around sunset, the pirates resumed the death ritual. The Leader began to chant, the others answered him, and Musso came over to complete the knots on my ropes. They stopped offering me food or water, which is what they'd done before the last time they strung me up. Any time they were getting ready to have a go at me, they cut off my rations.

My gut clenched up.

They began with the halal crap: *You can't touch this rope, don't touch your mouth, you must stand up, you must stand on the orange exposure suit.* I was hopping around trying *not* to stand on the orange suit and Musso, as usual, was getting fed up with me.

"Just stand on the orange!" he shouted. "You are crazy one."

He pulled on my hands, trying to stretch my arms out.

"Be a man!" he cried. "Military posture! Military posture! Sit up!"

I was sitting on the edge of the inboard seat. They were shining a flashlight from behind me so I could see a silhouette of my head on the far bulkhead. Tall Guy kicked my legs, trying to get my feet on the orange exposure suit. And every time the boat rolled to starboard, I heard the *click* of the gun, timed to the rocking of the ship.

I was scared to death. I was hiding it pretty well but it takes only one time for that *click* to become a *boom* and you're dead. I felt a rush of emotion and then a surge of strength, a totally primeval desire for more life. Nothing else, not food, not friends, nothing else. Just ten more minutes of life.

■ ■ ■ ■

Saturday was the hardest day for Andrea, as well. From what the State Department had told her, she'd expected to hear some big news on Friday. She'd geared herself up for that call. But it never came. That hit her hard, she told me later. She couldn't even eat. When Paige and Amber tried to make her oatmeal, she joked about being on "the hostage diet." There was more food than she'd ever seen in our house but she couldn't swallow a bite of it.

Our son, Dan, came home Saturday and Andrea wanted him and Mariah to keep their lives as normal as possible. Andrea was amazed by how strong the kids were. Surrounded by their friends, they kept up a brave front, without tears or hysterics. She told me a story about Dan that made me smile: Andrea was sitting on the couch early in the evening when my son, in his very Irish way, came and put his head on her shoulder. That's just something he does. It's his trademark.

"Mom?"

"Yes?"

"Do you think Dad's going to be okay?"

"Yes, Dan, I do."

338

He jumped up. "Good, I'm going to Luke's." Luke is a friend who lives down the road.

Andrea just laughed. "Of course, Dan. Go ahead."

Off he went.

But that was about her only moment of relief the whole day. Andrea was getting bulletins all Saturday: "The pirates want money and they want to go to land." Those were their two main demands. And she would say, "Can't you just give them those two things and get my husband back?" And the officials would say, "Well that's what we're working on. Because the fear is, if they get him on land, we may never find him." Andrea wanted to know if the company was going to pay up and, if the ransom was available, why not just hand it over right away? But she couldn't get an answer to that — things were too chaotic.

Andrea didn't care about the firepower or the money or the political message we were sending by negotiating with pirates. She just wanted me back. But it didn't seem to be happening. And people kept sending her e-mails about previous hostage situations in which the hostages always got killed. That's what the subject line on the e-mails said: "6 Hostages Killed in Bloody Shootout,"

"Grim End for Hostages as Kidnappers Open Fire." And Andrea was like, "Do you not realize what you're sending me?" She finally sent back an e-mail: "Happy thoughts only, please."

Andrea asked the State Department if they could get a message to me. They said they would try. So she wrote something out quickly. Someone in the U.S. government must be convinced that my wife is a nutcase, because what she wrote was "Richard, your family loves you, your family is praying for you, your family is saving a chocolate Easter egg for you unless your son eats it first." I knew why she wrote that. Dan *would* eat my Easter egg or anything chocolate, and she knew if she injected some humor into the note, I would know she was okay.

Andrea told me that one thought kept running through her mind that day: *Where do these pirates think they're going to go?* That really worried her. The pirates had three enormous navy ships surrounding them and they were still holding out, which told her how desperate they really were. So either they were going to give up or it was going to be a murder-suicide. That was the 50/50 in her mind. And the longer it went, the likelier the second outcome became.

"The feelings seemed to come in cycles,"

she said. "For a while, I'd believe I was going to see you again. And then the darker thoughts would come. A voice in my head would say, 'He could die, these things don't turn out well.' I would have to push those thoughts away, but they always came back."

By late Saturday night, the pressure and the disappointment got to Andrea. As much as she loved my sisters, the songs and the humor were wearing on her. Finally, she couldn't do the jokes anymore. She couldn't play along with the laughter. It just wasn't funny. One of my sisters said to her, "Oh, you're going to make so much money from this, you're going to retire." And Andrea snapped. "Do . . . you . . . really . . . think," she said, "that Richard got on that lifeboat so we could be *millionaires?*"

Saturday was a huge letdown for Andrea and the rest of my family because nothing happened. Now Sunday seemed like the last chance.

Back on the boat, all of a sudden I heard this electric sound, like a humming. It sounded like a drone or an electric engine. The tension in the boat ratcheted up in an instant. The pirates scattered and ducked away. I looked over at Young Guy and there was just abject fear in his eyes.

The pirates ran up and slammed the hatch doors closed.

It's coming, I thought. *They must see boats on the water aiming at us. Maybe whatever the navy ships had lined up to hide . . .*

The Leader barked something to Young Guy in Somali. He came over and sat across the aisle from me. That seemed to alleviate the fear in his eyes. He began clicking the AK-47 trigger and smiling with mad-dog eyes. Tall Guy began opening the gas cans and tying the hatch latches with bits of rope. Musso ran over with a rag and tied it around my eyes. I brought the side of my head down to my shoulder and managed to pull the blindfold down.

The Somalis were peeking through the hatches. I heard noises outside — the electric motor sound and engine noises. The pirates were getting their guns ready, pulling out the clips, checking them, slamming them back in. They clicked off the safeties. Fear was like a physical presence in that boat.

The Leader stayed away from the cockpit and all the pirates slunk back as far into the rows of seats as they could, pushing their backs up against the hull. They were trying desperately to get out of sight. Occasionally they would look out the windows, but almost immediately they'd duck back into their hiding places, as if they were afraid of being picked off.

Musso pulled into the shadows and saw me with the blindfold off. He slapped me, hard, across the face.

"You do that again, you be sorry!" he shouted.

My cheek was stinging, but I was happy to get a rise out of him. I smiled.

"What are you going to do," I said, "shoot me?"

We heard the noises again. Musso glared, but he was too scared to mess with me right then. He ducked down and slunk back into the second row of seats. Now all the pirates were out of sight, except for Young Guy. He didn't want to leave me. He was giving me serial-killer looks, with the gun pointed right at my chest. He put the blindfold on and again I pulled it down. The gun muzzle was within two feet of me.

I was in the third seat from the rear, port side, on the aisle. With the ropes, I couldn't get out of harm's way. I felt like a piece of beef in a butcher shop window. My fear was spiking. If the pirates were scared, there had to be a reason. It's strange to see people with guns show abject terror.

All of a sudden, I heard quick shots. It

sounded like an AK. I couldn't see who was firing, but it was close.

I realized the pirates had opened up the forward hatch and fired at a navy ship. The shots seemed to puncture the tension. Now they slowly came out of their hiding places. After a few minutes, Tall Guy even managed to fall asleep in the front of the boat.

I needed to take a piss.

"Hey, I need to go the bathroom," I said to no one in particular. "I need the bottle."

Ever since the escape attempt, they'd been making me piss in a bottle. They wouldn't let me near the door anymore.

"No," the Leader said.

"What did you say?"

The Leader waved his hand dismissively.

I screamed at the Somalis that they were going to pay for this, that they were going to die in this boat and they were nothing but pirates. They hated that word.

"Shut up, shut up!" the Leader screamed at me.

"I won't shut up. You're nothing but freaking pirates and that's how you're going to die."

He started the engine and revved it high. It was clear he knew where he was going.

The Leader erupted, screaming at me to shut up. The other Somalis began chanting again, just a brief version this time, as the Leader pushed the throttle forward and the lifeboat lurched ahead.

"When we kill you, we're going to put you in an unclean place," the Leader said. "That's where I'm taking you now."

"What does that mean?"

They explained that they knew about this shallow reef where the water was stagnant. It wasn't part of a tide pool that came in and washed the bay every twelve hours. Any body dropped there would rot and bloat and stink to high heaven.

"Very bad place," Musso said.

I couldn't hold it any longer. I felt a rush of wetness on my pant leg. They were letting me piss myself like a goddamn animal.

The rage just welled up in me. I felt degraded. I was screaming at the pirates, just cursing at them and telling them they were going to die.

The Leader yelled back, "Shut up! Shut up!"

The Leader arrived at our destination and killed the engine. I could see the *Bainbridge* out the aft hatch. It seemed like the navy ship was trying to catch up to us, but the pirates had outrun it.

Now the Somalis started giving me water

and food. The Leader insisted I eat Pop-Tarts.

"Fine, I'll eat the food," I said. They were reversing their normal rituals. It appeared I wasn't worthy of a clean death anymore.

"Eat more," the Leader said, practically force-feeding me the Pop-Tarts.

"Fuck you," I said.

"You're not halal, you're filthy, an animal," he cried. He forced food down my mouth, to make me dirty. He laughed at me. He walked away and went back up to the cockpit. Turning dramatically, he took his right hand and made a cutting motion, first across his throat, then both wrists and finally across his balls.

"You son of a bitch," I said. "If you kill me, I'll follow you. I'll come back and haunt you."

They tried to force my feet onto a blue bag lying on the floor. I was sitting on the outer edge of the seat arm, with my feet across the aisle on the opposite arm. I was still trussed up. It was too dark to identify who was doing what, but a pirate with an AK was behind me, shining a flashlight. All I could see was my head in silhouette against the far wall. There was another Somali lying by my side, another AK pointed up at my gut. The boat was really rocking in the swells.

"You can't die a clean death," someone said in the darkness.

I felt warmth on my leg again. I was pissing myself. It was so degrading, to have to sit there like a farm animal. I cowered, drained of strength, while the pirates were sniggering all around me.

This is the end, I thought. *It's over.* And something in me was happy about it. I wanted the navy to open up on the lifeboat with that .50-caliber gun and just end everything. I didn't care if I died at that moment — I just wanted the whole thing over with. My frustration boiled over and I was ready for the end.

But then I thought of my family and I told myself I had to go on.

My thoughts were going in two different directions at once. I believed the pirates were going to kill me and I didn't. I wanted this to be over and I wanted five more minutes of life. I think what was really confusing me was the pirates' motives. *Why would they try to intimidate me?* I thought. *I have no power to give them their ransom. What is this about? Could it really be just a test?*

I heard someone move behind me. It was so dark I couldn't even tell which of the

Somalis it was. He began dry-firing the AK-47 and he ordered me up on my feet. I staggered around, trying to stay upright. He was timing the click of the rifle to the starboard roll of the boat. It was this strange dance. It seemed to go on for three hours. "Sit," they cried.

I was ready for death. I straightened my back and sat up as tall as I could. The sweat was pouring down my face. My stomach was a knot, like I'd just done three hundred sit-ups at Four Corners back at the Massachusetts Maritime Academy.

"Military posture, verrrrry good," the Leader mocked.

This went on for hour after hour. I staggered around trying to get ready for a dignified death while the *click, click, click* beat like a metronome.

Finally, I'd had it.

"Get someone back here who can fucking shoot that thing," I said, collapsing on the chair, drenched in sweat. "I'm done. Do whatever you fucking want."

The Leader looked down at me from the cockpit. "Okay, that's it, no more action tonight, no action." The other Somalis relaxed and the tension drained away.

But for the remainder of the night, they started a bunch of new rituals. They put the gun on me and told me to move from this seat to that seat, to pick up this object — a cloth, a hatchet — and place it over there. They hit me if my halal line touched the deck. And I couldn't drag my ropes on the ground. All the while, they were calling me "animal . . . crazy . . . typical American." It was like I was dirty and they were trying to get me clean through these ceremonies. I was hopping from one place to the other, still bound. At one point, I just toppled over onto the deck when a swell hit the boat.

When morning came, I thought, *I won't make it through another day like this one.* Something had to give.

SEVENTEEN:
DAY 5, 0300 HOURS

Now most of the hostage situations we've seen off the Horn of Africa have ended with the hostages being released unharmed, and ransom being paid. However, just yesterday, one of these standoffs had a deadly outcome. French hostages . . . were freed yesterday after being held for almost a week. . . . It was four adults and a child. They'd been held aboard their yacht as it was seized in the Gulf of Aden Saturday. Now one of those hostages and two pirates died during the rescue operation. Three pirates, in fact, were captured. The French military made its move after the pirates refused several offers, including one to swap an officer for the mother and child who were being held on board. The pirates had also threatened to execute the hostages one by one. It's unclear if the hostage who died was caught in the

350

cross fire or if the pirates actually killed
him.

— *CNN, April 11*

When I woke up Sunday morning, the boat
was dark, gloomy. It matched my mood.

"Hey, Phillips," the Leader said. "I have a
new job now. I'm going to a blue Pakistani
tug and check it out for the navy, make sure
they're not Al Qaeda."

I just grunted at him.

"I'm going to help them, tell them where
to get food and fuel."

The navy came calling again. They wanted
proof of life, obviously. I saw them out the
back door, floating by on a Zodiac about
fifteen feet away, peering in at me. I gave
them a wave. The pirates were grouped near
the door, half shielded by the hull, their
guns pointed outward at the navy guys.

The corpsmen took a quick look at me
and asked if I was okay, and I said yeah,
and that was it. No James Bond stuff,
because there were very tense and paranoid
pirates standing three feet away from me.
"Here's our Al Qaeda contingent," one of
the navy guys said, almost joking with the
pirates. The Somalis were putting on their
tough-guy faces, really playing the part.
That feeling of familiarity was so clear. I

wanted to shout, "Do you know these guys?" But the Zodiac just passed back and forth a couple of times and left.

The Leader left the ship. I couldn't see where he went, or how he got there, but he claimed he was going to check out the blue Pakistani tug.

Young Guy took the opportunity to talk with me.

"When we get to Somalia, you want to go to the movies with me?"

"Oh, sure," I said.

"I'm going out with my girlfriend," Young Guy said. I looked over at him. The guy barely ever spoke, so this was new.

"You've got a date?"

"Yes, a date. With my girlfriend. And her mother's there. You can go out with her mother."

I raised my eyebrows.

"I will go with my girlfriend and you can go with the mother," he said. "We will go to the movies."

He leaned over to me. "And then, to a hotel."

I laughed.

I wondered, *Where am I? Are we close to land, sitting in a little navy anchorage?* It was strange to me that there were three navy ships and all this activity that the pirates were describing to me — tugs and other vessels — that wouldn't occur three hundred miles from shore. I was disoriented. Nothing about what was happening around me made sense.

All of a sudden, I saw a school of dolphins through the aft hatch. There must have been a hundred of them. I picked my head up and tried to track them through the water, but they were gone. A minute later, the dolphins reappeared right in front of the aft hatch. Surfacing and gliding through the water, spray shooting out of their blowholes.

To see a school of them swimming together gave my heart a lift. Maybe this would be a good day, I thought.

But the Somalis wouldn't leave me alone. They were obsessed with the knots again. They would tie a knot and tell me to undo it. If I touched the wrong string, they'd slap me in the head and tie a second knot. Then, if I didn't do things exactly right, a third. Pretty soon there were six knots I was trying to untie.

Even Young Guy got tired of the game. "What's the point?" he yelled at Musso and Tall Guy. They went right back at him.

"What's the matter? You want to be an American sailor? Huh? We're Somalis, we're twenty-four/seven."

The tension was mounting. The Somalis were arguing constantly, Young Guy vs. the other two. Around noon, the navy dropped off more food, but that didn't relieve the atmosphere on the boat.

The Leader had been off the ship for an hour. *He's bailing,* I thought. *He sees something is coming and he's selling these guys down the river.* I learned later that he went to discuss ransom and conditions with the navy, but I don't believe that. I think the Leader got off that boat because he saw bad shit coming down the pike.

All the while, the other three pirates were still continuing the tutorial on Somali knots. But I'd had enough of that, too.

"That's it," I said, "I'm done." It was 3 p.m. At that moment, I didn't care if they killed me, I wasn't going to tie another knot or take another command.

Suddenly, I felt weak. All the strength seemed to drain out of my body. I slumped back into my chair and things went blurry. I couldn't focus on anything, it was like my mind had let go. I felt dizzy and light-headed.

The pirates got nervous.

"You need doctor, you need doctor," Musso said. He got on the radio and demanded that the navy send one to the boat.

The Somalis brought water over to me and I drank some and I poured the rest over my head. They had gone from rationing my water to giving me all I wanted.

I was scared. I'd never felt this way before in my life. *My heart's giving out,* I thought. *This is how it happens.* It must have been heat fatigue. I'd always hated heat, but it'd never gotten to me like this.

The navy doctor arrived about an hour later.

"How are you doing?" he called to me from the inflatable.

"Well, I'm fine now. I think I just had a little heat stroke or something."

"How are the sanitary facilities?"

"Well, you're looking at it."

"Can you show me where you go? We want to make sure it's okay."

I didn't get it. I'd told them the pirates wouldn't let me near the door for anything.

What I didn't know was, at that moment, there were guns hidden under blankets on that Zodiac. The navy guys were trying to get me near the rear door, where they would have gestured for me to jump. Then they would have opened up on the Somalis. But the pirates weren't letting me anywhere near that hatch.

They also used the nonduress password

"suppertime." But I didn't know they had that code — Shane had given it to them.

Before the navy corpsmen left, they handed over more food, some fish and plums, and they told the pirates, "Make sure the captain gets this food. This is not for you. Captain only." So I tried to eat it, even though I still wasn't hungry. Those plums were the most delicious things I'd ever tasted. They'd brought four, one for each guy on the boat. I'd wolfed down two before I realized what I was doing.

"Oh, I'm sorry, did I eat yours?" I said to Musso. "Here, have my fish."

He just waved his hand. They were scared I was dying or something, so they were just happy I was eating.

The navy had also sent a pair of blue pants and a bright yellow shirt. I didn't want to put the clothes on, because I was filthy and the thought of getting this clean shirt dirty somehow offended me. I said to the pirates, "I'll put it on after I take a shower." But the pirates insisted. I put them on and the shirt immediately got wet and dirty from the water I was pouring over my head and the general filthiness of the boat.

It didn't occur to me that the navy gave me a bright yellow shirt so the sharpshooters could tell me apart from the pirates. My brain wasn't that sharp. I felt like a sluggish animal.

There also was a bottle of A.1. steak sauce. I didn't find out until later, but a navy crewman had written a message on the label: "Stay strong, we're coming to get you." I was devouring the plums and never saw it. And I didn't have my glasses, either, so I wouldn't have been able to read the message even if I had spotted it. I did wonder why they gave me A.1. sauce with fish — I think that's all they had aboard the ship as far as sauces go — but I quickly dismissed the thought and handed the bottle to the Somalis.

The Zodiac came back into view. "We're going to tow you," one of the navy guys called out.

"Tow us?" I said. I turned to Tall Guy. "What did you do, did you kill the engine? Is the rudder okay? What did you break now?"

The pirates quickly agreed to the tow, which was strange. Why would you want your adversaries to control your movement?

Unbeknownst to me, we were now within twenty miles of the Somali coastline. The navy didn't want us to land, because the Somalis could have called for reinforcements or tried to sneak me off the boat. But the pirates didn't want to land either because we'd drifted far from their home port and were nearing land controlled by a rival tribe. They didn't want to land there because they thought their reception would be a violent one.

By 5 p.m., we were tied up to the *Bainbridge*'s winch that sat on its fantail, a metal line connected to our bow.

Finally, before they left, the navy handed something to Tall Guy. "Give this to the captain," they said. He took it, gave it a glance, and handed it to me.

It was my watch.

"Where did you get this?" I said. The last time I saw it the Leader had it in his hand.

"From the pirate," the navy guy called.

My mind reeled.

The tension on the boat mounted by the minute. As we were being towed from the *Bainbridge*'s stern, we began to hear splashes, then saw black shapes floating by, one after the other.

"What's that?" the pirates cried into the radio. "No action, no action."

I couldn't make out what the shapes were, but I had an idea. Merchant ships can't dispose of plastics on the ocean, but the navy can.

The navy confirmed it. They told the pirates it was just garbage floating away.

With the Leader gone, the cohesion among the pirates frayed even more. Tall Guy and Musso turned on Young Guy. Maybe it was the stress or the fact that he didn't seem to be as gung-ho as they were — that had become clear when they were talking with the navy negotiators. Now they started to bully him.

"What, do you want to go drink a beer like an American? Do you?"

"No. I'm Somali."

"*We're* Somali sailors, we work around the clock. We don't stop. You're like one of those lazy Americans, drinking beer and going to the movies. You want to go to the movies?"

"Go to hell."

"You go to hell, American. We're here for the mission."

And then they called him a nigger. I was shocked.

"Do you want to be an American? Are you a nigger?"

The Young Guy shot back at them in Somali and English. All three of them were seething with anger. And they each had a gun within easy reach.

I fell asleep for a few hours and woke up with a start. The idiots were still arguing.

"I feel better now," I said. "But I want to go swimming." I did want to hit the ocean again. The memory of that cool water had stayed with me.

To my astonishment, the Somalis began to untie me. My hands were swollen and painful as they undid the ropes, but relief just flowed through my body. They left a loose tangle of ropes around my feet so I couldn't run and dive out the hatch.

"Come on, just let me dive in there," I said. I just wanted to cool off.

"No, you're too weak."

"I'll just jump in and jump out."

"Too weak, too ill. Just sleep."

Young Guy unraveled a couple of exposure suits and laid them out in the aisle next to me, making a kind of bed for me.

"Lie down," he said.

"I'm not lying down, I'm not doing anything you say. Let me jump in the water."

It was a standoff. I'd decided on total opposition. Cooperating hadn't gotten me anywhere with these thugs.

The pirates berated me for a few minutes, then they went away and sat in their usual seats.

I moved my feet, loosening the ropes as much as I could. Young Guy noticed and came down the aisle with his flashlight. The bindings got looser and looser.

"He's playing with the ropes."

"No, I'm just stretching out."

But then, I thought, *Enough.*

"I'm out of here, I'm not playing this game anymore." I kicked the ropes free from my feet and stood up. The pirates' heads popped up from fore and aft. I walked forward.

Musso jumped up. "Down, down! You can't leave."

"So shoot me," I said. "I've had enough. I'm out of here."

Musso dropped his gun and grabbed me around the waist. I felt Tall Guy come up behind me and grab hold of my leg.

"I'm sick of this." I took two steps toward the forward end of the boat.

BOOOM. A muzzle flash from the front of the boat. I reeled back and sat, landing on the third seat.

"What are you guys doing?" I shouted.

Young Guy had shot off a round from the front end of the boat.

"What's going on in there? What's the problem?" The voice was coming from outside and it sounded female.

The pirates were shouting at one another. "You can't shoot in here!" "What are you doing?!" "No shoot!"

"What's going on? What happened in there?" said the female-sounding voice, sounding urgent.

"No problem! Mistake!" The voices were coming from everywhere in the gloom of the boat. "Relax, okay, okay!"

Young Guy, pissed off for being cussed out, was in the cockpit now. Tall Guy was with him.

"It's okay," he was yelling at the woman who was outside the boat. "No problem now! All good."

I went to lie down on the makeshift bed. As I turned, I saw Musso and Tall Guy walk up toward the forward hatch. "Mistake, no problem! Okay, okay!" They were raising themselves up as I slid down to the floor.

I was exhausted. I just wanted to rest.

All of a sudden, shots rang out. *Bangbang-bangbangbangbang.* It sounded like six or seven in a row. As the noise echoed in the tiny boat, I dove into the row of seats, getting as low as I could. I felt something raining down on my face, jabbing my skin. *What now?* I thought. *What just happened?*

It seemed like the shooting went on for fifteen minutes, but I'm sure it lasted only a few seconds. I felt raw terror and confusion as I burrowed down as far as I could.

"What are you doing?" I shouted. "What

are you guys doing?"

I thought the pirates were shooting one another, and I was caught in the crossfire. They'd been arguing and it had escalated to gunfire. And now, after days of heat, punishment, and threats, there was complete silence.

All of a sudden I heard a voice. A male American voice. "Are you okay?" it said.

I couldn't understand who was talking.

"Are you all right?"

"I'm fine," I said. "But who are you?"

I looked up. Young Guy's face was a foot from mine. He'd fallen from his perch in the cockpit and he had dropped to the deck. His eyes were wide open and he was struggling for air.

"Hu-hu-huuuuuhh." I watched as he was taking his last breaths. He let out a moan, and I knew he didn't have long to live.

Then I saw the outline of a figure in front of me. He was dressed in dark clothes. That's all that registered. The SEALs told me later they heard a muffled shout after they'd fired on the pirates. They'd thought it was one of the Somalis coming after me. So a SEAL slid down the towrope to the bow and entered the lifeboat.

The SEAL checked the pirates. They were all dead now.

"Do you know how to get out of here?" the SEAL shouted.

I untied the rest of my bindings and stood up. I climbed over a barrier of rope the pirates had tied across the seats. My legs were weak. I staggered to the hatch and started to untie a rope the pirates had tied to secure the hatch from being opened from the outside. I could feel someone on the other side of the door pushing and pulling, trying to force it.

"Hold on, let me get it open," I yelled.

I got the rope free and the door was ripped open. A burly SEAL burst in and pushed me down into the boat. I could see his face hovering above me. Behind him I saw the enormous bulk of the *Bainbridge* looming above us. I felt like I could reach out and touch it.

"He's wounded, he's wounded," the SEAL shouted. My face must have been bleeding from the flying debris caused by bullets ripping into the boat.

"I'm fine, I'm fine," I said.

I stumbled toward the aft end of the boat and they gunned the engine. There were five navy guys onboard with me and they gave me the thumbs-up. The whole thing had probably taken all of sixty seconds.

There was another boat buzzing around.

The SEALs were yelling to their commanders, "He's okay. We got him!" A voice crackled on the radio, "Is he injured? Repeat, is he injured?" One of the SEALs radioed back, "Might be injured."

"I'm fine," I called out.

The launch zoomed toward the *Bainbridge.* I saw the big ship coming closer and closer and I thought, *My God, it's over. I made it. I'm out of there. I'm alive.*

Andrea was sleeping early Sunday morning when she thought she heard my voice, saying, "Ange, I'm okay. Don't worry, I'm okay." She woke up, went into the bathroom, and then got back into bed.

"Andrea," said Amber from the other side of the bed. "I just had an epiphany."

"What is it?"

"I really think Rich is going to be all right."

"Do you really think that? Because I was feeling the same thing."

She said she knew then that something was going to happen. It was Easter Sunday. Good or bad, Andrea felt that things were coming to a head.

Amber fell back to sleep, but Andrea couldn't. She kept thinking, *Enough talking. I have to do something. Rich has got to be tired and hot by now. How much longer can he hold on?* She wanted to send me some positive energy. But she was 7,500 miles away from her husband — what could she do?

Then it came to her. When the bishop of Vermont had called on Thursday, he'd graciously asked if there was any way he could help the family. All of a sudden, it seemed urgent to Andrea that she *do* something on Easter morning. And she knew exactly what it should be.

A few years ago, we'd gone to a mass out on Cape Cod with my family. The priest had just returned from Africa, where he worked as a missionary. And he talked about his work and how much it meant to him and he went into this homily that we always remembered. He would say, "God is good," and the response was "All the time." Then he'd say, "All the time," and the response was "God is good." This priest was trying so hard to get a crowd of very proper Catholics in stuffy Hyannis, Massachusetts, to really enter into the spirit of the thing, and it struck us as funny and moving at the same time.

That became one of our family sayings. We'd be saying good-bye to someone at the airport or we'd be hanging up the phone and one person would say, "God is good" and the other would answer, "All the time." It was just one of those codes every family has that binds you together. In times of crisis it was a reminder to be thankful for what we had.

Andrea lay in bed, unable to sleep. The minutes clicked by, 6 a.m., 6:30. She could have kicked herself. She was thinking, *Everyone, even the worst Catholic, goes to church on Easter morning. Why didn't I ask the bishop of Vermont to request all the priests to use that little homily in their masses? I could have had the whole state of Vermont saying it!* That image of thousands of people from Burlington to the college kids in Brattleboro to all the sleepy little farming communities repeating those simple words was very powerful to her.

"I had to do it," Andrea said.

She jumped out of bed, ran to Alison, and asked her if she could request that both Father Privé in Morrisville and Father Danielson in Underhill say the homily. Then she went about her morning routine. My mom arrived from Florida — she couldn't stay away any longer. And my sisters were getting ready to go home to their families.

Little did Andrea know, Alison called the priest and couldn't get a hold of him, so she jumped in her car and started driving. The GPS sent her the opposite way and she ended up driving mile after mile in the wrong direction, terribly afraid that she would miss the priest. But she finally turned around and made it to the church and Father Privé said he'd be happy to do it.

Around 11 a.m., Andrea thought, *Where the heck is Alison?* She'd been gone for five hours. Right then, her co-worker, Jonathan, walked in and said, "You've got to hear this." And he took his iPhone, hit "Speaker," and put the phone on the kitchen table. Alison, being Catholic herself, felt the need to stay at the church. And Andrea could hear a mass in progress, and it came to the homily and the priest began to sing, "God is good!" and the people in the church called back, "All the time." Father Privé had managed to put our family motto into a song. Andrea felt a huge wave of emotion sweep over her.

She leaned her head against the wall and started to cry. She thought of all those people who didn't really know me, doing this for our family. Through her tears, she looked up and out the dining room window. It had begun to snow, which is one of my favorite things in the world.

Andrea felt this was her sign. She turned

her face to the wall. And she said to herself, "Oh my God, he's really going to be okay."

EIGHTEEN:
DAY 5, 1945 HOURS

I am very pleased that Captain Phillips has been rescued and is safely on board the USS *Boxer.* His safety has been our principal concern, and I know this is a welcome relief to his family and his crew. I am also very proud of the efforts of the U.S. military and many other departments and agencies who worked tirelessly to secure Captain Phillips' safe recovery. I share the country's admiration for the bravery of Captain Phillips and his selfless concern for his crew. His courage is a model for all Americans.

— *President Barack Obama, April 12*

The navy lifted the Zodiac onto the *Bainbridge* with a davit. I was walking with my hand on the shoulder of the SEAL striding ahead of me. We walked into the back hangar, where navy guys called out, cheering and congratulating me. But it was still very tense — there were corpsmen running back and forth, with headphones and voice sets, obviously checking for more pirates and getting the situation on the lifeboat squared away. I waved and called "Thank you" as I was being led straight to the sick bay, where a medic was waiting.

Relief just flooded through me. Everything had happened so fast, it seemed like I'd been teleported out of that hellish boat onto this huge ship. The tension began to drain out of my body, slowly.

Thousands of miles away, Andrea hadn't heard a thing by Sunday morning. People were still coming and going and calling the house. She said good-bye to my sisters, who had to go back to their families, then went upstairs around 11:30 a.m., hoping to take a nap. Her bedroom was her safe zone, and it was understood that it was off-limits. Thinking she would fall asleep to the TV, Andrea turned to a movie channel and there on the bottom of the screen was a little ticker that said, "Captain Richard Phillips freed."

She didn't believe it. She went flying down the stairs and found Jonathan, screaming, "YOU HAVE TO FIND OUT IF THIS IS TRUE!"

In the jubilation and the excitement, everyone had forgotten to call my wife. They just assumed someone else had done it. I guess when information is so ubiquitous, you can't imagine anyone not knowing some important piece of news, especially when they're married to the central character. So Jonathan had to call Maersk and the Defense Department to get the scoop. Andrea didn't care — all she needed was to know that I was safe.

Jonathan got confirmation almost immediately. "I went running through the house shouting the news," Andrea remembered. "And then I called everyone I knew." Soon, the house filled with family and close friends.

Soon Andrea started to see pictures of me on TV. That was when she really knew I was okay — when she could see my face. She became glued to the set, not caring how many times they played the same tape. "I just couldn't get enough of it," she told me.

Around 3 p.m., the phone rang. Her friend Paige answered it. The farmhouse was getting so many media calls that she adopted a tough tone when she said, "Who is this?"

And I said, "You mean to tell me you don't recognize my voice?"

She screamed.

I could hear Andrea run over to the phone and I heard Paige blurt out, "It's Richard." I heard Andrea's voice saying, "Hello, hello?"

I did my usual, "Is your husband home?"

"No," Andrea said.

"Good. I'll be right over."

Andrea told me that she had tears in her eyes.

"I'm just so glad you're okay," she said, her voice thick with emotion. And then, "What were you *thinking* getting into that lifeboat?"

It was so good to hear her voice. That's all I needed, just to listen to her. The words hardly mattered. I asked her about the kids and she asked if I was hurt anywhere and if I'd had anything to eat. She went into nurse mode.

The call was cut off. Andrea told me later that she started flipping out because she finally had her husband back but couldn't speak to me. Paige called back a bunch of numbers and ended up getting a Navy SEAL onboard the USS *Boxer,* which was sailing near the *Bainbridge.* She told him how happy and overwhelmingly grateful they all were, and he said, "Oh ma'am, we're just doing our job." She invited him and the other SEALs to Vermont for a home-cooked Italian meal. It was exactly what Andrea wished she could have said to the SEALs. Paige was crying when she hung up.

The medic cut off my clothes. For the first time, I could smell myself. On the lifeboat, I hadn't realized how funky I'd become. I flashed back to the days onboard the *Patriot State,* the training ship at the Massachusetts Maritime Academy. That first summer, some of the other youngies and I had a contest to see who could go the longest without a bath or shower. There was no AC on that ship, so it was like a duel to our death. We called ourselves the Rude Family. I thought, *I would have won that competition.*

The medic gave me the okay, and I was taken up to the deck and straight onto a helicopter and flown to the USS *Boxer,* a big navy assault ship that had arrived after the *Bainbridge.* Two of the Navy SEALs came with me, still mission-minded and completely focused on what they were doing.

After I got on the *Boxer,* I went through another physical exam. I was given some new clothes — a T-shirt, a blue jumpsuit, and a baseball cap. I was then escorted to

VIP quarters. A guy came in. "Anything you need?"

"Yeah," I said. "I'd love a beer."

The guy nodded. "We can do that." I didn't know it at the time, but it was the captain of the *Boxer.*

He turned away and just as he began to walk off, I called out, "Hey."

"Yeah?"

"Think I can get *two* beers?"

The captain smiled.

"Yeah, you can have two beers."

The guy left and I stripped off my clothes and got ready for a shower. I was brushing my teeth buck naked when the captain returned, with two sailors hauling a huge cooler. It was full of beer.

"Holy crap," I said. "How long am I going to be here?"

They laughed at that, and the captain told me I could make a phone call. He also let me know President Obama wanted to talk to me. I finished my shower, jumped into my clothes, grabbed a beer, and followed the captain.

The sailors showed me to my room and I just sat on the bunk taking it all in, drinking my first beer. *I'm free, I'm alive, I'm safe.* It felt unreal. It seemed like I'd been taken from the living hell of that lifeboat to this clean, calm ship in a split second.

President Obama called. I picked up the phone and there was that familiar baritone voice congratulating me.

"I think you did a great job out there," he said.

"Well, all the credit goes to the military," I told him. "I can't thank them enough. And I want to thank you for the part you played." And I meant it. I knew the order for the rescue had to go all the way to the top, so in a way I was speaking to the man who'd gotten me out of that hellhole in the middle of the Indian Ocean.

"We're just glad that you're safe," the president said. Then we talked a little basketball — he's a hardcore Chicago fan and I'm a Boston diehard, so we chatted about how the Bulls matched up against my beloved Celtics. I couldn't believe I was chatting with the president from a navy ship halfway around the world, and talking about Kevin Garnett's jump shot.

The next day, the corpsmen asked me what I wanted to do. "I want to look around, see the ocean full around on the horizon," I said. I still had that feeling of confinement, of being trapped. They brought me up on deck and I just looked at the huge ocean all around me and the claustrophobic feeling started to dissolve. I could see the coast of Somalia and I realized how close we'd actually come to it. But I wouldn't feel totally free until I got off the water and felt land under my feet in Kenya.

Then I got to meet my rescuers. The SEALs gathered on the *Boxer* and I went through the entire line, shaking hands and saying thanks. I'd always respected the military, but now I really felt how selfless and duty-driven these guys were. They didn't want fame or money or recognition. They just wanted me safe and back with my family.

"You guys are the heroes," I told them. "You're the titans." And I believe that. What I did is nothing compared to what the SEALs do every day.

They were happy as hell, too. "Our missions rarely turn out this way," one of the SEALs told me. "We train for it to go down exactly as it did yesterday." I saw that I was a kind of good luck token for them, something tangible that had come out of all their years of training.

The leader of the team that had rescued me came to my room. He asked me how I was sleeping.

At first, I didn't want to tell him what had been happening with me. I was a bit ashamed, I guess. My first night after the rescue, I'd woken up in my quarters around 5 a.m., bawling my eyes out. I hadn't cried like that since I was a boy.

What am I, a wimp? I'd thought. *I'm lucky to be alive and here I am crying like a girl.*

I'd kicked myself in the ass and taken a shower. The crying went away, until the next morning, when the exact same thing happened. Wailing and sobbing right out of a deep sleep.

The SEAL leader listened to me, nodding. "You need to talk to our psychiatrist," he said.

"I'm not really into nut doctors."

He smiled. "It's accepted, we all do it. What you went through is a roller coaster of emotions. If you don't talk about it, it's going to stay with you." He wouldn't take no for an answer, insisting I see the psychiatrist.

Finally I did talk to the SEAL psychiatrist. I dialed him up and he explained to me that being a hostage had placed me between life and death, and when the body is faced with that kind of situation, it releases special chemicals to get you through the crisis. And these hormones were still surging through my body.

"Have you had episodes where you were crying?" he asked.

I was taken aback. "Exactly right."

"It's normal," he said. "Everyone goes through it. So how do you handle it?"

"I yell at myself, tell myself to stop being a wimp, splash water on my face, and get over it."

"Next time, don't end it. Just let it run its course."

I had my doubts. But the next morning, invariably at 0500, I woke up in my bunk crying. I swung my legs out and sat on the edge of my bed with my head in my hands, weeping. And I just let it go. For thirty minutes, tears streamed down my face and I didn't try to stop them. Waves of sadness and grief washed over me. And I let them. It was the strangest feeling.

And it never came back.

I spent the next four days back on the *Bainbridge.* I've never felt so old in my life. I was surrounded by eighteen- to twenty-four-year-old navy personnel, both men and women, who were highly proficient, eager, and pushing for more. There was a sense of professionalism, duty, and honor that could be felt throughout. But one thing the navy couldn't hide even if they wanted to: these men and women were dog-tired. I'm used to putting in long hours and I know the signs: coffee breath, bags under the eyes, tired-sounding talk, slow reactions. They'd been up for days, trying to rescue me. I learned later that Captain Frank had seldom left the bridge during the whole ordeal and I could see it in his face. That was dedication.

I went back to my quarters that night. As I was getting ready for bed, I noticed a painting hanging above my bed. It was an old-fashioned portrait and the man looked like an American sailor from the nineteenth century. I asked the captain about it later and he said, "Oh, that's William Bainbridge."

I laughed. The old pirate-hunter and Barbary captive was watching over me.

I had the run of the whole ship. I was there for the evening navigation briefing and listened to the men give the tide report for the upcoming docking at Mombasa. I was standing there for every promotion ceremony. I had seconds at the ice-cream social at 2100. I watched as the vessel met a supply ship in the middle of the ocean and brought on food, mail, and other cargo. Perhaps it would have meaning only for a guy who loves the sea and ships, but I felt privileged to see behind the veil of a great navy vessel.

I felt a little guilty. I explained to Captain

Frank that I'd become the guy I hated to have on my own ships. The guy who makes it to the mess hall for every meal, sleeps fourteen hours a day, and does absolutely nothing. The useless one. But for once in my life, I accepted the role.

The navy personnel tried to impress upon me the media storm that had broken over my hostage-taking, as did Andrea when I spoke with her. But it never got through to me. The first day on the *Boxer*, I was sitting in the mess deck when I heard voices I recognized, voices from back home. Startled, I turned around: On the ship's satellite TV, I saw the faces of my neighbors, my kids, Maersk officials. I turned my back to it. I didn't want to hear it. A navy pilot said, "Don't you want to see it?"

"I already know the story," I said, "I don't want to hear it again."

The night before the *Bainbridge* was supposed to make port at Mombasa, the message came across the PA that we'd changed course and were now under way to save another American ship, the *Liberty Sun,* which was under attack by pirates. I ran into Captain Frank, who began to apologize for not getting me to the rendezvous with my crew. I said, "Not at all, just go get 'em. Save those sailors." We met the *Liberty Sun*

381

and chased off the pirates, then turned back toward Kenya and docked amid high security and media scrutiny. I left the *Bainbridge* at 0400 on Friday morning.

The SEALs, meanwhile, had slipped off into the night, never to be seen again, without fanfare or recognition.

NINETEEN

At the farmhouse, the media frenzy ratcheted up again. Alison went out to make a statement, telling the journalists that it was Easter Sunday and the Phillipses needed family time. Calls poured in. Senator Patrick Leahy phoned and told Andrea they were dancing in the church parking lot where they heard the news. Diane Sawyer called to say she was doing cartwheels. Our Vermont senators and governor and everyone who'd been so good to my family called to express their joy at how things had turned out.

Late Sunday evening President Obama called Andrea.

"I just got off the phone with your husband," he said.

"You mean I got the *second* call?" Andrea said jokingly.

Obama laughed.

Andrea knew how big a part he'd played

in freeing me and she wanted to thank him warmly, but at the same time she knew this man is the president, and you want to have that respect and formality. The president told Andrea that "the whole nation has been praying for you" and how glad he was that it worked out — and that I sounded really good on the phone. "I couldn't thank him enough for what everyone had done for us," Andrea told me. "I remember saying at one point, 'My Easter basket runneth over.' " I thought it was amazing that he took the time to call not only me but my family in Vermont.

People were flooding into the house to celebrate. But the emotional release of my rescue had left Andrea drained. "It was like a plug had been pulled and all my strength and energy had flowed out," she said. "I needed to be alone with our kids." So she and Alison worked out an exit plan to get everyone back to their families. One of her friends knew she was back to normal when, hours after we got the good news, she heard Andrea's voice from another room: "WHO SPILLED SODA ON MY RUG?" Andrea doesn't remember that, but it sounds right. It was such a relief to be back to those kinds of things, she told me: Was everyone eating enough? And who was destroying my house?

The rescue restored Andrea's faith — or put back something that had been misplaced for quite some time, as she put it. "I don't believe in the God that punishes you or keeps track of every sin," she said, "but I do believe in a God of love. And afterward, I was like, 'Dear God, I haven't been your greatest follower, but I owe you a big one.' And I intend to be true to that obligation."

I was rescued on Easter Sunday and I flew home on the following Friday. The owner of Maersk provided his private jet, and a journey that usually took forty-five hours took only eighteen. I'd returned from the sea to Vermont so many times in thirty-odd years, flying in from all points on the globe, but this time felt completely different. Not only the luxurious jet and the direct flight, but the anticipation of seeing my family's faces again. I sat there sipping a Coke, looking down at the clouds and thinking of that moment when I finally caught sight of them.

Andrea told me that after my plane landed at Burlington airport, Dan, Mariah and she were walking up to the plane, and Mariah turned to Andrea and said, "Mom, I just have to run." She said, "Go ahead, run if you have to," and Mariah went tearing off. It was just like when she was a little girl. The next thing I saw was Mariah pushing through the customs guys and just hurling herself into my arms. I gave her a big hug and a kiss. I grabbed Dan in a bear hug and then I saw Andrea. She jumped into my arms and I was too overcome to speak. She said, "Oh, God it's so good to see you." The second thing she said was "You didn't change your clothes?!" Because I was dressed in the same jumpsuit I'd been in four days ago when she first saw me on TV. I laughed. I'd kept the clothes on to keep my connection with the *Bainbridge,* the *Boxer,* and the *Arleigh Burke.* I even wore the standard-issue white T-shirt the Navy gave me, something I rarely do. Then Andrea went into nurse mode: she started taking care of my wounds — months later, I still had scars on and numbness in my arms and wrists from the ropes — and cooking for me and making sure I got enough sleep.

It was like that time when I was almost crushed by a load in Greenland. You don't realize what you have until you come this close to losing it. And then it just seems so much more valuable.

At the airport, we were surrounded by crowds of people, by media, by well-wishers and government officials and everyone else. I could see on their faces how much they wanted to welcome me back. But I was just dying to get home. I wanted to go back to the life I loved, to the family I'd missed so much.

As we drove home, we saw people outside the airport holding up signs, people along the roads home, people in front of the house. They'd hung a sign up at the general store saying, WELCOME HOME, CAPTAIN PHILLIPS, and hundreds of people had signed it. When we pulled into the driveway, it was hanging on the barn across the road. I couldn't adequately express my thanks to all of them.

It wasn't until we got home that the full emotional weight of what I'd been through really hit me. And when it did, I went back to one particular moment on the boat. I remembered sitting there when I was saying my good-byes to my family and thinking about how Dan would say, growing up, that he didn't have a father and that his dad didn't love him because he was always away. That memory just pierced me through and through. I couldn't let another minute go by without doing something about it.

I pulled Dan aside, tears welling up in my eyes. "Dan," I said, "you know how you used to joke about not having a father?"

"Yeah," he said.

"Don't ever say that again, okay?"

He nodded. Just thinking about my son saying those words had hurt so deeply I didn't even want to joke about it. Now that I'd been given back my family, I didn't want to leave a single doubt in their minds about how much they meant to me.

Andrea and I knew how close we'd come to losing each other. We'd be sitting together alone in the house, on the couch, and I'd say, "You know, Ange, I really shouldn't have come out of this one alive." And she'd say, "I know." And I did know. Then she'd say, "The next time you are feeling lucky, could you please just buy a lottery ticket?"

Those first few weeks, Andrea was afraid to let me out of her sight. I'd wake up in the middle of the night and find her reaching out for me, afraid that my side of the bed would be empty. Andrea doesn't even remember doing that. I'd tell her, "It's okay, Ange. I'm right here. Go back to sleep." After a few days, I started telling friends, "She won't even let me go to the bathroom by myself!" That was an exaggeration. But not by much.

I still had no idea that the whole world had been watching my ordeal. I was totally amazed by how many people were caught up in it and touched by it: people who watched the situation unfold from a hospital bed, or who'd gone through something similar, or who just wanted to reach out and say that they were proud of me. There was a farmer out west who promised to carry feed or livestock wherever I wanted (I had to tell him I didn't own any cows) and a Vermonter who offered me the use of his hunting camp. People just wanted to feel connected to my story. I was floored.

"It restored my faith in people," Andrea said. "After sixteen years as an emergency room nurse, where you see people in terrible situations that rarely turn out well, your faith can get ground down. At times you forget there is good out there. But after how generous people were to us, how concerned they were about us, I saw that there really is good out there in unexpected places." It wasn't the celebrities that we met that made us feel differently, but the ordinary people like us. The neighbor who sent over the home-cooked meals day after day without wanting a word of thanks in return. And the Somali refugee living in Burlington who works at Andrea's hospital who came up to her to tell Andrea how happy he was for me and how he wanted to apologize for the bad people in Somalia. Andrea told him, "There are bad people everywhere."

And there are. But there are more good

people. I believe that now.

We did get to do things I'd never dreamed of doing. Going to the Washington National Opera, black-tie events, meeting some incredibly influential people. It was just unbelievable. There was a moment when we were sitting in the Oval Office, and Andrea whispered to me, "How did I get here?" It was a hard way to get a ticket on an unbelievable Ferris wheel ride, as Andrea put it. She was a Vermont girl who felt she'd been let into this huge amusement park. She kept telling me she was going to write a book on the "101 things you can do with Richard Phillips."

But the most moving event was a Navy SEALs reunion. The SEAL wives told Andrea they admired how she'd handled herself. She was in disbelief: They were saying how they admired her. "We knew our men were going to do their jobs," they said. "But you had to sit there and agonize about what was coming." All the while, we were in awe of them, young women in their twenties and thirties, some of them widows. A Navy SEAL wife never knows if her husband is coming home after a mission. Andrea had tears in her eyes, and so did I.

Everyone asks, "Did the experience change

you?" I'm stronger in my faith, no doubt. I'm not the kind of guy who makes pacts with God, and I never asked him to get me out of that boat in return for a lifetime of church attendance or anything like that. It's not an honest deal. But I did pray for strength. I prayed for wisdom. I didn't ask for an outcome, just for the ability to be my best self when I needed to.

I'll be grateful for what the SEALs did for me until the day I die. And these days I can't go to a ball game and listen to the "Star-Spangled Banner" without choking up. When other Americans risk their lives to rescue you, that anthem becomes more than a song. It becomes everything you feel for your country. The bond we all have with one another that is so often invisible, so often demeaned. I was lucky enough to experience it in a way that perhaps only soldiers do.

But the experience didn't change me. It only made me see things that had been in front of me all the time. Like the value of trying to see things through other people's eyes. During my career as a captain, whenever one of my crew members did something truly strange, I didn't just correct them. *I asked them why they were doing it that way.* Being interested in people's motives, the way they saw the world, helped me anticipate the moments of danger I faced later on. Especially onboard the *Maersk Alabama.* The crew and I were ready for each crisis not only because we'd drilled for exactly those kinds of situations, but because we thought three moves ahead of the pirates. I knew they'd want to talk to their leaders. I knew they'd want some reward, even if it was only a few thousand dollars. And I knew that they'd want to corral my men in one place. That helped immensely.

But what kept me alive was mental toughness. I just refused to let the pirates beat me. I've always loved winning when I wasn't supposed to. Even when playing basketball now and I know the other team is better. When the odds are against you, winning feels even sweeter. You have to train your mind never to give up.

The thing I saw the clearest was the lesson I learned on the lifeboat: we are stronger than we think we are. There were so many times during my ordeal that I was afraid that I didn't have what it takes to get through the next five minutes. Especially during the mock executions. That ultimate fear, of watching yourself die, was so terrifying that I thought I would collapse into a jibbering mess. But I never did. It taught me that I could handle far more than I'd given myself credit for.

We all set our endurance levels low, out of fear we will fail. We think, *So long as I have this job, or this house, or this partner, or this amount of money, I'll be okay.* But what happens when those things are taken away from you? And more — your freedom, your dignity, even things we take for granted, like your ability to use a bathroom? What happens when people try to take away even your life? You find that you are a larger and a stronger personality than you ever imagined you were. That your strength and your faith don't depend on how secure you are. They're independent of those things.

"You could do what I did," I tell people. "You just haven't had to yet." And they always say, "Well, I don't know about that." I do. Believe me. Every time I doubted myself, I came through it. Every time something was stripped away from me, I found I didn't really need it. We are stronger than we think.

And then, of course, there is the *H* word. "Hero." When I got home and the media left and friends said their good-byes and drove back to their homes and lives and the Hollywood agents stopped calling, I had a chance to sit down and read the letters that people had sent me. Some were addressed to "Captain Phillips, Vermont." I laughed about that, like I was Lindbergh or Abraham Lincoln — or Santa Claus at the North Pole! But I didn't feel different. I was a regular guy. Truly an ordinary person. And now people were using the word that I'd reserved for people like Audie Murphy and Neil Armstrong.

"You're my hero." It brought tears to my eyes. But they weren't tears of happiness. Honestly, I felt like an imposter, a phony. *I didn't do anything special,* I thought. *I don't deserve all this. I don't* want *all this.* I really don't take compliments well. It goes back to being raised with seven brothers and sisters in an Irish-Catholic home. I know how to deal with someone trying to kick my ass. But not with a compliment. In fact, the third night after I'd gotten back, I had a dream that the whole thing had been fake. There'd been no pirates, no hostage-taking, no rescue. And everyone was thinking I was a hero, but it was all made up, shot in a Hollywood studio. I was a flimflam artist, and everyone found out and hated me. I woke up in a cold sweat.

But I saw that everyone who's been through something extraordinary is called a hero. And they go on the talk shows and say, "You know, I don't think I am one." What they're really saying is, "If I'm a hero, it's by accident. You have this potential inside you, too. If fate put you in my shoes, you'd have done the same thing." And it's true. I didn't discover something about myself out there off the coast of Somalia. I discovered something about the potential of everyone who trains their mind to be strong. I'm an ordinary guy from Vermont who was given a glimpse of something very few people are lucky enough to see.

After all the interviews and the speeches and a kick-ass welcome-home party (five hundred of my closest friends and neighbors at the town park for a picnic), I'm back being a father and a husband. I finally got my new dog, Ivan, who is a mix of spaniel and mystery-dog DNA and is just as disobedient as Frannie. On hot summer days, he comes to the creek across from our house, the one that all the locals know about, and dives in after me. Then we walk back through the trees to my farmhouse.

It was there, weeks after I got back, that a neighbor who was pulling out of the dirt and gravel road across the way saw me putting wet clothes on the backyard line to dry. Ange was busy, so I was doing it for her. It must have struck him as funny that the hero, the guy with the movie deal, whatever, was back to doing the most ordinary things, as if I'd never been held hostage and come this close to dying.

He yelled across to me, and I turned and waved back. I laughed. I hadn't been thinking about how my life had come full circle. But that moment really brought it back to me. *I'm home,* I thought. I was finally back in my life again.

ABOUT THE AUTHOR

Captain Richard Phillips grew up in Winchester, Massachusetts, with seven brothers and sisters. He married Andrea Coggio, an emergency room nurse, in 1988, and they have two children. Phillips is a 1979 graduate of the Massachusetts Maritime Academy.